Global America?

STUDIES IN SOCIAL AND POLITICAL THOUGHT
Editor: Gerard Delanty, *University of Liverpool*

This series publishes peer-reviewed scholarly books on all aspects of social and political thought. It will be of interest to scholars and advanced students working in the areas of social theory and sociology, the history of ideas, philosophy, political and legal theory, anthropological and cultural theory. Works of individual scholarship will have preference for inclusion in the series, but appropriate co- or multi-authored works and edited volumes of outstanding quality or exceptional merit will also be included. The series will also consider English translations of major works in other languages.

Challenging and intellectually innovative books are particularly welcome on the history of social and political theory; modernity and the social and human sciences; major historical or contemporary thinkers; the philosophy of the social sciences; theoretical issues on the transformation of contemporary society; social change and European societies.

Global America?

*The Cultural Consequences
of Globalization*

Edited by

ULRICH BECK,
NATAN SZNAIDER
and RAINER WINTER

LIVERPOOL UNIVERSITY PRESS

First published 2003 by
Liverpool University Press
4 Cambridge Street
Liverpool
L69 7ZU

Copyright © 2003 Liverpool University Press

The right of Ulrich Beck, Natan Sznaider and Rainer Winter
to be identified as the authors of this work has been asserted by them
in accordance with the Copyright, Design and Patents Act, 1988

British Library Cataloguing-in-Publication Data
A British Library CIP Record is available

ISBN 0–85323–918-5 hardback
      0–85323–928-2 limp

Typeset in Plantin by Koinonia, Bury
Printed and bound in the European Union by
Biddles Ltd, Guildford and King's Lynn

Contents

Contents

List of Contributors

Ulrich Beck is Professor of Sociology at the University of Munich and Visiting Centennial Professor of the London School of Economics and Political Science. His books include *Risk Society* (1992), *Reflexive Modernization* (1994, with Anthony Giddens and Scott Lash), *Ecological Politics in an Age of Risk* (1995), *Ecological Enlightenment* (1995), *The Normal Chaos of Love* (1995, with E. Beck-Gernsheim), *The Reinvention of Politics* (1996), *Democracy Without Enemies* (1998), *World Risk Society* (1999), *The Brave New Work* (2000), *Individualization* (2000).

Gerard Delanty is Professor of Sociology at the University of Liverpool. He was Visiting Professor at York University, Toronto in 1998 and in 2000 Visiting Professor at Doshisha University, Kyoto, Japan and has taught at universities in Ireland, Germany and Italy. His books include *Inventing Europe: Idea, Identity, Reality* (1995), *Rethinking Irish History: Nationalism, Identity, Ideology* (1998, with Patrick O'Mahony), *Social Science: Beyond Constructivism and Realism* (1997), *Social Theory in a Changing World* (1999), *Modernity and Postmodernity: Knowledge, Power, the Self* (2000), *Citizenship in a Global Age* (2000), *Challenging Knowledge: The University in the Knowledge Society* (2001), *Nationalism and Social Theory* (2002, with Patrick O'Mahony).

Eva Illouz is Senior Lecturer in Sociology at the Hebrew University of Jerusalem. She is the author of *Consuming the Romantic Utopia: Love and the Cultural Contradictions of Capitalism* (1997). She is currently working on *Oprah Winfrey and the Glamour of Misery* (Columbia Press) and *Flat Identities and Thick Relations: The Rise of Homo Communicans* (University of California Press).

List of Contributors

Yu Keping is Professor and Director at the China Center for Comparative Politics and Economics in Beijing; Concurrent Professor at Peking University, Nankai University, Fudan University and Shengzheng University. He was Guest Professor at the Free University Berlin, April 1995–Febuary 1996, and Visiting Professor at Duke University, Durham, NC, January 1994–July 1994. His books include *Politics of Public Good or Politics of Rights* (1999), *Antinomies of Globalization*, ed. (1998), *Socialism in the Global Age*, ed. (1998), *China's Political System Nowadays* (1998).

Rob Kroes is the Chair of American Studies at the University of Amsterdam. He is a past president of the European Association for American Studies (1992–96) and the author, co-author, or editor of 31 books, including *The Persistence of Ethnicity* (1992), *If You've Seen One, You've Seen the Mall: Europeans and American Mass Culture* (1996) and, most recently, *Them and Us: Questions of Citizenship in a Globalizing World* (2000). He is the general editor of two series, published in Amsterdam: European Contributions to American Studies, and Amsterdam Monographs in American Studies.

Richard F. Kuisel is Professor of History at the Center for German and European Studies, Georgetown University; formerly Professor of History, State University of New York at Stony Brook (1980–2000) and Assistant Professor of History, University of California, Berkeley (1970–80). Awards include the New York State Association of European Historians prize for best book in European History (1995), and the Gilbert Chinard Prize (1993). His books include *Le miroir américain: 50 ans de regard français sur l'Amérique* (1996), *Seducing the French: The Dilemma of Americanization* (1993), *Le capitalisme et l'état en France: modernisation et dirigisme au XXe siècle* (1984), *Capitalism and the State in Modern France: Renovation and Economic Management in the 20th Century* (1981), *Ernest Mercier: French Technocrat* (University of California Press, 1967).

Jan Nederveen Pieterse is Professor of Sociology, University of Illinois at Urbana-Champaign. He was Associate Professor in Sociology at the Institute of Social Studies in The Hague. He has taught in Ghana and the United States, has been a visiting professor in Japan and Indonesia and has lectured in many countries. His books include *Development Theory: Deconstructions/ Reconstructions* (2000), *White on Black: Images of Africa and Blacks in Western Popular Culture* (1992) and *Empire and Emancipation* (1989), which received the 1990 J.C. Ruigrok Award of the Netherlands Society of Sciences. Edited books include *Global Futures: Shaping Globalization* (2000), *Globalization and Collective Action* (2000), *World Orders in the Making: Humanitarian Intervention* *and Beyond* (1998), *The Decolonization of Imagination* (1995, with Bhikhu Parekh), *Emancipations, Modern and Postmodern* (1992) and *Christianity and Hegemony* (1992).

Aihwa Ong is Professor of Anthropology, University of California at Berkeley, Center of SE Asian Studies. Her books include *Flexible Citizenship: The Cultural Logics of Transnationality* (1999), *Ungrounded Empires: The Cultural Politics of Modern Chinese Transnationalism* (main editor, 1997), *Bewitching Women, Pious Men: Gender and Body Politics in Southeast Asia* (main editor, 1995), *Spirits of Resistance and Capitalist Discipline: Factory Women in Malaysia* (1987).

Motti Regev is Senior Lecturer at the Department of Sociology, Political Science and Communication, The Open University of Israel. Publications include *Popular Music and Israeli Culture* (forthcoming, co-authored with Edwin Seoussi, University of California Press), 'Rock Aesthetics and Musics of the World', *Theory, Culture and Society* 14 (1997), 'Producing Artistic Value: The Case of Rock Music', *The Sociological Quarterly* 35 (1994).

George Ritzer is Professor of Sociology at the University of Maryland, where he has been a Distinguished Scholar-Teacher and won a Teaching Excellence Award. George Ritzer has held a Fulbright-Hays Fellowship, has been a Fellow at the Netherlands Institute for Advanced Study and the Swedish Collegium for Advanced Study in the Social Sciences, and has held the UNESCO Chair in Social Theory at the Russian Academy of Sciences. His major publications are *Sociology: a Multiple Paradigm Science* (1975), *Toward an Integrated Sociological Paradigm* (1981) and *Metatheorizing Sociology* (1991). He has written *The McDonaldization of Society* (1993), *Expressing America: A Critique of the Global Credit Card Society* (1995), *The McDonaldization Thesis: Explorations and Extensions* (1998) and *Enchanting a Disenchanted World: Revolutionizing the Means of Consumption* (1999). His work has been translated into many languages: *The McDonaldization of Society* alone has been, or is being, translated into more than a dozen languages. He has co-edited the *Handbook of Social Theory* with Barry Smart (2001).

Roland Robertson is Professor of Sociology at the University of Aberdeen. He was Professor of Sociology and Religious Studies at the University of Pittsburgh. He has authored or co-authored a number of books, including *Meaning and Change, International Systems and the Modernization of Societies, The Sociological Interpretation of Religion* and *Globalization*.

List of Contributors

Todd Stillman is a graduate student in the Department of Sociology at the University of Maryland, College Park. His major interests are social theory and consumption. He has co-authored essays on Guy Debord and the Situationists, Las Vegas casinos, and customer service.

Natan Sznaider is Associate Professor of Sociology at the Academic College of Tel-Aviv in Israel. His publications revolve around theoretical questions regarding moral sentiments, popular culture and collective memory. He has published a study on the social history of sentiments, *The Compassionate Temperament: Care and Cruelty in Modern Society* (2000). He is the author of *Über das Mitleid im Kapitalismus* (2000). Together with Daniel Levy, he has recently completed a comparative study on the relationship of Holocaust memory and globalization (*Erinnerung im globalen Zeitalter: Der Holocaust*, 2001).

John Tomlinson is Professor of Cultural Sociology and Director of the Centre for Research in International Communication and Culture (CRICC) at the Nottingham Trent University. He is the author of *Cultural Imperialism* (1991) and *Globalization and Culture* (1999), both of which have been extensively translated.

Rainer Winter is a sociologist, Professor of Media Theory and Cultural Studies and Director of the Institute of Media and Communication Studies at the University of Klagenfurt. He is author and editor of a number of books and articles in social theory, sociology of culture, cultural and media studies. His recent books include *Die Kunst des Eigensinns: Cultural Studies als Kritik der Macht* (2001) and as co-editor *Kultur, Medien, Macht: Cultural Studies und Medienanalyse* (1999, 2nd edn), *Widerspenstige Kulturen: Cultural Studies als Herausforderung* (1999), *Politik des Vergnügens* (2000), *Die Fabrikation des Populären* (2001) and *Die Werkzeugkiste der Cultural Studies* (2001).

Acknowledgments

We hope to have shed light on new perspectives for researching Americanization and the cultural consequences of globalization. This volume presents contributions which grew out of a conference on 'Global America' held in Schloss Elmau, Germany in October 2000. We gratefully acknowledge the generosity of the director of Elmau, Dietmar Müller-Elmau, who made the conference possible.

Introduction

Natan Sznaider and Rainer Winter

'Caution: objects in this mirror may be closer than they appear.' This warning appears at the beginning of Jean Baudrillard's book *America* (1988: 1) – in its way, a type of travel journal, in which Baudrillard defines the USA as the centre of the world. In his opinion, the USA represents the first truly modern society, which, through radicalness and indifference, has become a model for the rest of the world, as it is for Europe. He analyses the shaping of everyday life by film and television, the central importance of surface and speed, the inspirational experience of the American landscape, in particular the emptiness of the deserts, and the cultural and social features of city life. This analysis leads him to diagnose the 'death of the social'. Wim Wenders also reflects critically, after his travels in the US, on the American icons and myths and the threat of advertising and of Hollywood on experience and imagination. This can be seen in his films such as the road movie, *Paris, Texas* (1984). However, Wenders' fascinating images of the landscape in the south-west USA and the cities of Los Angeles and Houston, as well as of the symbols of American popular culture, reveal the ambivalence of his views. Hence his views do not seem as pessimistic as Baudrillard's. While in his theoretical works Wenders warns of the colonization of fantasy by products of the American culture industry (Wenders 2001), *Paris, Texas*, as well as some of his other films, portrays American society as a complex and multifaceted phenomenon. Wenders has himself developed a cultural identity as a film-maker through encounters with the image of America found in Hollywood. In addition, rock music made it possible for him to turn away from German post-war culture. Together with comics, John Ford films, Dashiell Hammett and Raymond Chandler novels, this music provided Wenders with the view of an imaginary America that positively shaped his own fantasies, wishes and

1

utopian dreams. Earlier, it was Alexis de Tocqueville who visited America in the nineteenth century and started this European tradition of self-reflection through the prism of the USA. De Tocqueville emphasized equality as the fundamental cultural trope of America – in spite of slavery and existing inequalities. He was also one of the first to dwell on the potentially destructive forces of individualism in an increasingly democratic society, making him the mentor of many critics of the so-called 'mass-society'. De Tocqueville also stressed the religiosity of modern society, in that individualism is turned into a faith, as is liberty. He knew that despotism is not in need of faith, but liberty needs it more than anything else.

The concept of *Americanization* might be the key to understanding these matters. Both within Europe and outside it (in Israel, for example), many people both on the 'old Left' and on the 'old Right' (two rapidly fading formations) were and still are used to blaming the decline of virtue, culture, tradition and citizenship on Americanization. It is true that America is, alas, very good in matters of mass consumership, but this perception considers consumer culture as some sort of imported, contagious disease, rather than intrinsic to mass prosperity.

These different, yet connected, perspectives of European intellectuals provide a good starting point from which to consider the difficult issues dealt with in this book. Starting from the phenomenon of Americanization, it deals with the cultural consequences of globalization. Up to now, the discussion has taken place, as a rule, amid the tense relationship between staunch criticism and pessimistic judgements on the one hand and ambivalent, even at times positive, evaluations on the other. Other than in the case of Wenders, these could even be described as approving of the phenomenon of Americanization. These conflicting points of view leave no room for compromise and return again and again. They determine public discussion because they express hopes and fears concerning social development and the future. Against this background of conflicting positions, our book aims at contributing to a sophisticated debate of the question of a global America. Theoretical analysis and empirical studies will help to avoid rash judgements, thus clarifying ideas and distinguishing facts. Alongside the (apparently) familiar phenomenon of Americanization, there are a number of connected questions and problems which should be understood analytically, investigated empirically and discussed critically. The contributions in this book show that it is possible to provide a precise and neutral definition of the globalization processes that seeks in addition to bring the cultural consequences more clearly into focus.

The increasing popularity of the idea of globalization in sociology is connected to the fact that many of today's problems cannot be grasped adequately on the level of nation states, but only through the analysis of global (trans-national) processes. In this way, the influence of Hollywood, McDonald's or Burger King fast food and Nike sports shoes and accessories refers to global processes of production, circulation and reception of cultural commodities, where there is no doubt that American products dominate. In one critical interpretation, a 'culture-ideology of consumerism' (Sklair 1998) has been analysed, which aims to include as many social groups and cultural identities as possible worldwide. Participation in consumption does not take place in a Fordistic scenario whereby cultures become more uniform and standardized, as Max Horkheimer and Theodor W. Adorno believed in their famous theory of the culture industry (1972). Rather the (global) market actually demands differences which are the basis for the development of marketing strategies. Critics believe that flexible and mobile organizations offer every Western social group the very consumer commodities that they demand to develop and to express their identity in the framework of the 'politics of identity' (Hardt and Negri 2000: 152ff.). Even counter-cultures are deeply integrated into the trans-national consumer world, which penetrates into our everyday lives. According to Fredric Jameson (1998: 64), evolving within this consumerism there are 'developing forces that are North American in origin and result from the unchallenged primacy of the USA today and thus the "American way of life" and American mass media culture'. His interpretation suggests that the 'new world culture' is dominated by the USA.

Anxieties regarding the global in our time repeat similar anxieties regarding Americanization a century ago, which are being replayed with different notions and actors. Then and now, the theme of a global culture has become the object of political, ideological and academic controversies. Many of these debates are posed in dichotomous terms, juxtaposing national and post-national models: the former perceives globalization to be a shallow replacement for national values. In times of post-nationality these so-called 'national values' are often termed 'authenticity'. Similarly, earlier modernization scholars and more recently post-nationalists also operate with mutually exclusive categories. The former perceived local/regional/ethnic bonds as primordial remnants soon to be abolished by the nationalization of the masses. It is argued pervasively, however, that the global does not replace the national (or the local), but stands in a dialectic relationship to it. Globalization involves the simultaneity and the interpenetration of what are conventionally called the global and the local, or – in more abstract vein – the universal and the particular (or if you will the 'American' and the 'local').

When processes of consumption are no longer analysed from the point of view of production or marketing, it is rapidly apparent that cultural

3

commodities, when they are received and usurped, are subject to contextualization and, at the same time, localization processes, which can acquire their own weight (Robertson 1995). This also applies to worldwide products such as Coca-Cola, burgers from McDonald's or Barbie dolls, as anthropological studies show (Miller 1994). It would be only too easy to dismiss this as banal and trivial in comparison to the 'big' issues of global justice, human rights, compassion and so on. Nevertheless, it has become increasingly clear that these processes of contextualization and localization are also at work when it comes to the emergence of a global ethics and even global memory (Levy and Sznaider 2001).

While diversification and the corresponding product marketing aim to manage differences globally, various creative forms of appropriation develop in the processes of localization. These forms give specific meaning to cultural – ideal or material – commodities circulated around the world. They effectively take over these commodities and make them resources for creating and developing a personal identity. At the same time, 'tactics' to rework and creatively use these resources can be discovered (de Certeau 1984) which were unforeseen by their producers. Optimistic interpretations speak of a 'variety from below' (Fiske 1996) which is based on processes of 'excorporation' (Grossberg 1997) and of usurpation of (global) products for independent purposes. In this way, people can make their own culture out of resources provided by global flows (Winter 2001). Above all, Néstor García Canclini (1995) has shown how, in the case of Latin America, the eclectic, playful and creative treatment of global products can lead to the development and proliferation of new cultures which are distinguished by 'impurity', syncretism and hybridity. According to James Lull (2001: 157), the power of the hybrid is actually the essential characteristic of contemporary cultural activities. We construct 'supercultures' in the global age of communication which is distinguished by growing and 'complex connectivity' (Tomlinson 1999) and apparently unlimited access to cultural resources from (sometimes very) distant places. These supercultures make orientation, formation of identity and agency possible. They assume various forms, are openly in favour of change and can lead to the formation of new communities, for example using electronic networks. The Internet is a perfect example. According to Lull (2001: 144ff.), it was originally a typically American cultural phenomenon, but it is now used by groups across the world which differ in language and culture. Its communicative power enables (apparently) limitless cultural possibility (Poster 2001).

Even if we sceptically oppose this positive assessment, it is obvious that a differentiated theoretical and empirical analysis in local contexts can provide deeper insights into processes of Americanization. Hence, the idea of a homogeneous global culture turns out to be a simulacrum. Globalization and localization must always be dealt with together. They are part of the massive and radical processes that Roland Robertson (1992: 100) described as 'the interpenetration of the universalization of particularism and the particularization of universalism'. At the same time, we must not only observe the global flows of capital, technologies and images but also, as Arjun Appadurai (1996) has shown, the flows of migrants for whom images of America can also hold a cosmopolitan promise. Is this cosmopolitanism defined primarily by aesthetics, focusing on pleasurable reception and experience (Lash and Urry 1994: 256), or can it also be oriented cognitively and ethically? John Tomlinson (1999: 202) points out that the development of semiotic skills and a hermeneutic reflexivity do not lead inevitably to a 'responsibility for the global totality'. Nevertheless, there are signs of a 'global citizenship' (Held 1995) which distinguishes itself by its potential openness and sensibility towards groups, cultures and problems across the world. It opposes the interests, both 'de-nationalized' and limitless, of global ventures. Varied forms of exchange and interaction produce a 'cultural and social interconnectedness', which does not jibe with the homogenization scenario that some critics have outlined. What consequences it has remain open and contribute to the 'cultural complexity' (Hannerz 1992) of the present. At the same time, the shape of a global civil society is apparently emerging.

A more crucial aspect in this context which Appadurai emphasizes is the (new) role of the imagination and its significance as a social power (Castoriadis 1975). On one hand, imagination is defined and disciplined by the influence of states, markets, media and consumption. On the other hand, however, it is also the basis for the development of protest, dissent and new forms of collective life (Appadurai 2000: 6). It is the requirement for a political agency and for the formation of new forms of social activities. At the same time, Appadurai stresses 'the mobility and malleability of those creative forms of social life that are localised transit points for mobile global forms of civic and civil life' (2000: 6). His perspective makes it clear that a process such as Americanization does not run uniformly and is not imposed from above. It leads to heterogeneous answers and different accentuation. Even the capacity of making a personal image of America and taking over its imagery has become a global phenomenon. By means of plural constructions, the picture of America has also become reflexive. It becomes clear that even the US-American idea is a construction and that it can be changed in many ways by ethnic groups such as Asian-Americans or Hispanic-Americans.

Appadurai (2000: 15) believes that a sociology that examines this new vantage point and the social forms linked to these developments (transnational networks, organizations, movements, and so on) is needed. He appeals for an examination of globalization 'from below', which would also analyse the 'grassroots' organisations interested in counter-globalization. This approach argues in favour of new fields of subpolitics (Beck 1994) and shows that globalization and Americanization do not only run in one direction, but rather there are deviations, lines of flight and counter-movements, which are also dealt with in this book. These processes are, without doubt, affected by an emerging new structure of temporality generated by the quickening pace of daily life on the one hand and by the acceleration of media images and information on the other. Speed destroys space, and erases temporal distance. 'Speed' in the nineteenth-century imagination was always connected to degeneration, the breakdown of tradition, the metropolis, which in the words of one of the leading sociologists of the beginning of the twentieth century, Werner Sombart (1911), was nothing else but the natural continuation of the desert. It was Baudrillard (1988) again in his stimulating analysis of America who drew attention to America as a desert enabling speed and a particular kind of memory, namely forgetfulness. Does this argument really hold up? Old-fashioned modernists operate under the assumption that identity is based on continuity and slowness, the counter-principle of America. Collective cultural identity is identified with those feelings and values that perpetuate a sense of continuity, shared memories and a sense of common destiny among a group with common experiences and cultural attributes. America, without 'history', has no identity in the minds of those rejecting it. In the words of Baudrillard, who considered this a compliment, 'Americans are the only true primitive people'. The contempt for America and the philistine quality of American cultural life became popular with the mid-nineteenth century depoliticized avant-garde, for whom Americanization was synonymous with the vulgarization of life. This is of course also the approach of the Frankfurt School. Nevertheless the distinction between the avant-garde and popular art, between high and low culture, also sustained the old distinction between aristocratic and peasant culture. A society without a nation state, without the old cultural hierarchies, was and still is conceived as a society without culture as a principle of order. America, on the other hand, may stand therefore for the liberation of the masses from the cultural tutelage of the elites who dictate canons of 'good' and 'bad' taste.

Primarily, however, the postcolonial discussion has emphasized how the colonization strategies of Western powers, including their attempts to order the world 'ontologically', have been undermined in a number of different ways. Various practices produce differences that call into question essential identities, static conceptions of culture and homogeneous world-views. The postcolonial situation leads us to question, reconsider and differently express familiar and well-known positions. As Iain Chambers (2001) shows, postcolonial theory also challenges traditional Western images of science and conceptions of humanism. In certain ways, it is a symptom of the Second Modern Age in which self-evident truths disappear because modernization and the processes linked to it have become reflexive (Beck et al. 1994). For our purposes, this means that an analysis of the cultural consequences of globalization must not start from the belief that cultures are 'organic bodies'. Rather, they are based on the (political) articulation of historical links and limitations, on the connection and disconnection of elements. Culture can be understood as a continuing, open and unfinished process which is intensified in the course of globalization and which is increasingly reflexive.

The title *Global America? The Cultural Consequences of Globalization* formulates a research question that is more closely examined by theoretical conceptualizations in Part I of this book. Ulrich Beck argues that the idea of Americanization suggests a national understanding of globalization that is poorly adapted to the transnational world of the Second Modern Age. Rather, he proposes 'rooted cosmopolitanism', a cosmopolitanism that draws equally on the local. This serves to dispel the binary thinking that still tends to characterize discussions on postcolonialism. The 'otherness' of others is recognized, and at the same time the sociological imagination can be freed from its methodological nationalism and can embrace a cosmopolitan perspective, with all the consequences this implies for the field. Not only Beck's, but most of the other contributions to this volume point in this direction of a new methodological cosmopolitanism.

George Ritzer and Todd Stillman also attempt to provide theoretical grounding for the notions of Americanization and globalization. They relate these to McDonaldization, that is, the increasing rationalization of society. Fast-food restaurants are associated all over the world with the American way of life. The McDonaldization process linked to this is defined by increased efficiency, and the ability to predict and calculate the production process. This process is not necessarily one of Americanization but refers to the forms of standardization typical of the present late modern age, the same forms that characterize the field of consumption. Ritzer and Stillman view both Americanization and McDonaldization as specific and not identical expressions of globalization and emphasize the homogenizing effect of Americanization.

John Tomlinson focuses on the relationship between culture, modernity and immediacy. For a conceptual analysis of globalization's cultural consequences, he relates cultural phenomena to the globalized texture of modernity, using the key feature of 'immediacy', characterized by speed and immediate access, as the salient feature of the globally modern cultural experience. Tomlinson argues for a culturally critical imagination which can examine the emerging processes of globalization in an unbiased way.

In Part II these theoretical explanations are put to the test by national case studies. Jan Nederveen Pieterse analyses 'American exceptionalism' and its role in the 'US hegemony' as a means of better grasping globalization. This not only impacts on the field of consumption and popular culture but also has a decisive influence on economic and development policies, international politics and questions of security. Nederveen Pieterse believes that a coalition of progressive powers from Europe, Asia and America is needed to influence the development of globalization and its cultural consequences.

Taking France as a proving ground, Richard Kuisel analyses the process of Americanization there, one part of which is importation of the 'American' products, images, technologies and practices by non-Americans. Although Kuisel rejects the view held for example by Pierre Bourdieu and Loïc Wacquant (1999), that this is a form of cultural imperialism, he considers it obvious, like Ritzer and Stillman, that Americanization means a transformation of the present world towards homogenization. His examples show that France is doubtless more American today than in the 1930s.

On the other hand, Gerard Delanty shows the limits of Americanization by analysing the example of Japan. Americanization succeeds within the structures of the Japanese culture yet paradoxically helps to support that very culture. For instance, the introduction of 'conspicuous consumption' leads to a strengthening of group identities and to the founding of a self-identity within the respective group. According to Delanty, Americanization prompts an enlargement of the available cultural resources (for example in the field of 'popular culture'), as a tool through which meaning is created in the framework of the existing cognitive, symbolic and normative structures.

Yu Keping shows as regards present-day China that Americanization and anti-Americanization exist at the same time. McDonald's, Donald Duck and American films are popular, and China trusts Western, and above all American, science, technology and products. On the other hand, China is also striving towards a revival of Chinese tradition after a parallel 'Sinification' of Western civilization.

In Part III the theme of 'Global America?' is dealt with from a transnational perspective. Aihwa Ong examines the role of Asiatic techno-migrants in the network economy, especially in California and Vancouver. The vision of freedom and the hope for a good life have brought generations of Asian migrants to North America. Ong reveals how today neo-liberal 'migratory regimes' direct the flow of people. Investors, managers and 'high-tech' experts are favoured.

She critically opposes the democratic visions and the optimism that are linked by some commentators to the cosmopolitan project.

Using the example of the Americanization of the Holocaust, Natan Sznaider shows how a global memory has arisen which is based on mass-mediated forms of communication that transcend territorial and linguistic borders. This however does not mean that it is uniformly structured. Because global culture is characterized by processes of hybridization and individualization, the experience of time is heterogeneous, fragmented and plural. Ethnic minorities in the USA (such as African-Americans, Jews and others) have developed – beyond the nation state – their own forms of memory in which collective identities are expressed. Even here the outlines of a cosmopolitan global project are revealed.

Eva Illouz discusses suffering as a form of collective identity, where transnational culture contains not only utopian possibilities, as Appadurai shows, but also makes a spectacle of private and public grief. In an analysis of the *Oprah Winfrey Show*, she illustrates how American forms of suffering are exported successfully to the rest of the world and create transnational 'communities of fate' (David Held). Illouz views this process as 'globalization from within' as defined by Ulrich Beck, but is sceptical whether it can, through individualization and standardization of suffering, develop a cosmopolitan solidarity, which has the 'glocal' in mind and would be an expression of 'globalization from below'.

Rainer Winter examines the processes of 'glocalization' (Robertson 1995) in the reception and appropriation of popular American media products. Through a number of examples, including an ethnographic examination of hip-hop culture in Germany, he shows how hybrid formations arise. The transnational culture of hip-hop also demonstrates that a globally anchored cultural identity and local identification are not mutually exclusive but rather are two sides of one process.

Motti Regev analyses the influence of the Anglo-American-defined 'rock aesthetic' on 'world popular music'. Its eclectic character makes it possible to link it to various musical styles. Regev explains that this American cultural form has become the dominant habitus across the world, to produce local music that expresses rebellion against traditions and authoritarian regimes. This produces a dual identity, which is both local and cosmopolitan.

Rob Kroes examines whether the Internet acts an instrument of Americanization, by spreading American cultural values and mental disposition. He concludes that there is an elective affinity between the logic of the Internet and American values which enables individual consumers to break apart coherent wholes and combine them creatively into new ones.

Global America?

In his epilogue Roland Robertson takes an in-depth look at definitions of Americanization and anti-Americanism. He concludes that 'anti-Americanism' reflects the fact that the USA is becoming a transnational society. Robertson states the case for circumspection and analytical accuracy in dealing with the crucial issue of Americanization.

This volume was completed with America and the world facing a period of deep crisis as a result of the terror attacks on New York and Washington DC on 11 September 2001. Was the attack aimed at American power or global culture? Was it both? The USA decided that it was an attack on its national security. The response was an assertion of sovereignty as the attack on Iraq in 2003 demonstrated. However, if the attack had been defined within the framework presented here – that is, as an attack against global culture, a crime against humanity – then the reaction would have been global as well. This was not the case. International tribunals can serve as a model.

Americanization, in the final analysis, will also be tested by America's willingness to submit itself to a newly regulated process of globalization. The terror attack on 11 September and the war against Iraq correspond to uncertainties about our own world and in particular the discontinuities that exemplify the transition to global modernity. It is precisely the abstract nature of 'good and evil' that symbolizes this new global world, which contributes to the extra-territorial quality of cosmopolitan memory and life. The contributions to this volume (with the exception of the epilogue) were written well before these attacks and before the USA decided to go to war. Recently we have witnessed a shift from 'global culture' to a not very global politics in which the USA is affirming its hegemonic aspirations. Is this the limit case for global America? Furthermore, do recent events in world politics show that culture does not equal politics after all, and that cultural globalization has not created the 'end of history'? Whether it has produced the so-called 'clash of civilizations' remains to be seen.

References

Appadurai, Arjun (1996), *Modernity at Large: Cultural Dimensions of Globalization.* Minneapolis: University of Minnesota Press.
— (2000), 'Grassroots Globalization and the Research Imagination'. *Public Culture* 12(1): 1–19.
Baudrillard, Jean (1988), *America*. London: Verso.
Beck, Ulrich (1994), 'The Reinvention of Politics: Towards a Theory of Reflexive Modernization', in Beck, Giddens and Lash (1994): 1–55.
Beck, Ulrich, Anthony Giddens and Scott Lash (1994), *Reflexive Modernization: Politics, Tradition and Aesthetics in the Modern Social Order.* Cambridge: Polity Press.

Bourdieu, Pierre, and Loïc Wacquant (1999), 'On the Cunning of Imperialist Reason'. *Theory, Culture and Society* 16(1): 41–58.

Castoriadis, Cornelius (1975), *L'institution imaginaire de la société*. Paris: Editions du Seuil.

Certeau, Michel de (1984), *The Practice of Everyday Life*. Berkeley: University of California Press.

Chambers, Iain (2001), *Culture After Humanism: History, Culture, Subjectivity*. London and New York: Routledge.

Fiske, John (1996), 'Hybrid Vigor: Popular Culture in a Multicultural, Post-Fordist World', *Studies in Latin American Popular Culture* 15: 43–59.

García Canclini, Néstor (1995), *Hybrid Cultures: Strategies for Entering and Leaving Modernity*. Minneapolis: University of Minnesota Press.

Grossberg, Lawrence (1997), *Dancing in Spite of Myself: Essays on Popular Culture*. Durham, NC, and London: Duke University Press.

Hannerz, Ulf (1992), *Cultural Complexity*. New York: Columbia University Press.

Hardt, Michael, and Antonio Negri (2000), *Empire*. Cambridge, MA, and London: Harvard University Press.

Held, David (1995), *Democracy and the Global Order*. Cambridge: Polity Press.

Horkheimer, Max, and Theodor W. Adorno (1972), *Dialectic of Enlightenment*. New York: Herder and Herder.

Jameson, Fredric (1998), 'Notes on Globalization as a Philosophical Issue', in Fredric Jameson and Masao Miyoshi (eds), *The Cultures of Globalization*. Durham, NC, and London: Duke University Press: 54–77.

Lash, Scott, and John Urry (1994), *Economies of Signs and Space*. London: Sage Publications.

Levy, Daniel, and Natan Sznaider (2001), *Erinnerung im globalen Zeitalter: Der Holocaust*. Frankfurt: Suhrkamp.

Lull, James (2001), 'Superculture for the Communication Age', in James Lull (ed.), *Culture in the Communication Age*. London and New York: Routledge: 132–63.

Miller, Daniel (1994), *Modernity: An Ethnographic Approach. Dualism and Mass Consumption in Trinidad*. Oxford and New York: Berg.

Poster, Mark (2001), *What's the Matter with the Internet?* Minneapolis: University of Minnesota Press.

Robertson, Roland (1992), *Globalization: Social Theory and Global Culture*. London: Sage Publications.

Robertson, Roland (1995), 'Glocalization: Time-Space and Homogeneity-Heterogeneity', in Mike Featherstone, Scott Lash and Roland Robertson (eds), *Global Modernities*. London: Sage Publications: 25–44.

Sklair, Leslie (1998), 'Social Movements and Global Capitalism', in Fredric Jameson and Masao Miyoshi (eds), *The Cultures of Globalization*. Durham, NC, and London: Duke University Press: 291–311.

Sombart, Werner (1911), *Die Juden und das Wirtschaftsleben*. Leipzig: Dunker und Humblot.

Tomlinson, John (1999), *Globalization and Culture*. Cambridge: Polity Press.

Wenders, Wim (2001), *On Film*. London and Boston: Faber & Faber.

Winter, Rainer (2001), *Die Kunst des Eigensinns: Cultural Studies als Kritik der Macht*. Weilerswist: Velbrück Wissenschaft.

PART I

THEORETICAL PERSPECTIVES

CHAPTER 1

Rooted Cosmopolitanism: Emerging from a Rivalry of Distinctions

Ulrich Beck

US presidents, including Bill Clinton and George W. Bush, tend to declare that the USA is the guiding light of the world. All draw on a long tradition, since Abraham Lincoln once described America as 'the last best hope of the earth'. There are, however, many people, even in the USA, who would take the opposite stance. Whereas Clinton saw America as a vector for expansion of the free market and democracy throughout the world, others see corporate globalism dotting the landscape with McDonalds and filling the airwaves with Disney. Recently, protesters have been massing in the streets every few months against the system they see embodied in the WTO, the IMF and the World Bank. Each time this happens, commentators point out that the protesters present a bewildering array of demands. Nevertheless it would not be too much of an oversimplification to say that in a certain way all their demands oppose the three facets of American hegemony: its military power, its market power, and its power to influence other countries' political agendas and cultural ideas.

Thus global America is indeed highly controversial. European intellectuals have also criticized it deeply (see Bohrer and Scheel 2000, or Bourdieu and Wacquart 1999). But is Europe an entity with a competing vision? Or, to be harsh, does it have a vision at all? Do Europeans want, for example, to expand to include Eastern Europe and Russia? Or do they want to draw a line and 'Latin-Americanize' these countries? Do Europeans have any strong feelings that are not inspired by fear – fear of losing their national sovereignty, a decline in their quality of life, a drop in their global clout? There is some justification in saying that Europe's lack of a positive vision leaves the USA with a world-view monopoly, although it is surely a great irony that the United States – a republic whose individual citizens are so relatively lacking in xenophobia and arrogance

– can feel comfortable presenting itself as if it were a missionary to the heathens.

In this chapter I would like to clarify some conceptual oppositions. My claim is that the concept of *Americanization* is based on a national understanding of globalization. The concept of *cosmopolitanization*, by contrast, is an explicit attempt to overcome this 'methodological nationalism' and produce concepts capable of reflecting a newly transnational world. Things are made even more complicated by the fact that it is very difficult to draw a clear-cut line between these concepts, which is what makes the theme of this book so tricky and exciting.

Why 'Cosmopolitan'?

I begin my overview with a seemingly minor query; namely into the nature of the term 'cosmopolitan'. From a national perspective 'cosmopolitan' or 'cosmopolitanism' is viewed pejoratively, as an enemy image. 'Cosmopolitan' refers to the 'global player', the 'imperial capitalist' or 'middle-class intellectual without local roots', and as such is a loaded concept. The term has a long history in the social sciences, going back to ancient Greek philosophy (Diogenes) as well as to the Enlightenment (Kant, among many others). However, there is a 'new cosmopolitanism' in the air since, through criticism, the concept has been rediscovered and reinvented. Since the late 1990s there has been a sharp increase in literature that attempts to relate discourse on globalization (in cultural and political terms) to a redefinition of cosmopolitanism for the global age.

For this reason it is worth pointing out that etymologically, cosmopolitan is a combination of 'cosmos' and 'polis'. Thus 'cosmopolitanism', interestingly enough, relates to a premodern ambivalence towards a dual identity and a dual loyalty. Every human being is rooted (*beheimatet*) by birth in two worlds, in two communities: in the cosmos (namely, nature) and in the polis (namely, the city/state). To be more precise, every individual is rooted in one cosmos, but simultaneously in different cities, territories, ethnicities, hierarchies, nations, religions, and so on. This is not an exclusive but rather an inclusive plural membership (*Heimaten*). Being part of the cosmos – nature – all men (and even all women) are equal; yet being part of different states organized into territorial units (polis), men are different (bearing in mind that women and slaves are excluded from the polis). Leaving aside for one moment the issue of women and slaves, 'cosmopolitanism' at its root includes what was separated by the logic of exclusion later on.

'Cosmopolitan' ignores the either/or principle and embodies '*Sowohl-als-auch* thinking', the 'this-as-well-as-that' principle. This is an ancient 'hybrid', 'mélange', 'scape', 'flow' concept that is even more structured than the new offshoots of globalization discourse. Thus cosmopolitanism generates a logic of non-exclusive oppositions, making 'patriots' of two worlds that are simultaneously equal and different.

What makes cosmopolitanism so interesting for social theory of 'second' modern societies is its thinking and living in terms of inclusive oppositions. Nature is associated with society, the object is part of subjectivity, otherness of the other is included in one's own self-identity and self-definition, and the logic of exclusive oppositions is rejected. Nature is no longer separated from national or international society, either as a subject or as an object; 'We' are not opposed to 'Them'. This was the dominant mode of social and political theorizing and political action in the first modern nation-state societies and sociologies.

Kant defined cosmopolitanism as a way of combining the universal and the particular, *Nation und Weltbürger* – nation and world citizenship. As regards the concept of 'globality' (see Robertson 1992; Albrow 1996), cosmopolitanism signifies *rooted* cosmopolitanism, having 'roots' and 'wings' at the same time. This definition also casts aside the dominant opposition between cosmopolitans and locals, since there is no cosmopolitanism without localism.

In the social sciences, methodological cosmopolitanism is opposed to methodological nationalism; that is, it rejects the state-centristic perspective and sociological (lack of) imagination. It attempts to overcome the naive universalism of early Western sociology (which has nevertheless been quite productive in creating Eurocentric sociological frames of reference, which up to now have defined global realities very powerfully). Methodological cosmopolitanism implies becoming sensitive and open to the many universalisms, the conflicting contextual universalisms, for example, of the postcolonial experience, critique and imagination. Methodological cosmopolitanism also means including other ('native') sociologies – the sociologies of and about African, Asian and South American experiences of 'entangled modernities' (Randeria 2002) in the European perspective. 'Entangled modernities' replaces the dualism of the modern and the traditional, pointing to and again creating the image of a deterritorialized mélange of conflicting contextual modernities in their economic, cultural and political dimensions. This, of course, does not answer the basic question; namely, is 'cosmopolitanism' a cosy word for Americanization and the new economic imperialism?

17

Nationality, Internationality, Transnationality

Any discussion of Americanization should include the question of what, or who, or where, is 'America'. The Latin-Americanization of the world would mean something completely different. It is odd, to say the least, that this difference should be overlooked by the same people who decry Americanization. Even if we are more precise, and refer to the US-Americanization of the world, a more thorny issue remains. Do we have a firm grasp of what it means to be 'US-American'? Or is the USA yet another country that has been cosmopolitanized from within? If so, what impact does this have for a framework using this as a model?

Anthropologist Louisa Schein has suggested one plausible response (1998). She examined a Hmong Symposium held in St Paul, Minnesota, a city located in the north of the United States, near the Canadian border. There are approximately 25 million Hmong scattered throughout the world, and the Congress was festooned with flags. There were four on one side of the table (China, the USA, Vietnam and Canada) and five on the other (Argentina, Australia, France, Thailand and Laos). Schein's original goal was to see how the attempt to form a transnational Hmong identity would be affected by the rivalry between the United States and China.

To understand her analysis, we need to make a distinction between nationality and internationality, on the one hand, and transnationality and cosmopolitanism on the other. Nationality and internationality are not opposed to one another. On the contrary, they presuppose each other. A single nation, whose borders and sovereignty are not recognized by other nations, is just as inconceivable as a global nation state. Neither of them has the unity that defines a nation state. One lacks it from the outside, the other from within. Nations can only exist in the plural. Internationality makes nationality possible. They are two sides of the same state system.

Transnationality and cosmopolitanism, on the other hand, undermine this system and presage a Copernican revolution in both political thinking and social theory. Let me explain what I mean briefly in terms of Kant. Kant believed that powerful cosmopolitan sentiments would emerge in eighteenth-century Europe from the universalization of commerce and the dissemination of republican principles. When cosmopolitan sentiments became strong enough to cancel out the tendency of states to act as self-regarding autonomous units, all individuals would be seen 'as though' they were co-legislators in a single moral community. Kant assumed, to put it in Habermasian terms, that the decisive political inspiration of future centuries would be the development of a universal communication community. The Eurocentrism that discolours

18

Kant's universalism makes it look somewhat antiquated in light of postmodern and postcolonial critiques. However, part of his reasoning is still timely; namely his theorizing of the ways in which cultural and political communities could be shaped to achieve higher levels of respect for cultural difference.

Thus nationality excludes and transnationality includes the national Other – in terms of both political philosophy and experience. Transnationality refers to a revolution in loyalties. From a transnational perspective, national societies exclude along three axes (see Linklater 1998). The first is what Walzer (1983) calls the 'distribution of membership', the principles that determine who belongs and who does not. The second is what Aihwa Ong (1999) calls 'flexible citizenship' – living under conditions of transnationality, who defines the notion of individual rights? The third axis concerns the distribution of responsibilities and identities across national borders. Natan Sznaider addressed this issue in the *Süddeutsche Zeitung* (October 2001) when he asked why the television picture of the murder of the Palestinian boy Muhammed Al-Durrah in the arms of his father did not set off a politics of compassion among the Israeli public.

To sum up, what is transnationality? It is a general term for ways of life and responsibility that replace the national 'either/or' with a multinational 'this as well as that'.[1] To come back to Louisa Schein's analysis, this is precisely the goal set by the Hmong, who wanted to strengthen and elevate their group identity above the differences imposed by living in different nation states. Schein's question was how much room there would be for such an attempt amid the great power rivalry of China and the USA. Wouldn't national interests end up dominating the proceedings, as they did in similar cases during the Cold War? The surprising finding was that exactly the opposite emerged. Rather than using the conference as a means of furthering national interests, China and the USA both used this Asian diaspora to redefine their own national identities. To put it differently, both states decided that transnationality served their interests. For the Chinese, supporting the aims of the conference was a way of displaying their openness, which furthered their aim of increasing their economic interdependence with the West. For the USA, the conference was both a means of celebrating a globalization that it considers one of its greatest successes, and emphasizing that 'the America dream' was also an Asian one. This oft-mentioned American dream – the idea of a place where immigrants can come and be at home – may be more of an ideal than a reality. When set in the context of modern communications and transportation, where immigrants can keep in constant touch with their compatriots around the world, it turns into a radically transnational ideal and practice.

1 In Beck 1997, I elaborate on this distinction between 'the age of either/or' and 'the age of "and"'.

If there is a US-Americanization of Asia and Europe, is there also an Asiatization of the USA? Or at least can we examine how the deterritorialization of Asian identities is changing the core of US identity? For that matter, didn't the US-Americanization of Europe grow out of the Europeanization of America? When the USA liberated Europe from Nazism, did it Americanize Germany, or Europeanize it? Isn't America everywhere – and therefore nowhere specific? Hasn't Americanization as a strategy transformed itself into an uncoordinated and unconscious self-cosmopolitanization of the world? Isn't the alternative everywhere; namely, the cosmopolitanization of the nation and the state which is contradicted by national structures and (ethnic) national consciousness, a very dangerous situation?

These are the sorts of questions that grow out of a cosmopolitan perspective. All of our existing political categories presume the nation state as the ultimate political reality, and this methodological nationalism is clearly at work in our conviction that the way to clarify any mixture is to segregate out which nation is the influencer and which one is influenced. In cases like these, however, such analyses produce nonsense. They separate influences that make more sense together. The world is generating a growing number of such mixed cases, which make less sense according to the 'either/or' logic of nationality than to the 'this-as-well-as-that' logic of transnationality. Our intellectual frames of reference are so deeply ingrained that this transnational way of thinking has been comparatively undeveloped.

Another feature that Schein's study of the Hmong conference makes clear is that these two paradigms – nationality/internationality on the one hand and transnationality on the other – are not mutually exclusive. We already know, of course, that cosmopolitanization acts pervasively behind the façade of nationality. The extension of state power into the realm of the transnational has caused a further redefinition of the nation. This is especially clear in Europe, where many politicians play a double game, building transnational institutions at the same time as they stage pageants of national power and togetherness.

This lack of mutual exclusiveness does nothing to alter the fact that transnationality undermines the naturalness of ethnicity, both at the level of the nation state and at the level of cultural identity. It is precisely this feature that can make room for an immigration policy that goes beyond the ideal of integration. Noble as it is, integration still turns on the logic of either/or. Groucho Marx once joked that he refused to belong to any club that would accept him as a member. A cosmopolitan immigration policy might reverse the phrase and say 'Foreigners who just want to be like us we don't need'.

Cosmopolitanization

Second Modernity is characterized by ways of life that scramble the one-to-one correspondence that once existed between language, birthplace, citizenship, nationality and physical appearance. There are now pluralistic and multi-ethnic complexes combining elements that would formerly have been kept apart by national and cultural barriers. Indiscriminate mixing of national identities is no longer a nationalist nightmare or a utopian dream. It is an everyday fact and a trend that will increase. This was the initial definition of cosmopolitanization: inner globalization, globalization from within – the blurring, through migration, telecommunications and transport, of the foundations of nationhood. The root cause is competition in a world market, especially in a world labour market. The conflicts produced by the resultant clash of incommensurable world-views, and the creativity that arises from trying to synthesize them, has become an everyday feature of the human condition.

There are at least two ways of conceptualizing globalization. On the one hand is what David Held (1995) calls interconnectedness. This view highlights the way in which interdependencies, networks and flows are increasing in the modern world. This view still presumes that national units, which are being interconnected, are the ultimate reality, which is the central principle of what I call 'methodological nationalism'. Cosmopolitanization, on the other hand, which is my own tradition, highlights how far social structures and institutions are becoming transnationalized. The premise here is that the national is ceasing to be the national. Once we take this point of view, we need a systematic distinction between the national manifestation and the cosmopolitan reality of 'global fluids' – the flows of information, symbols, money, education, risks and people.

The British sociologist Michael Billig (1995) has developed the concept of 'banal nationalism'. He means that we are constantly and unconsciously defining and confirming our national identities as we engage in mundane activities. The opposite is true as well. We often experience what could be called 'banal cosmopolitanism'. This seems obvious when we look at pop music or fads, although youth culture is tricky. As John Tomlinson (1999) has done, let us look at something more central to existence: food. Is it even possible to eat nationally nowadays? From yoghurt to meat to fruit – and let's not even talk about the global mishmash that is *Wurst* – our consumption is the consummation of a global process of production. The workers of the world may not yet be united but their food certainly is. Foods now found side by side at the neighbourhood supermarket used to be separated by great distances. This is banal cosmopolitanism in a nutshell. It is the expression and the means of an everyday culinary eclecticism that is celebrated in cookbooks and treated as the most normal thing in the world on TV cooking programmes. Here world society comes into the kitchen and literally melts in the pot. Anyone who wants to hoist the national flag over the kitchen table is going to have to plant it on the existence of national dishes which are, in any case, being constantly reinvented. These are clearly only islands in the broad stream of banal cosmopolitanism, and this example could be multiplied a thousandfold.

A common objection to all this is that many people are sedentary, and they are therefore untouched by the process of cosmopolitanization. As John Tomlinson (1999) and John Urry (2000) have shown so well, staying at home is becoming yet another way of getting around. Television is only one example. The word means to see things far away: television abolishes distance and sees through walls. Movie stars, senators and the folks from the local bar, drug lords, porn queens and the president of the United States – all of them visit our living room whenever we turn on the TV. An everyday life in which television plays an integral part – and perhaps soon one into which the Internet will be just as integrated – is not one in which walls or physical distance do much to separate a person, even a sedentary one. In a sense, all individual monads occupy simultaneously the same undivided space, consuming the news of the world together. When this goes on long enough, our acquaintances from the news start to become part of our lives, like spirits haunting a house. In the end, even immobile individuals, by virtue of occupying the same simultaneous global present, become like Leibnizian monads, in whom the complexity of the world is reflected.

Banal nationalism is being constantly eroded by this torrent of banal cosmopolitanism. This process of inner globalization is exemplified perhaps most surprisingly in military organization. It is difficult to criticize people whose first instinct is to view NATO's current attempts at cosmopolitan renewal with distrust. After all, we all know that each country treats its national security apparatus as though it were a holy of holies. Yet the leadership of NATO really is pushing forward the process of denationalization. A particularly striking case is the transnationalization of production of weapons such as the Panzer, new warplanes and transport carriers, new information systems, and so on. This means sharing weapons secrets, although it was only a decade ago that secret weapons were the national analogues of sacred relics, things that sanctified the border-barriers that preserved them. These are rapidly turning into their opposite and no one seems to think it worthy of comment. The result is that national security and national power have come to depend on international cooperation. National sovereignty itself has had to become transnational in order to preserve itself.

The main conclusion to be drawn from all these examples of banal cosmopolitanism is that the experiential space and horizon[2] that distinguished First Modernity – that of national societies bounded off from one other, each distinguished by its own language, identity and politics – are rapidly becoming a myth. Precisely those institutions that were thought to best define the nation are becoming progressively more transnational and cosmopolitan. That means that our most basic categories for understanding the social world will have to be altered.

Society and politics are shedding their national form even while the new organizational forms of the cosmopolitical are still struggling to be born. From this ontological change must follow an epistemological one. However, we must not fall from one fallacy into its opposite, from an imagined homogeneity of the nation state to an imagined homogeneity of cosmopolitanism. Empirically the process of inner cosmopolitanization appears to run up against quite obvious limits. On the one hand, a transnational space and horizon of experience have entered the seemingly closed confines of the nation state and recentred social life. On the other hand, social acts are still given tangible shape by the institutions of the nation state through such ordinary things as passports, labour markets, migration policies, and political parties. To the extent that people are aware of denationalization, many have reacted to its strangeness with fear and xenophobia (as is the case currently in Germany, but not only there). The resulting situation is thus highly contradictory. The decisive question may be whether this subterranean cosmopolitanization will finally become something people become conscious of and support, or whether it will only set off national reflexes. Regardless, let us turn to a more technical question. Why is this process better understood as banal cosmopolitanization, rather than as banal Americanization, banal multiculturalism or banal universalism?

Universalism and Cosmopolitanism

The question that really distinguishes one doctrine from another is where they stand on the otherness of the other. The answer seems simple enough: cosmopolitanism affirms it; neo-liberalism, globalization and Americanization deny it. In fact this simple answer will take a while to dissect.

Discourse on modernization and development has come in for a lot of criticism, especially from thinkers in the Third World. Several writers, above all postcolonialists, have shown that the doctrine of universal values is honeycombed with interpretations that regulate how Europeans are supposed to

2 R. Kosselleck makes a systematic distinction between these two concepts in his book *Vergangene Zukunft* [*Futures Past*] (1989).

conduct themselves towards people defined, in cultural terms, as the Other. The discovery of 'humanity' as an empirically redeemable social entity occurred historically at the same time as the discovery of 'savages'. Barely had the progress of navigation and trade brought forth the promise of a world society – what Jean Bodin called *res publica mundana* – than the genus humanum began to be divided according to the dictum that 'equal' means 'of equal worth' and 'different' implies 'of lesser worth'.

My thesis, which owes a lot to my reading of the postcolonialists, is that the production of knowledge about the Other is a necessary preparation for, and an invariable accompaniment to, colonial rule. From this perspective, the European doctrine of universally valid claims is, still today, a strategy of power. Every concept of modernization implies a traditionalism against which it can be measured, and every assertion that modernization is good entails a claim that the traditionalism it is replacing is worse. In this context, claiming that modern science and modern economics are value-free approaches to universally valid knowledge, while at the same time identifying these approaches with modern society, amounts to elevating the assertion that traditional societies are inferior into an indisputable dogma. In this sense, the discursive strategies of the present differ only in their sophistication from those of 500 years ago, despite the fact that the institutional landscape has changed entirely.

The Finnish political scientist Teivo Tievainen (1999) discusses in detail a conference held in 1550 in Valladolid to determine an answer to the question of whether Indians were different from, and therefore of lesser worth than, Europeans. He points out that there are interesting parallels between the positions staked out there and the postulates that guide the IMF and the WTO. In Valladolid the two main positions were represented by Bartolome de Las Casas, a Dominican priest who devoted most of his life to the cause of the Indians, and the Aristotelian philosopher Juan Ginés de Sepúlvida. Tzvetan Todorov (1984) argued that the polarity expressed there between Civilization and its Other has defined European thinking ever since. The philosopher started from the assumption that society is naturally hierarchical. The priest started from the assumption that all men are naturally equal. The former emphasized the differences between Spaniards and Indians – for example, that the latter ran around naked, made human sacrifices and had never heard of money or Christianity or beasts of burden. From this the philosopher deduced a great chain of humanity whose 'links' were living on different cultural levels. In this scheme, it seemed obvious that different meant lesser. Two consequences arose from this position. In the first place, the differences between barbarians and Europeans seemed to Sepúlvida to be not only as great as the distance between Europeans and God, but similarly ordained. Given this, the role of education was to make the natives understand that they served God's will by serving the higher societies – in other words, to reconcile them to their exploitation and repression.

The Dominican priest was eloquent in his defence of the Indians. He argued that the Indians were like the Europeans in surprising ways. They lived up to the ideals of the Christian religion, which makes no distinctions based on skin colour or place of birth. He said that the Indians were friendly and modest, and obeyed the rules that should regulate relations between societies. They cared about their families and their traditions. He summed up by saying that, taken as a whole, the Indians were if anything better suited than most other societies to hear the word of God and to put his teachings into practice. For the priest, the Indians were no different in essence from Europeans, and therefore of no less worth.

Since that time, both the racism of the philosopher and the progressivism of the priest have been subjected to many critiques. From a cosmopolitan viewpoint, the most interesting thing is what they have in common. Neither of them entertained the possibility that the Indians could be both different and of equal worth. Thus both positions presuppose a universal scale of values that necessarily transmutes difference into superior/inferior. Even good Father Las Casas only accepts the equality of the Indians because they are capable in his eyes of accepting the universal truth of Christianity. He believes that the split between Christians and heathens can be resolved because it can be overcome. The barbarians can be baptized, and then they can partake of true religion. This is not that far from saying that 'underdeveloped countries' and 'traditional societies' can be 'modernized' – that they can be baptized in the truth of democracy and market economics, and thereby achieve salvation through Western universalism.

There are two sorts of power at work here. In the first place, when universalism identifies difference with lesser value and similarity with equal value, history shows that in the end this is used to justify physical force. In the second place, the missionary perspective that is still present in concepts such as 'modernization' and 'development policy' makes a pedagogical goal out of justifying authority. It was this pedagogical aspect that Gramsci had in mind when he wrote that hegemony was always justified in part through the educational process, and that this was not only true for domestic authority, but also between nations and between world cultures. Michel Foucault (1982) called this the 'ritual of truth'. It grows out of the duty to normalize the truth: to deny the otherness of the Other, and to convert the latter to the universal truth – which Europe and the USA just happen to possess.

It is worth highlighting that both of the Valladolid positions – that humanity is divided into a hierarchy of different races of different worth, and that humanity is by nature equal – are examples of metaphysical realism. Both take as a fundamental assumption that their characterizations of humanity are ahistorical, and that they are valid for all societies past or future.

I began this section by saying that the core of cosmopolitanism is the recognition of the otherness of the Other. I can now make this proposition more precise. It affirms what both of the Valladolid positions rule out: that the Other is both different and equal. Cosmopolitanism therefore sets itself against both racism and universalism. Cosmopolitanism is the struggle to keep this seemingly timeless racism from enduring into the future. This includes making clear the extent to which the ethnocentric universalism of the West is an anachronism that can be overcome. Cosmopolitanism is an antidote to ethnocentrism and nationalism. It should not be mistaken for multicultural euphoria. On the contrary, cosmopolitanism starts from the hard-won insight that there is an invariable connection between ethnocentrism and the hatred of foreigners, and tries to advance beyond this sort of 'common sense'. For a similar reason, cosmopolitanism is an advance over the concept of 'hybridization', because it avoids the dangers inherent in using biological metaphors for human difference.

Internationality and Transnationality

To summarize, the dualism that lies at the base of cosmopolitanism is conceived in very different ways by the competing conceptual schemes of internationality and transnationality. Between these two ways of thinking a new kind of existence is taking shape. The First Modern world was a national world. There was a clear division between inner and outer, between domestic and foreign. In that world, the nation state was the principle of order. Politics were national politics, culture was national culture, labour, class formation and class conflict were all primarily features of the nation state. International politics was a multiplication of nation states, each defining one another's borders and mirroring one another's essential categories. National and international were two sides of an interdependent whole. It was as impossible to conceive of a nation state in isolation as to imagine an inner without an outer. This social ontology defined territories, defined identities, and largely defined history as the clash of national projects, much of it bloody.

The reality of transnationality is quietly turning this entire structure of meaning inside out. When we examine the world from a transnational perspective, it is obvious that national and international are becoming harder and harder to distinguish. The defining parts of the nation are becoming denationalized. The national is becoming a zombie-category – an example of the living dead. Up to now, our political coordinates have mapped everything onto national space and time. The dissolution of these coordinates justifies describing this as the beginning of a new era. First Modernity was national modernity. Second Modernity is transnational or cosmopolitan modernity. Second Modernity is when society ceases to be a synonym for the nation state, and when all social development – economic, cultural, political and techno-logical – becomes first and fundamentally transnational. As more process shows less regard for state boundaries – people shop transnationally, love trans-nationally, are educated transnationally (that is bilingually), live transnation-ally (that is combine multiple loyalties and identities) – the paradigm of societies organized within the framework of the nation state loses touch with reality.

At this point I should caution against a possible cosmopolitan fallacy. The fundamental fact that the experiential space of the individual no longer coincides with that of the nation may give the impression that we are all going to become cosmopolitans. However, cosmopolitanization does not automatic-ally produce cosmopolitan sentiments. It can just as naturally give rise to the opposite, to the rebirth of ethnic nationalism, the rise of the Ugly Citizen. This can happen at the same time as cultural horizons are expanding and sensitivity to different lifestyles is growing; neither of these things necessarily increases the feeling of cosmopolitan responsibility. To study cosmopolitanization is to study a dialectic of conflict between cosmopolitanization and its enemies.

Thus the opposition between transnational and international is neither logically nor temporally exclusive. Instead there is an uneasy coexistence be-tween the two realities and the two ways of thinking. Furthermore, their com-bination is not a zero-sum game. It is possible for both to wax simultaneously. It is during this transitional period that rooted cosmopolitanism emerges.

Rooted cosmopolitanism is defined against the two extremes of being at home everywhere and being at home nowhere. It refers, as Roland Robertson (1992) and John Tomlinson (1999) argue, to an 'ethical glocalism'; that is, to be engaged in the local and the global at the same time. It is opposed to ethno-centrism but also to universalism, whether from the left or the right. Familiar with the violent realities that grow out of mutually exclusive certainties, it is suspicious of the false euphoria and the covert essentialism of multiculturalism. When it comes to the critique of imperialism, rooted cosmopolitanism points out that in a postcolonial world there is no pure, pre-colonized nation to go back to. The only way forward is into a cosmopolitan world beyond both nationalism and imperialism.

The situation is similar with regard to struggles over class, gender, ethnicity and sexual preference. All of these started as national struggles, but all have overflowed and networked beyond the boundaries of the nation state. The cosmopolitanization of social movements is one of the most striking

27

developments in recent years. It also seems clear that these movements now embody claims and conflicts that make more sense when understood in transnational terms – not least of all because a cosmopolitan perspective is the only thing that preserves them from falling back into postmodern ethnocentrism and ethnic nationalism.

These are the realities that challenge modern thought. How can the social sciences – sociology, political science, history, anthropology and geography – elevate themselves beyond the national viewpoint, overcome their methodological nationalism and develop a cosmopolitan perspective? What does a cosmopolitan social science look like? What will it mean to cosmopolitanize all of our basic concepts and methods of comparison? And how can we carry out social, historical and political analysis on this new basis?[3]

References

Albrow, Martin (1996), *The Global Age: State and Society beyond Modernity*. Cambridge: Polity Press.

Beck, Ulrich (1997), *The Reinvention of Politics: Rethinking Modernity in the Global Social Order*. Cambridge: Polity Press.

— (2000a), *What is Globalization?* Cambridge: Polity Press.

— (2000b), 'The Cosmopolitan Perspective: Sociology of the Second Age of Modernity', *The British Journal of Sociology* 51(1): 79–106.

— (2000c), *World Risk Society*. Cambridge: Polity Press.

— (2000d), 'The Cosmopolitan Society and its Enemies', Public Lecture, LSE (February).

Beck, Ulrich (in conversation with J. Willms) (2000), *Freiheit oder Kapitalismus – Gesellschaft neu denken*. Frankfurt: Suhrkamp.

Billig, Michael (1995), *Banal Nationalism*. London: Sage Publications.

Bohrer, K. H., and K. Scheel (eds) (2000), *Europa oder Amerika? Zur Zukunft des Westens*, special issue of MERKUR 9–10 (September–October).

Bourdieu, Pierre, and Loïc Wacquart (1999), 'On the Cunning of Imperialist Reason', *Theory, Culture and Society* 16(1): 41–58.

Foucault, Michel (1982), *The Archaeology of Knowledge*. New York: Pantheon.

Held, David (1995), *Democracy and the Global Order*. Cambridge: Polity Press.

Kosselleck, Reinhardt (1989), *Futures Past: On the Semantics of Historical Time*. Cambridge, MA: MIT Press.

Linklater, Andrew (1998), *The Transformation of Political Community*. Cambridge: Polity Press.

Ong, Aihwa (1999), *Flexible Citizenship: The Cultural Logics of Transnationality*. Durham, NC, and London: Duke University Press.

Randeria, Shalini (2002), 'Entangled Histories of Uneven Modernities: Civil Society, Caste Solidarities and Legal Pluralism in Post-Colonial India', in Yehuda Elkanan, Ivan Krastev, Elísio Macamo and Shalini Randeria (eds), *Unravelling Ties: From Social Cohesion to New Practices of Connectedness*. Frankfurt/New York: Campus.

Schein, Louisa (1998), 'Importing Miao Brethren to Hmong America: A Not-So-

---

3 See Beck 2000a, 2000b, 2000c, 2000d; Beck with Willms 2000.

Stateless Transnationalism', in P. Cheah and B. Robbins (eds), *Cosmopolitics – Thinking and Feeling Beyond the Nation*. Minneapolis: University of Minnesota Press: 169–91.

Tievainen, Teivo (1999), 'Globalization of Economic Surveillance, Passages', *Journal of Transnational and Transcultural Studies* 1(1): 84–116.

Todorov, Tzvetan (1984), *The Conquest of America*. New York: Harper & Row.

Tomlinson, John (1999), *Globalization and Culture*. Cambridge: Polity Press.

Urry, John (2000), *Sociology Beyond Societies*. London: Routledge.

Walzer, Michael (1983), *Spheres of Justice: A Defense of Pluralism and Equality*. New York: Basic Books.

CHAPTER 2

Assessing McDonaldization, Americanization and Globalization

George Ritzer and Todd Stillman

The Globalization Debate

New or changing cultural phenomena ignite competition among traditions of social theory. These contests often result in a plurality of descriptions of the defining characteristics of the contemporary scene. Most recently, contending perspectives on the globalization debate have emerged and seem unresolvable. The macro-phenomenology of globalization has had tremendous contemporary resonance.[1] *Globalization* is a fully fledged buzzword, referring, as often as not, to the blending of cultures in the global marketplace and in the transnational media.[2] The idea of *McDonaldization* has also had a profound cultural resonance. Students, activists and the general public (not to mention social thinkers: see Smart 1999; Alfino et al. 1998) have found the idea of McDonaldization useful for describing everything from religion (Drane 2000) to the university (Parker and Jary 1995) to museums (Kirchberg 2000). Finally, the idea of Americanization has mobilized debate and resistance in Europe, Asia and South America (Kuisel 1993). In this essay, we discuss the relationships among these three perspectives and analyse the degree to which they can be integrated.

The ideas of McDonaldization and Americanization are at odds, to some degree, with the characterizations of globalization that have the greatest cachet today. There is a gulf between those who see the consequence of global capitalism as an increasingly Americanized and/or rationalized world and those who

---

1 This tendency is counterbalanced by a pronounced strain of realist political and economic analysis (see, for example, Chase-Dunn 1989).
2 'Globalization' also refers to the increasing power of capitalism – bolstered by neo-liberal economic policy – on the world scene. It can also refer to the growth of transnational governance. In this essay, however, we focus on the culture of globalization.

prefer a characterization of contemporary society as pluralistic and indeterminate, in which rationalization and American culture are only two trends among many. At the risk of being reductive, this divide amounts to a difference between a vision of a world that is becoming increasingly American, rationalized, codified and restricted and a vision of the world as ever more diverse, effervescent and free.

The three concepts are rooted in competing visions of modernity. Specifically, McDonaldization is reminiscent of a top-down, 'iron cage' version of modern social theory. With roots in the Weberian tradition, it asserts the progressive sway of rationalized structural constraints over agents, especially in the sphere of consumption. Americanization is cousin to a neo-Marxian conception of economic imperialism and cultural hegemony. This perspective asserts that America's aggressive exporting of media and commodities amounts to a crypto-imperialist attack on national sovereignties. Finally, most of globalization theory embraces the postmodern emphasis on diversity, hybridity, velocity and agency. Citizenship, tradition, and status hierarchies each decline in relative importance to the ability of the individual to fashion a self from a bricolage of commodities and media.

Initiating a dialogue of theory integration, we draw some lessons from the globalization literature for understanding McDonaldization and Americanization. George Ritzer has already argued that an appreciation of the extent of McDonaldization can expand our understanding of globalization (Ritzer 1998; Ritzer and Malone 2000). This essay will show how the insights of globalization can provide new insights into the diffusion of McDonaldization. A second task is to uncouple McDonaldization from Americanization by underscoring the Weberian roots of the former and the Marxian heritage of the latter. Such an undertaking can only be partly successful: at this point in history, McDonaldization and Americanization go hand in hand. Third, we contrast the globalization perspective with the Americanization perspective. Finally, we propose a hierarchical model of the relationships among McDonaldization, Americanization and globalization.

Globalization

Globalization most often refers to the growth of transnational politics, the integration of the world economy, and a subsequent blending of cultures around the world. While there might be remote areas still untouched by free trade, television, or migration, the scope of globalization's impact is by definition global. There are few regions of the world unaffected by the global flows of investment, tourists, pollution, people, crime, and so on. The thrust of globalization theory suggests that global forces will eventually influence even the most remote 'corners' of the globe. The rainforests of South America, to name a seemingly improbable example, have already become a tourist destination, a source of natural resources for the lumber and pharmaceutical industries, a centre of migration for people from more populated regions and a key area for drug manufacturing. As the pressure for land increases, rainforest regions will doubtless be further shaped by global influences.

As the primary engine of globalization, capitalism drives the movement of people, the exploitation of resources, the opening of markets, and the diffusion of technology. Capitalism extends commodity chains across the planet in search of the lowest price for labour, the greatest expertise, the cheapest materials, and the largest markets (McMichael 1996). But capitalism has been a globalizing force for centuries (Gunder-Frank 1978; Wallerstein 1974). One novelty of the current experience of globalization is found in technological advances in media and transportation that generate a heightened awareness of the world filtered through the international media and commodity culture (Gray 1998). More people, in more places, watch more Julia Roberts movies, World Cup soccer matches, papal visits, and guerrilla wars than ever before. The international media direct attention to AIDS in sub-Saharan Africa, mad cow disease in Great Britain, human rights abuses in China, the ozone hole over Antarctica, and the ballot counts in Palm Beach. More of the world wears tennis shoes, drinks Coca-Cola, eats pizza and egg rolls, and drives Honda cars.

Much of, but not all, the world imbibes the spirit, to say nothing of the products, of globalization. Manuel Castells (1996) reminds us that the experience of globalization is divided between cosmopolitans, who are in a position to partake of the experience of globalization, and provincials, who are either ignored or exploited. Those most disposed to take advantage of the fruits of globalization live in core urban areas and work in the new economy, but others – workers, military personnel, students – also experience globalization at first hand.

What does globalization mean for those who experience it? Commentators have asserted that globalization, above all, creates cultural possibilities that might have been impossible in the modern era when state, economy, culture and people were more tightly aligned. The effect of globalization is to increase the number of choices for actors to the extent that '[m]ultiple identities and the decentering of the social subject are grounded in the ability of individuals to avail themselves of several organizational options at the same time' (Nederveen Pieterse 1995: 52). In other words, globalization generates a host of new organizational forms that increase the options for local actors, rather than damaging or displacing traditional forms. Reasoning along this line, some observers have concluded that global culture is additive to local culture. By this logic, actors throughout the world effectively become bi- or poly-cultural.

The idea of globalization has spawned more than its share of theory. Thomas Friedman (1999) sees globalization as the dreamed-of opportunity for economic development and political liberalization for 'backward' peoples around the world. Postcolonial scholars smell crypto-imperialist motives in the exploitation of subaltern labour markets and natural resources (Antonio and Bonanno 2000). Arjun Appadurai (1996) sees globalization as the unravelling of the quintessential modern project of nation-building, undermined by a myriad hybrid identities and cultures.

The question becomes 'which globalization?' The answer, according to Roland Robertson (1992), is that globalization deserves to be considered in terms of the intellectual and practical terrain on which actors draw their conclusions about globalization, thereby leaving open the possibility of multiple images of globalization. From our perspective, Robertson is right to acknowledge the variety of images of world order with resonance in contemporary society. Yet, despite the wide variety of theory on globalization, it is possible to distill a few key propositions concerning contemporary global culture:

- The world is more pluralistic than the hegemonic world-views of modern social theory had previously allowed. Globalization theory is exceptionally sensitive to differences within and between its analytic categories.
- Individuals have more power to adapt, innovate and manoeuvre within a globalized world than the top-down perspectives of modern social theory had previously allowed. Globalization theory takes individuals into account as self-creating agents.
- Social processes are relational and contingent. Cultural globalization provokes a variety of reactions – ranging from nationalist entrenchment to cosmopolitan embrace – that feed back on and transform globalization.
- The key cultural changes of the late twentieth century are the increasing commodification of social life and the increasing velocity and centrality of media. Commodities and media became the material of self-creation as well as legitimate objects of social scientific inquiry.

McDonaldization at Large

McDonaldization is also a new process although it has, as we learn from Weber, deep roots in the historical process of rationalization. McDonaldization has a profound effect on the way individuals experience their world. The term describes the rationalization of society – the places and spaces where people live, work and consume – using the fast-food restaurant as a paradigm. The process is a direct consequence of the ascendance of four related processes: a push for greater efficiency, predictability, calculability, and replacement of human with non-human technology (Ritzer 2000a). McDonaldized venues, then, emphasize standardized products and quantity over quality. These practices and values give McDonaldization a competitive advantage over other models of organization; they make it possible to manage large numbers of people (be they employees or customers) in an efficient way. A fifth consequence of McDonaldization is the irrationality of rationality; that is, its principles tend, among other things, to devalue consumers and workers.

While its roots are in the (fast-) food industry, McDonaldization implies much more than changes in cuisine. For example, hotels/motels with a local flavour and flair tend to disappear, to be replaced by McDonaldized chains like Holiday Inn. In the system of higher education, colleges and universities tend to lose their distinctive local characteristics as they all increasingly converge on the model of McUniversities. Much the same could be said about political campaigns that everywhere come to be dominated by polling, media ads, sound bites, and the like. Thus, McDonaldization is occurring not only across the landscape of consumption but also across a broad range of social settings.

The McDonaldization thesis asserts that rationalized systems are penetrating throughout social life, thereby fundamentally changing the way people work, consume and interact in a wide variety of settings. Although rationalization has been a compelling fact of modern life for a very long time, its newest incarnation – McDonaldization – has made great inroads into consumer culture both in America and abroad since the 1960s. Internationally, McDonald's has 30,000 branches in 130 countries today – up from 3,000 in 1990. This says nothing about the success of the McDonaldization *model*, which has diffused through other successful American fast-food chains (KFC, Pizza Hut) as well as through indigenous versions of McDonaldized means of consumption (for example, Russkoye Bistro in Russia, Nirulas in India). This worldwide growth has had an undeniable effect on traditional ways of life, often to the detriment of local practices, and its influence is likely to increase in the future as more people become more habituated to efficient and predictable settings. Yet many areas of the world have not been McDonaldized. They continue to use more traditional, or less rationalized, means of consumption, modes of production, and ways of interacting. While one can predict a long-term trend towards increasing McDonaldization in these areas, it may be a very long time before many of them see even the first signs of this process.

What is clear, nevertheless, is that McDonaldization deserves a place in any thoroughgoing account of globalization. There can be little doubt that the logic of McDonaldization generates a set of values and practices that have a competitive advantage over other means of consumption. The McDonaldization model is not only more efficient; it also reproduces more easily than other models of consumption. The success of McDonaldization in the USA over the past half century, coupled with the international ambitions of McDonald's and its ilk, as well as indigenous clones, strongly suggest that McDonaldization will continue to make inroads into the global marketplace not only through the efforts of existing corporations but also via the diffusion of the paradigm. Fast, cheap and clean is a winning recipe that is, and will be, widely imitated.

It should be noted, however, that competitive advantage through efficient production and service does not equate with an insurmountable competitive advantage. There are limitations to McDonaldization based on the desires and expectations of consumers. On the one hand, McDonaldization keeps costs low, allowing McDonaldized businesses to extract profit from a broader base of consumers. A three-dollar lunch at a fast-food restaurant is within the means of many who cannot afford to eat steak at finer restaurants. On the other hand, this base of consumers is limited by the fact that some consumers who can afford fast food still choose to eat it only occasionally or not at all. They may find that efficient eating cannot satisfy all (substantively rational) reasons for eating or they may simply find fast food distasteful. For this reason, the rise of fast food has not diminished the popularity of traditional-style, full-service restaurants in the USA (Nelson 2001).

Americanization

Americanization can be defined as a powerful one-directional process that tends to overwhelm competing processes (e.g. Japanization) as well as the strength of local forces that might resist, modify and/or transform American models into hybrid forms. Moreover, the notion of Americanization is tied to a particular nation – the USA – but it has a differential impact on many specific nations.

Americanization is inclusive of McDonaldization to some degree, but it also includes other forms of American cultural, political and economic imperialism. We can capture under the heading of Americanization the worldwide diffusion of the American industrial model in the post-Second World War era; the worldwide diffusion of the American consumption model in the 1990s; the marketing of American media, including Hollywood film, popular music and NBA basketball, abroad; the marketing of American commodities, including cola, blue jeans and computer operating systems, abroad; extensive diplomatic and military engagement with Europe, Asia and South America, including

Table 1: Attributes of globalization, Americanization and McDonaldization

	Globalization	Americanization	McDonaldization
Definition	'[T]he compression of the world and the intensification of consciousness of the world as a whole' (Robertson 1992: 8).	The propagation of American ideas, customs, social patterns, industry and capital around the world (Williams 1962).	'[T]he process by which the principles of the fast food restaurant are coming to dominate more and more sectors of American society as well as the rest of the world' (Ritzer 2000a: 1).
Vision of the World	Multi-directional circulation of persons, information, resources and commodities.	American exploit-ation of world markets and resources.	Emphasis on efficiency, predictability, calculability, and the replacement of human with non-human technology.
Economy	Extension and intensification of world trade.	Dominance of the American industrial model. Hegemony of American corporate interests.	Diffusion of rationalized models in service and production. Increasing control and dehumani-zation of workers and consumers.
Politics	Growth of trans-national governance and social move-ments.	Increasing unilateral political action by the USA and its allies.	State activity based on cost–benefit analyses. Political engagement increasingly routinized – McCitizens (Turner 1999).
Culture	Increasing oppor-tunities for self-transformation and bricolage.	Dominance of American consumer and media culture on the world scene.	Consumer culture, especially, but also religion, education, justice and health care, become subject to standardization.

efforts to support democratization; the training of military, political and scientific elites in American universities; and the development and use of the international labour market and natural resources by American corporations.

The reach of Americanization is great. Take the case of one aspect of Ameri-canization: the global reach of Hollywood films. [The American film industry has overpowered many national film industries in Europe and elsewhere, to the detriment of national artistic expression] The blockbuster films of Julia Roberts and Harrison Ford not only flow through an official distribution system, but they are also pirated and sold on the streets of Third World cities. While several nations, including India and China, continue to produce large numbers of commercial films, even in these countries, American films are also often featured on the marquee. Similarly, many films that are less successful in America find a global market, and this can hold true for art films as well as action movies (Kael 1985). The result is not simply a general familiarity with American cultural products (the sort of secondary identity described by Nederveen Pieterse); American films have stifled other national cinemas.

Yet this is only one part of the problem with contemporary cinema. The other side of the equation is that the grammars of other national cinemas are being transformed for American distribution. The Chinese, for example, have bemoaned the fact that their leading directors (including Zhang Yimo and Chen Kaige) make films that exoticize (or in Said's [1978] terms 'orientalize') Chinese culture and history for Western audiences. The most recent example is Ang Lee's *Crouching Tiger, Hidden Dragon*, which won many international prizes, but reportedly was unsuccessful in mainland China. In short, Chinese films are being tailored to American sensibilities in order to gain prestige and sales. As a result, American film culture in some sense has become world film culture. This is not to say that American cinema is not subject to diverse interpretations depending on the cultural context in which it is viewed, but only to suggest that American cultural artefacts are an increasingly central element of global culture.

McDonaldization and the Lessons of Globalization Theory

The McDonaldization thesis is, in some ways, the antithesis of the global culture perspective. Globalization theory, as we have seen, tends to subscribe to an increasingly pluralistic view of the world. As we noted above, the globalization perspective envisions, among other things, an increasing variety of organizational options. But McDonaldization is chiefly a homogenizing process. It tends to reduce diversity in the means of consumption insofar as they are incompatible with efficiency, predictability, calculability and the replacement of human with non-human technology. Thus, a McDonaldized society tends towards 'organizational isomorphism' (DiMaggio and Powell 1983). DiMaggio and Powell argue that three related processes make competing organizational structures look more and more similar. First, organizations are coerced by cultural expectations. Second, organizations tend to model themselves on other organizations in an environment of 'symbolic uncertainty'. Third, the process of professionalization develops formal credentialling systems that generate strong norms among managers. An additional process that DiMaggio and Powell exclude from their account, but which plays an important role in McDonaldization, is the competitive advantage that rationalized systems have over other contending models of organization.

In the current transnational milieu, all four processes contribute to a general convergence of organizations around the McDonaldized model. Here cultural expectations, imitation, managerial norms and competitive advantages play out across national borders. In addition, one need only look at the effects of long commodity chains on the spread of McDonaldization. McDonald's virtually requires its suppliers to rationalize their operations (Schlosser 2001). For imitation, it may be that the influx of widely diverse consumer goods and cultural materials creates the symbolic uncertainty that pushes consumers to adhere closely to familiar models. This situation would then enhance the competitive advantages that McDonaldized systems already enjoy. The growing number of international MBA graduates experiencing similar curricula contributes to isomorphism. And finally, but most importantly, McDonaldized systems simply out-do traditional models of organization by lowering labour and training costs.

Conflict between globalization and McDonaldization theory on the relative emphasis of agency is also evident. McDonaldization theory tends to see individuals as manipulated by the formal rationality of a means of consumption; that is, consumers tend to behave in ways in which the model intends them to behave: in the fast-food restaurant they queue in an orderly fashion, eat quickly, and clear their own tables.[3] Globalization theory would emphasize the agency of consumers when they encounter means of consumption.

Yet the cultural perspective on globalization raises important questions about the limits of McDonaldization that cannot be adequately answered in the terms of the latter thesis. How universally does the ideology of McDonaldization penetrate the lives and values of people who operate within and between McDonaldized structures? How thoroughly does McDonaldization change the cultures with which it comes into contact? Is McDonaldization definitive and irreversible or will alternative logics of consumption remain viable (or emerge)? These questions are fundamental to understanding the limits of McDonaldization as a perspective and as a process.

Indeed, if we apply the lessons of globalization theory to McDonaldization, we arrive at such limits. The McDonaldization perspective accords only a limited role to agency, is suspicious of excessive claims of pluralism, and asserts

---

3 For a more nuanced view of consumer behaviour in McDonaldized settings see Ritzer and Ovadia 2001.

the probable continuation, even acceleration, of rationalization within the means of consumption and elsewhere – views that are called into question by globalization theory. Yet the central claim of the perspective – that efficiency, calculability, predictability, and the replacement of human with non-human technology define the structures of the new means of consumption – has not been called into question. The effect of these structures on consumers, the reach of this model across the globe, and the teleological implications of this sort of rationalization theory are secondary considerations. Even if they are essential for understanding how McDonaldization operates on the global scene, they clearly go beyond the project of describing the rationalized contours of the new means of consumption (and elsewhere).

McDonaldization is not a strict analogue of globalization. Globalization theory has a much greater scope than McDonaldization. The concept of globalization is designed to capture the increased interpenetration of global culture across a variety of nations, regions and spheres. While globalization can refer to the influence of McDonaldized means of consumption or American consumer goods on the world scene, it can also capture, say, the influence of Japanese culture on contemporary Asia or the effects of German philosophy on Russian politics.

Despite such differences the McDonaldization thesis can be clarified in the light of globalization theory. McDonaldization is subject to the forces of pluralism in at least three senses. First, when McDonaldized models are exported, they are always subject to a degree of indigenous adaptation (Watson 1997). Second, McDonaldized models can develop indigenously in a process of emulation that tends towards isomorphism. Third, a McDonaldized model can accommodate a variety of ends. One need only consider the diversity of settings that have been McDonaldized to see that this is the case. Thus, while structural diversity in means is increasingly limited, both real and cosmetic diversity of ends persists.

While McDonaldized models may be designed to control agents (consumers), there are limits to the power of the model to control agency. Individuals retain the ability to negotiate the terrain of McDonaldized settings, to make meaning of McDonaldized processes, and to forge identities out of the elements of McDonaldized organizations.

Thus, the power of McDonaldization to homogenize is limited. Reactions to McDonaldization, as well as its unintended consequences, create contingencies that force the constant adaptation of any McDonaldized organization. While the first principles remain constant, McDonaldized organizations are continually adapting and evolving.

McDonaldization and Americanization

McDonald's is an American icon regardless of the analytic distinctions we have employed in this essay. For this reason, in Europe, China and other countries around the world, protesters have attacked McDonald's as a symbol of America and American cultural imperialism (Daley 2000; Watson 2000). In short, McDonald's carries American connotations as both a process and an icon. In terms of the former, it involves the exportation of a particularly American style of organization, service and consumption. For the latter, it serves as the symbol of American economic affluence (and political power) throughout the world.

Fast-food restaurants are emblems of the American way of life. The close association with Americanization has both enabling and constraining effects on the diffusion of McDonaldization. McDonaldized means of consumption can be taken as an exotic import, valued for their novelty by the nouveau riche and the young as a way of asserting a cosmopolitan identity or a high social status. In this regard, McDonald's close association with America probably aids the diffusion of the model by minimizing the tendency for the rationalized model to disenchant consumers (Ritzer 1999). As the novelty wears off, however, McDonaldized means of consumption around the world will need to make efforts to re-enchant their rationalized cores to attract repeat customers. If the experience in the USA is any indication of how this process will progress, we can expect that McDonaldized means of consumption across the globe will capitalize on consumer nostalgia for the worlds they have displaced by creating simulations of local traditions. It will be a poignant irony when, sometime in the future, a McDonaldized setting in Paris or Beijing recreates the ways of eating and living it displaced.

The close association of McDonaldization with Americanization may, in some circumstances, impede the reception of McDonaldized models of consumption. In this scenario, consumers eschew McDonaldized systems not because they find speed, efficiency and predictability particularly disenchanting or distasteful, but rather, because McDonaldization represents cultural imperialism. Such is the case with activists targeting McDonald's restaurants in France, India, and many other countries. So long as the association of McDonaldization with Americanization remains strong, we can expect that efforts to adapt to local practices will be of limited efficacy in areas where anti-American sentiment is strong. However, as indigenous means of consumption learn to emulate McDonaldized systems, the close association of McDonaldization with Americanization will diminish. Efficiency, predictability, calculability and the replacement of human with non-human technology will continue to enjoy a competitive advantage over other organizational principles long after the association with America has been severed.

The competitive advantages enjoyed by McDonaldized systems in the USA do not completely apply to the worldwide diffusion of the model. Price, for example, can be less of a competitive advantage in some international settings than it is domestically because locally produced goods are often less expensive than exotic imports. Furthermore, taste remains a significant limitation on the international demand for fast food, as is clear from the concessions that McDonald's and others have made to the vagaries of local tastes (for instance, curry burgers in New Delhi or teriyaki burgers in Tokyo). Thus, the potential for McDonaldization to homogenize consumption is limited by the ability (price) and willingness (taste) of consumers in the USA and abroad to countenance rationalized means of consumption.

It must also be noted that Americanization implies a process by which things American are affecting more and more of the world, but the impact of McDonaldization is not simply outside the USA. Consider the increasing McDonaldization of the United States, including the disappearance of regional differences leading to greater homogenization across that country. One could not describe this as Americanization; it seems odd, to say the least, to think of the Americanization of America. However, we can clearly think in terms of the McDonaldization of America.

The McDonaldization of America may be regarded as the 'de-Americanization of America'. Although America has long been associated with a mélange of cultural and regional traditions, the well-known melting-pot, McDonaldization can be seen as driving out cultural and regional traditions and replacing them with a single, homogeneous system. Thus, the local delicatessen, Italian pizzeria, lobster shack, taco stand and so on tend to disappear as they are swamped by McDonald's and other fast-food restaurants; or these cultural and regional traditions are themselves McDonaldized and transformed into chains of Nathan's Hotdogs, Pizza Hut, Red Lobster and Taco Bell. These bear little trace of their origins in local and regional enclaves and their food has been 'watered down' so that it suits the tastes of a great many different consumers.

Thus, Americanization and McDonaldization are linked but not coupled. It may be that McDonaldization is only temporarily a subset of Americanization. Already today, McDonaldized systems are being created throughout the world and some of them are being exported back to the USA (for example, the UK-based Body Shop). It is already clear that McDonaldization is *not* only a process of Americanization. As more countries develop and export their own McDonaldized systems, we can expect to associate McDonaldization more with globalization (and less with Americanization), in the sense of it becoming increasingly multi-directional with the best adaptations and most novel forms successfully competing on the world stage. It is also likely that McDonald-ization will become so ubiquitous and codified that it will exist as a process independent of any particular nation. Indeed, it could be argued that McDonaldization is fast becoming an independent force as models for efficient and rational consumption diffuse into new areas. Such a situation would force us to rethink whether McDonaldization is a global or an American process.[4]

Americanization and Globalization

The differences between the Americanization and the globalization perspec-tives cut across the world economy, global culture and transnational politics. No subscriber to a globalization standpoint would ever deny that the USA is a dominant force in the world. Thus, the issue becomes a matter of relative emphasis, first, and then a question of effect. The thrust of globalization theory asserts that Americanization is only one of many global forces. Furthermore, even if US activity makes up a large portion of transnational activity, it poses less of a threat to local and national cultures than others might think. From this perspective, a fundamental flaw of images of Americanization is that they fail to take account of the power of local agents to selectively appropriate American influences while retaining cultural, political and economic autonomy.

In the economic sphere, the question of Americanization would seem to be an empirical one. If a large number of national economies are exploited by American corporate activity to a greater degree than they are by corporations from other countries, then the Americanization of an economy becomes a simple fact. However, corporations formerly identified with America are now often owned and operated by foreign interests (for instance, Chrysler, Seagram's and Burger King). Furthermore, international powers also have a great influence over American markets (automobiles, cellular phones and home electronics all have powerful competitors based outside the USA). Nevertheless, America is by far the world's largest economy and, as such, its reach and influence are strong.

In the area of consumer culture, the Americanization perspective would seem to be less ambiguous. The world is awash with American products and brands that together constitute a kind of cultural imperialism (Klein 2000;

4 Indeed, McDonaldization is a dominant contemporary model for rationalization but models from other nations have been influential in other periods. For example, the Mandarin bureaucracies of the Ching dynasty gripped the imagination of European state-builders in the eighteenth century. Another example, of which Max Weber was doubtless aware, was the effect of the Prussian model of military rationalization which became the model for modern armed forces.

Tomlinson 1991). Nike, Levi's, Coca-Cola and McDonald's are recognizable symbols around the world. Yet Rick Fantasia (1995) and Richard Kuisel (1993) are quick to point out that many nations – they use the example of France – have an ambivalent relationship with American products. When products are understood as American products, they are treated differently than they would be if they were simply seen as ubiquitous. As Coca-Cola became the global soft drink of choice it lost the distinction of being an American product, but until it did it was mainly thought of, and treated as, an exotic import. The exoticism with which it was understood served to temper its hegemonic effects – to be hegemonic, something must be both familiar and natural. Coca-Cola has already achieved that status in some places but many American products are still too contentious to have reached that degree of penetration.

On politics, the Americanization perspective is critical of heightened American international influence whereas globalization sees the dominant trend as the waxing of transnational governance and the waning of the nation state. Here it seems clear that the globalization perspective has perhaps glimpsed the future but also has overstated the case for the present. Nation states are by no means on the verge of disappearing; in fact, in nearly 50 regions of the world, separatist groups are struggling to create new ones. Of the transnational organizations, the most influential – including the World Trade Organization and the United Nations – are organizations of states, designed to help them cooperate more closely but not to displace territorial power structures.

On the other hand, Americanization is a political reality. Militarily, the United States is active in Europe, the Middle East, Latin America and South East Asia. It seems that not a month goes by without an incident involving American forces in some far-flung locale. Diplomatically, the United States has taken a place as a key mediator (or interested party) in regional conflicts between Ireland and Britain, Israel and the Palestinians, China and Taiwan, and North and South Korea. In terms of development, the United States offers economic aid, technical assistance and student exchanges with other nations. However, other nations have taken the lead from the USA on a spectrum of political issues. On some key issues, such as land mines and the environment, the US position has been repudiated in international circles. Nevertheless, the USA is obviously an influential political player on the world scene.

Thus, the case can be made that Americanization is an important form of globalization. Divergences between the perspectives are centred on the question of the degree to which American influence is hegemonic or, conversely, one of many. The McDonaldization model is of particular interest in this context. As more and more nations engage the USA diplomatically, economically and

43

culturally, they may feel coerced to develop compatible (McDonaldized) organizational models. Furthermore, these models have hegemonic character-istics; that is, they tend to be seen as natural means for organizing consum-ption, production and social life, rather than particularistic, American imports.

Modelling the Relationships: A Hierarchy of Processes?

Charting the geography of globalization, Americanization and McDonald-ization (see Table 1), it is immediately clear that globalization has the broadest scope simply because it encompasses a greater variety of transnational and international exchanges. McDonaldization and Americanization are neverthe-less phenomena with great influence in the Western world and growing influence worldwide. This essay is not merely an attempt to juxtapose terms in order to exploit the tension among them. Assessing the 'fit' among different concepts is the first step in integrating their insights. Thus, we see this section as the beginning of an attempt to reassess the relationships among globaliza-tion, Americanization and McDonaldization. We will try to show how, rather than being competitors, they fit together and complement one another.

A beginning point is the idea that globalization, Americanization and McDonaldization constitute a hierarchy, with globalization encompassing, at least in some sense, the other two. If globalization includes all processes affect-ing large portions of the world, then Americanization and McDonaldization can be seen as specific cases of globalization. From this perspective, globalization is the broadest process, Americanization is a specific, powerful globalizing force, and McDonaldization is (among other things) a constituent part of Americanization.

The idea that globalization, Americanization and McDonaldization fit together into a hierarchy of processes is an attractive proposition because it averts the kind of paradigm conflicts that have characterized other debates in sociological theory including the modernity/postmodernity and the macro/micro debates (Ritzer 2000b). Such a hierarchy would give credence to the idea that globalization is a blending of economies, cultures and peoples as well as to specific examples of crypto-imperialism and homogenization that would seem to challenge the ideals of hybridity. The hierarchy acknowledges that Americanization and McDonaldization, however powerful, are not totalizing processes; that is, neither exhausts the process of globalization. Rather, this hierarchy suggests that Americanization and McDonaldization are significant subsets of globalization, with strong influences on the global scene, perhaps having a greater influence on other regions of the globe than cultural forces from these areas are able to exert in response.

Yet the notion of a hierarchy of global processes is problematic. First, globalization is at least a partial rejection of both the Americanization and the McDonaldization perspectives. While American cultural materials may be flooding international markets, globalization theory asserts that they are more likely to supplement than to displace indigenous products. Globalization is also ordinarily conceived of as a multi-directional process emanating from a variety of sources and with consequences that have an impact on the entire planet. In other words, globalization involves not only Americanization, but also Japanization, Brazilianization, and so on.

It may be that globalization and Americanization are mutually exclusive images of world order. Furthermore, a sophisticated view of globalization acknowledges the role of local inputs in addition to global forces leading to hybrid cultures, or what Roland Robertson (1992) calls 'glocalization'. Such an image may be incompatible with the idea of Americanization: the question comes down to a subjective judgement of whether hybridity is an adaptation of an existing model or culture or something more novel. If, for example, a hybrid of American production techniques and Japanese-style labour relations produced the Japanese automobile industry, should this be termed Americanization or is this hybrid better understood as a novel mode of production? To force Americanization into this framework would radically transform the imperialistic valency of the concept.

There are also problems with the assertion that McDonaldization is a constituent part of Americanization. While some elements of McDonaldization are indelibly American (an emphasis on speed and efficiency), the core processes transcend national affiliation. It is true that McDonaldization is quintessentially American because the process was created in the USA and its dominant manifestations remain American in origin. While Americanization may always redound to the benefit of the United States, McDonaldization will not always do so. In fact, it is very likely that other nations will soon wrest the lead in the process of McDonaldization from the United States (just as America's lead in assembly-line production has long since disappeared). At some point, the greatest force in the further McDonaldization of American society could come from the importation of successors to places like Russkoye Bistro and Nirulas. Even now, the expansion of Burger King in the United States benefits its British owners.

Thus, the promise of a hierarchy of global processes would need to overcome the fact that globalization, McDonaldization and Americanization are in some senses mutually exclusive.

Conclusion

We began with the suggestion that in spite of their conceptual differences the simultaneous resonance of globalization, McDonaldization and Americanization deserves further exploration. We then went on to map the terrain of the three perspectives (see Table 1), suggesting points of difference and convergence. Last, we suggested that the three ideas can be made more compatible, but not completely so, by conceiving of their interrelations less as competing perspectives and more as a hierarchy. Thus, while it may be inappropriate to set McDonaldization on an equal footing with globalization as world-historical processes, it will nevertheless continue to have a broad impact. The fact that McDonaldization carries with it a set of formally rational principles that not only outdo competitors but also diminish respect for substantive values in the process makes it a corrosive force for homogenization. Anything can be made more efficient, calculable and predictable, but only at the expense of individual creative energy and traditional arts of living. More and more aspects of our lives are subject to McDonaldization.

A similar case can be made for the perils of Americanization. While there is no question that the reach of American cultural products is long, globalization's insights into the diversity of other 'global flows' and the ability of agents to manipulate the meanings of American products are a useful corollary. Yet Americanization has an overall homogenizing effect on world culture, either by muscling out local products or by encouraging emulation. The result may temporarily increase the options of local individuals in search of new identities, but in the long run the isomorphic convergence of culture around American tastes and ways of doing things will have a negative impact on cultural heritage.

We conclude by noting that these judgements are made at a particular historical moment when McDonaldization is in ascendance and America enjoys global hegemony. As time passes, other models for organizing social life, dealing with new exigencies, will develop, though they too are likely to suffer from an excess of formal rationality. Nations throughout the world may become restless with American dispositions, and turn their attention either back to their own traditions or towards forging new models and tastes out of alternative elements in the global mélange.

References

Alfino, Mark, John Caputo and Robin Wynyard (1998), *McDonaldization Revisited: Critical Essays in Consumer Culture*. Westport, CT: Greenwood Press.

Antonio, Robert J., and Alessandro Bonanno (2000), 'A New Global Capitalism? From

"Americanism and Fordism" to "Americanization-Globalization"', *American Studies* 41(214): 33–77.

Appadurai, Arjun (1996), *Modernity at Large*. Minneapolis: University of Minnesota Press.

Castells, Manuel (1996), *The Rise of the Network Society*. Oxford: Blackwell.

Chase-Dunn, Christopher (1989), *Global Formation: Structures of the World Economy*. Oxford: Blackwell.

Daley, Suzanne (2000), 'French Turn Vandal into Hero Against U.S.', *The New York Times* (July 1): A1.

DiMaggio, Paul J. and Walter W. Powell (1983), 'The Iron Cage Revisited: Institutional Isomorphism and Collective Rationality in Organizational Fields', *American Sociological Review* 48 (April): 147–60.

Drane, John (2000), *The McDonaldization of the Church*. London: Darton, Longman and Todd.

Fantasia, Rick (1995), 'Fast Food in France', *Theory and Society* 24: 201–43.

Friedman, Thomas (1999), *The Lexus and the Olive Tree*. New York: Farrar, Strauss, and Giroux.

Gray, John (1998), *False Dawn: The Delusions of Global Capitalism*. London: Granta Books.

Gunder-Frank, Andre (1978), *World Accumulation, 1492–1789*. New York: Monthly Review Press.

Kael, Pauline (1985), 'Why Are Movies So Bad? or, The Numbers', in Pauline Kael, *State of the Art*. New York: Dutton: 8–20.

Kirchberg, Volker (2000), 'Die McDonaldisierung deutscher Museen', *Tourismus Journal* 4: 117–44.

Klein, Naomi (2000), *No Logo: Taking Aim at Brand Bullies*. New York: Picador.

Kuisel, Richard F. (1993), *Seducing the French: The Dilemma of Americanization*. Berkeley: University of California Press.

McMichael, Philip (1996), *Development and Social Change: A Global Perspective*. Thousand Oaks, CA: Pine Forge.

Nederveen Pieterse, Jan (1995), 'Globalization as Hybridization', in Mike Featherstone et al. (eds), *Global Modernities*. London: Sage: 45–68.

Nelson, Joel (2001), 'On Mass Distribution: A Case Study of Chain Stores in the Restaurant Industry', *Journal of Consumer Culture* 1: 141–60.

Parker, Martin, and David Jary (1995), 'The McUniversity: Organization, Management and Academic Subjectivity', *Organization* 2: 1–20.

Ritzer, George (1998), *The McDonaldization Thesis: Extensions and Explorations*. London: Sage.

— (1999), *Enchanting a Disenchanted World: Revolutionizing the Means of Consumption*. Thousand Oaks, CA: Pine Forge.

— (2000a), *The McDonaldization of Society*. New Century Edition. Thousand Oaks, CA: Pine Forge.

— (2000b), *Sociological Theory*. New York: McGraw Hill.

Ritzer George, and Elizabeth Malone (2000), 'Globalization Theory: Lessons from the Exportation of McDonaldization and the New Means of Consumption', *American Studies* 41(213): 97–109.

Ritzer, George, and Seth Ovadia (2001), 'The Process of McDonaldization is Not Uniform nor are its Settings, Consumers, or the Consumption of its Goods and Services', in Mark Gottdiener (ed.), *New Forms of Consumption: Consumers, Culture and Commodification*. Lanham, MD: Rowman and Littlefield: 33–49.

Robertson, Roland (1992), *Globalization: Social Theory and Global Culture*. London: Sage.

Said, Edward (1978), *Orientalism*. New York: Pantheon.

Schlosser, Eric (2001), *Fast Food Nation*. New York: Houghton Mifflin.

Smart, Barry (1999), *Resisting McDonaldization*. London: Sage.

Tomlinson, John (1991), *Cultural Imperialism*. Baltimore: Johns Hopkins University Press.

Turner, Bryan S. (1999), 'Citizens: Risk, Coolness, and Irony in Contemporary Politics', in Barry Smart (ed.) *Resisting McDonaldization*. London: Sage: 83–100.

Wallerstein, Immanuel (1974), *The Modern World System*. New York: Academic Press.

Watson, James L. (1997), *Golden Arches East: McDonald's in East Asia*. Stanford, CA: Stanford University Press.

— (2000), 'China's Big Mac Attack', *Foreign Affairs* 79(3) (May/June): 120–34.

Williams, Francis (1962), *The American Invasion*. New York: Crown.

CHAPTER 3

Culture, Modernity and Immediacy

John Tomlinson

Reconceptualizing Cultural Globalization

In what follows I shall try to depart quite radically from a form of discourse that has, I believe, become a constricting way of talking and thinking about the cultural implications of globalization. This discourse is elaborated around the assumption, baldly stated, that cultural globalization inevitably takes the form of a spread of cultural practices – and habits, values, products, experiences, ways of life – from certain dominant *places* to others. We might call this general pattern of critical thought the 'geopolitical conception of cultural influence'. It appears in particular forms in the ideas of Americanization or Westernization – ideas that are frequently conflated – as both are with the notion of the spread of global capitalism as a form of cultural imperialism.

Now it is not as though this way of thinking is necessarily in every case misguided or wrongheaded, or that the issues it foregrounds are unimportant.[1] However, it *does* direct us towards thinking around a fairly familiar set of critical concerns and, moreover, within a conceptual framework that may limit the scope of understanding of emergent cultural phenomena. For even in criticizing or radically qualifying the more robust articulations of the cultural imperialism thesis, we find ourselves reproducing a style of thinking about culture in terms of these compelling spatial power metaphors: metaphors of territory and borders, of flows and the regulation of flows, of invasion and protection(ism). Even the most sophisticated cultural-critical discourses that

---

1 What is at stake here is not so much the rights and wrongs of the cultural imperialism, McDonaldization, Westernization, Americanization or global homogenization theses, but the tendency to read the broad process of cultural globalization through these lenses. For critiques of this tendency see, *inter alia*, Beck 2000a; Robertson 1992; Thompson 1995; Tomlinson 1999.

have emerged around the ideas of hybridity or transculturation – though they challenge the implicit close mapping of culture on to nation – fail to break with the dominant imagery of cultural territories, liminalities, cross-border flows, fusions, and so forth.

Hence, the result of much recent cultural-theoretical activity has been to rescue culture from the subservient, instrumental position within which it has been placed in traditional political-economic accounts (still, it has to be said, by far the most common way in which globalization is figured), and to prise it away from its anchoring within (increasingly empirically implausible) conceptualizations of the ethnically integrated, bounded and sovereign nation state. But it has *not* been to detach culture sufficiently from a fundamentally territorial imagination. If we take seriously the idea that globalization involves *deterritorialization* – in Néstor García Canclini's sense of 'the loss of the "natural" relation of culture to geographical and social territories' (1995: 229) – then there is a good argument for attempting to reconceptualize cultural processes so as to produce more adequate accounts of cultural experience within global-modern societies.

Ulrich Beck coined the wonderfully evocative phrase 'zombie categories' to describe the growing inadequacy of normal social science concepts in grasping the rapidly changing empirical condition of globalizing modernity. Citing Kant's dictum, 'Concepts without observations are empty, observations without concepts are blind', Beck writes '[N]ormal social science categories are becoming *zombie* categories, empty terms in the Kantian meaning. Zombie categories are living dead categories, which blind the social sciences to the rapidly changing realities inside the nation-state containers and outside as well' (Beck 2000b: 5).

Taking my lead here from Beck, what I want to explore is another way of thinking about the cultural implications of globalization – a way that associates cultural phenomena less with territorial influence than with shifts in the *texture of the modernity* that has become globalized. Are there emergent cultural phenomena that are better thought of as entailments of a generalized global modernity – particularly as mediated through new communications technologies – rather than as the hegemonic projects of dominant national cultures or as the homogenizing effects of a rapacious commodity capitalism?

I want to suggest that we can see such phenomena in the connections between a global-modern institutional/technological context of increasing 'connectivity' and emergent cultural styles, imaginations, sensibilities, practices and values. However, I shall not attempt a general argument about how global connectivity gives rise to such phenomena but shall, more modestly, offer one example as illustrative of the type of emergent phenomenon I have in mind, and as indicative of possible alternative approaches to cultural globalization. The example I shall explore is the principle of 'immediacy', which I take to be an increasingly general feature of the broad global-modern cultural experience – certainly in the developed West and arguably increasingly in non-Western societies. But I shall deliberately *not* be concerned with the issue of the provenance and spread of this phenomenon. Instead I shall try to sketch out an argument as follows:

1. Immediacy stands as a cultural principle in relation to the technological – and particularly the communicational – bases of our particular era of global modernity as 'mechanical speed' stands to those of the preceding era.
2. Immediacy can in this sense be thought of as the 'end' of conventional speed in a number of ways which associate technological transformations – particularly new globalizing media and communications technologies – with a distinct, broadly distributed, emergent cultural imaginary.
3. To grasp its cultural-imaginary significance, immediacy needs to be conceived within a vocabulary that breaks its intuitive link to older 'early-modern' ideas of speed and mobility. Rather than thinking of 'immediate' events in strictly temporal terms – as things occurring without delay – we should see this as just one aspect of a broader meaning, related to the core idea of mediation – what I shall call the abolition or redundancy of the middle term. This broader meaning grasps something of the cultural experience and sensibility of our current era of modernity, closely related to, though not reducible to, the rapid diffusion of deterritorializing technologies.
4. Examining the cultural-imaginary principle of immediacy may help us to understand the link between cultural values and rapid social-technological change – a link that has too often been conceived in terms of cultural pathology models and articulated from an explicit or implicit standpoint of cultural conservatism. Resisting the drift to conservatism may, in turn, help us to understand the cultural process of globalization in fresh ways, breaking with the geopolitical conception of cultural influence.

Immediacy, Communication and Speed

I begin with an example – perhaps a slightly extreme one – of what I understand by immediacy. Researchers at Roke Manor Research, a part of the Siemens technology group, have predicted the commercial development, within the current decade, of a technique to embed microsensors in the optic nerves of television journalists – enabling them to 'transmit' what they see, live, to our television screens. The technology, they claim, already exists to do this (Radford 2000).

51

This sort of research is most obviously provocative on account of its 'cyborg' connotations: the rather troubling implications of a body modification carried out for an instrumental – worse, a commercial – purpose. And, speaking as an old-fashioned humanist, I am personally rather reassured by the unlikelihood that such technology will find a ready market – the unlikelihood, that is, of any imminent vogue for radical surgical intervention as a career development option within the chapels of the National Union of Journalists.

However, this aspect of the example is not the most significant one for my purposes. For in a sense an implant can be understood – qualms about penetration of the surface of human flesh as the breaching of a liminal point in our humanistic culture notwithstanding – as simply a more sophisticated form of communicational prosthesis on a continuum with headphones or lapel microphones: in Marshall McLuhan's famous but now unfortunately gendered phrase, media technologies as 'extensions of man' (1964: 41).

The deeper point then becomes the *cultural principle* that drives such technological developments: the principle that helps answer the obvious question of why anyone should *want* to produce and market – should see a need for – such things. And this principle, at first glance, looks like a pretty familiar one: the convention – so obvious that it escapes examination – of the *immediate* delivery of news. This quintessentially modern cultural assumption that 'the news' – indeed all sorts of communication – should be delivered as quickly as possible makes obvious sense of the trajectory of increasing acceleration in media technologies: the telegraph, the telephone, the communications satellite, the networked computer and current CMC convergences (for instance 'WAP' [Wireless Application Protocol] technology linking mobile phones with news services via the Internet). In most of these recent developments, speed of delivery becomes associated with social ubiquity: the instant, context-independent availability of information.

This context-independence of news dissemination – particularly its dissociation from the authoritative discursive position of the national culture – is typified in the development of 'Ananova', a computer simulation bearing a close resemblance to the *Tomb Raider* video game heroine Lara Croft. Billed as 'the world's first virtual cyberchick newsreader', Ananova was sold in July 2000 by the Press Association's new media division to the (then British, now French-owned) mobile phone operator Orange for £95m for use on its Internet portal (Hyland 2000).[2]

2 Doubts have, however, recently emerged over the industry-predicted smooth take-up of so-called '3G' (third generation) technology utilizing increased bandwidth to facilitate web connection, video and so on. With a European market for 'conventional' voice and text mobile phones reaching saturation point, this raises interesting questions over consumer discrimination in relation to perceived communications 'needs'. The economic corollary to this can be seen in

Add to these technological developments recent innovations in media institutions themselves – for instance 24-hour television news services, on-line news services with web pages updated every minute and click-to-vote 'inter-activity' – and we get a sense of immediacy as a principle of speed and instantaneity of access; that is, access to information, but also to business, to consumption (for instance on-line shopping), to entertainment, or simply to one another (mobile phone chat as a defining feature of contemporary youth culture). Put this all together and we might begin to see our early twenty-first-century Western culture as dominated by a technology-driven obsession with speed, ubiquitous availability and instant gratification along with decreasing attention spans (the so-called 'three-minute culture') and so forth. Immediacy thus becomes associated with what James Gleich (1999) has called 'the acceler-ation of just about everything'.

This binding of immediacy to speed is, I think, part of a very typical modernist story which we all probably know quite well. It is a story that begins optimistically around the end of the eighteenth century with speed linked to the Enlightenment values of progress, order, increased efficiency, cosmopoli-tanism and so on, which reaches a kind of watershed at the end of the nineteenth century in the Futurists' celebration of speed as creative icono-clasm (Marinetti 1973), and which then gradually loses confidence in itself. So the emancipations and the exhilaration of speed become accompanied by anxieties over control (its tendency to run away with us: modernity as, in Anthony Giddens' [1990] resonant phrase, a 'Juggernaut') or even by moral panics over its pathological effects on culture or on values. So, this is a familiar narrative following the contours of the broader cultural critique of modernity. But the point is that it is *one* single story, in which there is a continuous coupling of modernity to speed and on to immediacy, or to what Paul Virilio (1997) calls the 'absolute velocity' of cyberspace.

I am actually rather dubious about this single continuous story, and so what I want to do now is to explore the idea that there may be a *discontinuity* between present-day immediacy and earlier modernist speed.

Solid and Liquid Modernity

To help make this comparison, I am going to draw on Zygmunt Bauman's recent suggestive distinction between what he calls a 'heavy', 'solid', 'hardware-

---

the string of announcements of losses, reduced second- and third-quarter revenue predictions, employment cutbacks, plant closures and panicky management sackings and replacements affecting many of the sector's biggest names (Cisco Systems, Motorola, Ericsson, Phillips, Yahoo, BT, Siemens, Alcatel) in the early months of 2001.

focused' modernity and a new 'light', 'liquid', 'software-based' modernity. Putting this very briefly, according to Bauman we are currently witnessing the end of an era of heavy modernity, in which, 'size is power and volume is success: the epoch of weighty and ever more cumbersome machines, of ever more populous factory crews, of ponderous rail engines and gigantic ocean liners' (Bauman 2000: 114). Apart from the obvious characterization in terms of heavy industrial and labour-intensive production, Bauman links heavy modernity with a relative fixity in time-space location – or at least a tendency in hardware to be 'sluggish, unwieldy and awkward to move'. As a consequence, 'heavy modernity' is a period in which power is concentrated in physical locations: 'embodied and fixed, tied in steel and concrete'. Expanding power means expanding the ownership and control of these geographically fixed locations and so Bauman associates heavy modernity with simple territorial expansion: the increasing possession of space and the control of time. It is the era of territorial conquest, of colonization, of the regulation (the clocking and hence the uniformity) of time and of the coordination of time-space: the era of the survey, the schedule, the timetable, the control plan.

By contrast, our emergence into 'light', 'liquid' modernity is into a world where solidity, fixity and sheer extension of possessed location is no longer automatically an asset: a world where capital is fluid and entrepreneurs travel light; where production methods are plastic, sourcing is variable, employment is temporary, planning is flexible and adaptable; where logics are fuzzy. This contrast in the realm of business cultures – Microsoft or Yahoo as opposed to Ford or Renault – flows over into the broader culture. The valuing of fixity, permanence and location – in everyday lifestyles, in attitudes and values – gives way to the valuing of mobility, flexibility and openness to change. Constructing, planning and regulating give way to coping with uncertainty, and 'going with the flow'; durability cedes to transience, the long term to the short term. Above all, in liquid modernity, distance is no object: 'In the software universe of light-speed travel, space may be traversed literally in "no-time"... Space no more sets limits to action and its effects' (Bauman 2000: 117).

Like all big heuristic distinctions – of which Bauman is a master – this one is vulnerable to criticism in all sorts of ways. There are of course many problems with epochal views of social and cultural change[3] and there are well-known

---

3 See Albrow 1996 for a view of globalization based on a sophisticated epochal analysis and Tomlinson 1999: 32ff. for a discussion. But really I think that Bauman's distinctions need to be read in the same context as Beck's use of the ideas of first and second ages of modernity (Beck 1997; 2000a): that is to say for their *critical-heuristic* value rather than as 'new problematic evolutionary forms(s) of periodization based on either–or epochal "stages"; when everything is reversed at the same moment, all the old relations disappear for ever and entirely new ones come up to replace them' (Beck 2000b: 5).

difficulties in dualistic thinking. However, there is little to be gained from picking away at the details of Bauman's distinction because this misses the point, which is not to provide precise descriptions but to help us think creatively about processes happening around us. So for the most part I want to take the contrast between solid and liquid, heavy and light modernity as a viable and suggestive one.

The application of this contrast to an understanding of speed is quite straightforward. Despite Bauman's stress on the 'ponderous', gargantuan nature of heavy modernity, he understands how important speed, as the conquest of space (in Marx's famous phrase, 'the annihilation of space by time') is to this era. Modernity, he says, 'is born under the stars of acceleration and land conquest' (Bauman 2000: 112). In heavy modernity what I shall call mechanical velocity is crucial in overcoming the 'natural' resistance of physical space to the fulfilment of desire: it is intimately tied to the early-modern narrative of scientific-technological progress.

To illustrate the cultural imagination associated with mechanical velocity we can consider a cultural product of the era of heavy modernity, the documentary film *Night Mail*, made in 1936 for the British GPO Film Unit.[4] Produced by John Grierson, directed by Basil Wright and Harry Watt and featuring verse by W. H. Auden and a score by Benjamin Britten, this short film has become a classic of the British documentary film movement and arguably a definitive early-modern cultural text. The film is, in a sense, both a documentation and a celebration of mechanical velocity in the delivery of modern communication and also in the territorial 'binding' of the nation as one culture, by means of communications technologies. What it shows is the journey of the overnight mail express – the 'TPO Down Special'[5] – from London Euston to Glasgow, on which mail from intervening stations and locations is collected and sorted as the train speeds north.

---

4 During the 1930s the GPO Film Unit, under the directorship of John Grierson, became a focus for leftist artists and intellectuals, employing, among others, W. H. Auden, Benjamin Britten, the painter William Coldstream and the directors Basil Wright, Alberto Cavalcanti and Humphrey Jennings (one of the co-founders of the 'Mass Observation' movement).

5 'TPO' for 'Travelling Post Office'. The first travelling post office – a converted horsebox utilized to enable the sorting of mail while the train was on the move – ran on the Grand Junction Railway in 1838. By 1852 the mechanical bag exchange system was introduced which remained in use on the British railway system, little modified, until its eventual withdrawal in 1971. Although the improved acceleration and braking capabilities of modern locomotives, along with other developments in postal delivery practices, made the mechanical exchange apparatus obsolete, the TPO continues to run as a mobile sorting office; see Blakemore 1990. The 'Up-Special TPO' – running in the opposite direction to the Night Mail – achieved fame in 1963 when it became the victim of the 'Great Train Robbery', an event chiefly remembered in the person of colourful fugitive criminal Ronald Biggs.

As the mail express's journey proceeds, so the film unfolds most of the main characteristics of the cultural imaginary of mechanical velocity. First, there is an obvious focus on the exercise of mechanical power overcoming – 'eating up' – distance: the locomotive, in the words of Auden's verse, 'shovelling white steam over its shoulder', emphasized in recurrent images of the pistons and wheels, the rush of wind and the pulsating, accelerating rhythm of Britten's score. This is speed tied to effort and the overcoming of obstacles – for example the steep gradients of the Pennines on the later part of the journey. It is a pretty basic image of work in Bertrand Russell's famous definition of 'moving things around at or near the surface of the earth'. But the exercise of power is shown here within the context of other quintessentially early-modern (heavy-modern) themes. For instance, goal orientation, organization and time-space regulation are continually stressed in the sequences showing the precise timetabling of the Night Mail and its coordination with connecting trains, or in the routines of sorting the letters, or the famous sequence showing the high-speed mechanical collection and delivery of mail bags from the trackside. These sequences also display an ideology of teamwork and the disciplined coordination of mechanical and labour power in the achievement of a common goal. And related to this is a heroic image of labour and a sense of the exhilaration of velocity which, though it appears here in a more muted and disciplined key, has at least distant echoes of the Futurists' obsession with the heroics of machine speed.

But if we were to identify the central theme of *Night Mail*, we could say it is, above all, a film about the *closing of the gap* between a point of departure and a point of arrival. The goal, the effort, the technologies, the exhilaration of mechanical velocity that are celebrated here all constellate around this key element in the modern imagination: demolishing distance, bringing the news, connecting localities. For the Night Mail's journey crucially documents and affirms in its dependable, precisely organised regularity, both the connectedness and the cultural unity of the nation state: not just across distance, but across rural and urban, class, regional, and even 'national' divides:

> Dawn freshens. Her climb is done
> Down towards Glasgow she descends,
> Towards the steam tugs yelping down a glade of cranes
> Towards the fields of apparatus, the furnaces
> Set on the dark plain like gigantic chessmen.
> All Scotland waits for her:
> In the dark glens, beside pale-green lochs,
> Men long for news. (Auden 1966)

The relevance of speed here is defined by the manifest concrete realities of space, distance, separation: these are the obstacles that technologies of speed promise to overcome and *here lies speed's value*: in the *gap* between departure and arrival, desire and its fulfilment.

The crux of my argument is that this sort of speed is categorically different from immediacy. Mechanical velocity is still with us in abundance; indeed, the Night Mail still runs. Just as globalization has not literally shrunk the world, so distance and the physical effort to overcome it still stubbornly persist. But now we have something else. Now we also have the phenomenon of immediacy which, in its light, effortless, easy ubiquity, has more or less displaced both the laborious and the heroic cultural attachments of an earlier speed. And with this displacement comes a shift in cultural assumptions, expectations, attitudes and values.

One way to point up this contrast is to think of the cultural production that is elaborated around one of the cultural icons of the early twenty-first century: the mobile phone. Without taking a specific example, it is obvious that much of the marketing imagery associated with this technology trades on a very differ-ent set of cultural assumptions to those of *Night Mail*. Frequently aimed at a young audience, advertisements for mobile phones stress leisure and playful-ness as opposed to labour, consumption rather than production, a software insouciance as contrasted with a hardware work discipline. But, again, if we press to the core of immediacy as exemplified in such cultural production we can see that there is a principle involved that constellates all the other impressionistic features. And this, I would say, is that, in contrast with mech-anical velocity, here in a sense *the gap is already closed*. Immediacy makes speed redundant.

Closing the Gap: The Redundancy of the Middle Term

Why is this? This is a matter of cultural imagination and perception rather than of precise technological function. The *impression* we get from the use of new communications technologies – when they are working properly that is – is one of a general effortlessness and ubiquity. Things – and particularly people – do seem to be pretty much immediately available. There is no apparent effort in communicating; there seem to be no great obstacles to overcome. The silent, invisible 'soft' technology appears to have done all that for us: it has closed the gap between here and elsewhere, now and later. If we view the use of com-munications technologies as an aspect of consumption, it is even tempting to say that it has closed that most significant gap of all for capitalist modernity, the motor of the market economy, the gap between human desire and its fulfilment. The fact that it has not *quite* done this – that it has simply reduced the duration of the cycle of consumption (that is, increased its frequency) – is, of course, reassuring for the immediate high-consumption system. But it may be more perplexing in the longer term, posing as it does the threat or promise (depending on your perspective) of an ultimate generalized market saturation: not merely a 'post-scarcity' economy, but a sort of technologically achieved equilibrium between supply and demand – a culture, in the high-consumption societies, of generalized immediate satisfaction, diminishing the supposed infinite reservoir of wants. How, it must be wondered, would even the near approach to such a balance affect the dynamics of capitalism?[6]

Although immediacy has not quite closed this most fundamental of gaps, it seems to have closed others that could be seen as constitutive of the early-modern cultural imaginary. Paul Virilio observes that the effect of the transport revolution of the nineteenth century was to reduce the significance of a journey to two points, Arrival and Departure – a fundamental shift in the cultural meaning of travel which is still preserved for us today in the architecture of railway stations[7] and now even more strongly emphasized in the spatial design of airports. But the coming of new communications technologies, Virilio says, means that 'departure now gets wiped out and "arrival" gets promoted, the *generalized arrival of data*': 'The key notions of (radio, video, digital) signal input and output have overtaken those usually associated with the movement of people and objects traditionally distributed throughout the extension of space' (Virilio 1997: 56). Early-modern speed was heroic precisely because it displayed the force and the effort involved in overcoming the extension of space. Its terminals – solid markers of the achievement of the defeat of distance – were suitably conspicuous and monumental.

By contrast, new 'soft', 'immediate' technologies – technologies of 'generalized arrival' such as mobile phones and personal computers – seem to trade on an opposite aesthetic and set of values: the redundancy of effort, the ubiquity of presence, discretion and miniaturization in the 'terminal'.[8]

---

6 It is probably premature to worry about (or anticipate) such a generalized economic plateau, given the considerable scope for capitalist expansion in relation, for example, to the market in health care provision as it shades into the extension of the span of active human life. Nevertheless even an approach to equilibrium in *some* sectors of the market – some clusters of consumer goods – would have a profound effect on the confidence structures of the global economy.

7 The idea of railway terminals as significant factors in the social reconceptualization of space was a matter of cultural debate in the nineteenth century. For example, the British cultural critic, John Ruskin, a famous enemy of the railways, described passengers as 'human parcels who dispatch themselves to their destination by means of the railroad, arriving as they left, untouched by the space traversed' (Schivelbusch 1980: 45).

8 The question of the significance of the miniaturization of new communications technology is interesting in that there remains ambiguity over whether this is explicable in purely functional

What these observations amount to is the suggestion that there is a broadly viable distinction to be made between the cultural imagination elaborated around, on the one hand, solid modernity and mechanical velocity and, on the other hand, liquid modernity and immediacy. It is a distinction based on the sort of general cultural assumptions, dispositions and aesthetic judgements that seem to correlate with the rise of different time-space organizing technologies. It is agnostic as to issues of causality and it is rather impressionistic. But despite this, the distinction seems to be suggestive enough to warrant a little more conceptual probing of the idea of immediacy. And we can do this by separating immediacy as a cultural principle more completely from its historical entanglement with speed.

In fact, in terms of definition, immediacy has only a second-order relation to speed. In the *Oxford English Dictionary*, its most general meaning is that of 'having direct effect, without an intervening medium or agency'. This meaning clearly applies to speed in the sense of 'occurring or done at once or *without delay*' (thus without the intervening medium of time). But it also applies to the bridging of distance (and thus to much of the cultural impact of globalization) in the sense of immediacy as *proximity*, 'nearest, next, not separated by others'. But what lies at the conceptual and etymological heart of the term is the general sense, from the Latin *immediatus*, of being without a mediating presence. Immediacy – closing the gap – is therefore most generally the redundancy or the abolition of the middle term.

This more abstract and general principle can, plausibly, be applied to a range of contemporary cultural practices, experiences, values and attitudes. The redundancy of space gestures to the lived experience of globalization: proximity, deterritorialization, and the penetration of localities by distant forces. The promise of the (virtual) abolition of the medium of delivery of communication underpins a dominant cultural style: 'televisual immediacy' and transparency as media production values; live and continuous news reporting and so on. It is in this sense also (which involves the rather deeper idea of uninhibited, direct access to reality) that we can understand the cultural rationale behind interventions such as optic nerve implants – practices that Virilio (1997: 57) sees more darkly as the colonization of the last *territory* – 'the tragedy of the fusion of the "biological" and the "technological"'. Perhaps most obviously, abolishing time – or more properly, abolishing *waiting* – refers

---

terms – related to convenience and mobility – or whether the associated aesthetic value connects with a changing cultural conception of the body–machine interface. Actual body modifications (such as optic nerve implants) do not however seem to me an inevitable extension of what Virilio (1997) refers to as 'the law of proximity', precisely because the aesthetic satisfaction of possession – the independent existence, the 'thingness' – of technological goods would seem lost in literal incorporation.

us to all those critiques of cultural acceleration and generalized *impatience* with which we are familiar today: notions of 'instant gratification' or the 'three-minute culture', instanced by fast-food restaurants, scratchcard gambling, the concept of *time poverty* as a correlate of professional success, even road rage.

Notice, however, that these critiques can now be understood not as critiques of speed as such – of the acceleration of culture – but as responses to the abolition of the middle. (Road rage then is not really about the desire for speed, but about the perception of other drivers as 'barriers' – intervening terms – to the achievement of immediate goals.) Recognizing this broader, more general meaning of immediacy is, I think, important to avoid that constant temptation for the sociologist or the cultural analyst: the rush to critical judgement.

Interpretation before Critique

If immediacy is a genuinely original feature of a globalized, electronically mediated culture, then we should not be surprised to find that we do not yet possess an adequate analytic and critical vocabulary with which to address it. Bauman scarcely exaggerates in saying that 'the advent of instantaneity ushers human culture and ethics into unmapped and unexplored territory' (Bauman 2000: 128). Nevertheless, the temptation is often to try to use the old maps to find our way: to compare new experiences and values with older, more familiar ones and, usually, to find the new ones wanting.

Thus in trying to come to critical terms with immediacy, it is understandable that it is often approached as at least a deficit condition, if not a form of cultural pathology. There is a ready-to-hand strain of cultural critique which implicitly draws on the idea that, to put it in a rather homespun way, 'patience is a virtue'. Thus the idea of closing the temporal (if not the existential) gap between desire and satisfaction may mean the loss of a dimension of cultural life that has been traditionally valued. This dimension could include the complex cultural-aesthetic-psychological qualities of anticipation or of deferral – of 'living towards the future' – that were typical of earlier periods of modernity. Or it could refer us to the social-ethical values of restraint: the inhibition – perhaps according to a green agenda – of constant impulsive consumer desire. Or, again, it may relate to the rather more subtle idea – which we find in Bauman and in critics such as Castoriadis – that what is threatened is a cultural sensibility that values the *long durée* (duration, durability and the eternal) over the immediate.[9]

9 See particularly the final part of Castoriadis's essay 'Reflections on "Rationality" and "Development"' (1991). My conception of the 'cultural imaginary' significance of immediacy owes much to Castoriadis's key concept of the 'social imaginary signification' (Castoriadis 1987).

These are genuine and significant concerns, of course, but they can be easily exaggerated. Bauman, for example, voices some familiar cultural anxieties when he goes on to claim that '[i]nstantaneity means ... on-the-spot fulfilment – but also immediate exhaustion and fading of interest ... liquid modernity is the epoch of disengagement, elusiveness, facile escape and hopeless chase ...' (Bauman 2000: 120). One way of avoiding this slide towards the 'going-to-hell-in-a-handcart' school of critique[10] is to properly historicize and contextualize the value assumptions against which such deficits are implicitly assessed. Thus we might want to scrutinize the value of 'patience' itself. For patience is a virtue surely only in relative, context-dependent terms – it is not an absolute value. Patience, defined as 'calm endurance of hardship, pain, delay', or as 'tolerant perseverance', has its root in a cultural response to suffering (from the Latin *patiens*). In this basic sense it is a good example of a virtue made out of necessity. 'What cannot be cured must be endured' and so patience valorizes the dignified endurance of pain, illness and hardship. It is not difficult to see why such a cultural value loses its grip with the broad affluence of modernity, where expectations of technological solutions to an increasing number of life's vicissitudes are constantly growing.

Does this mean that the cultural principle of immediacy has made the value of patience obsolete? Well, not quite, perhaps. But it has certainly displaced and marginalized it. For it is hard to defend the idea of deferral of satisfaction or toleration of hardship or deprivation without fetching up in a certain questionable asceticism. What is more, the appeal to patience cannot be entirely cleared of an ideological suspicion: as the counsel of the powerful to the subordinate – underlined in religion – to tolerate their lot. The problem is, of course, that with the marginalization of patience in this ideological sense, may come also the marginalization of the concomitant values of a more general tolerance, forbearance, endurance and respect for the long term. Values are often not so much clear-cut, precise, moral-cultural instruments as they are clusters of (sometimes ambiguous and contradictory) moral attachments constellating around broader cultural principles.

The principle of immediacy thus faces us with new cultural-ethical problems. However, the response to these cannot be to cleave to the values of a previous era which we expect to pass down, pristine and intact, from one context to quite another. So, on the one hand, our critical disposition ought to be one that always avoids the danger of the slippage towards an unsupportable cultural conservatism. This does not mean, on the other hand, that we are faced with the bleak prospect of complete value relativism. It is rather a

10 Not, of course, that I accuse Bauman specifically of anything so crass. I merely observe that the slide towards this sort of critique is always a potential danger in the analysis of cultural trends.

question of recognizing the context-embeddedness of values in the different relationships that have been historically established between technological change and cultural experience. What this suggests is that the meanings people attach to the integration of new technologies into their everyday lives need to be much more thoroughly interpreted and understood.

Such an interpretation may reveal underlying meanings quite distinct from the driven, Sisyphean pursuit of euphoria that Bauman describes. These may include, for example, the inchoate expression of an existential desire – submerged in a culture of possessive individualism – for greater human connectedness, completion and fullness of social experience. Such a desire might be read in the frequent reports of users of 'immediate' technologies such as cellphones of the need to be constantly 'in touch' with other people. We could either read such reports of experience in this way, or, in a more pessimistic mood, as the compulsive pursuit of endless (in both senses) social stimuli. What matters then is to get the interpretation right before building the critique. The values we lack and the moral dispositions we might want to foster thus need to be searched for in the sensitive practice of cultural hermeneutics.

Conclusion

This discussion of immediacy and some of its cultural-aesthetic and moral implications has obviously been a rather rough freehand sketch, and has left all sorts of questions unresolved and even unposed. However, my aim here has only been to present in the idea of immediacy an *example* of a cultural principle which seems to be generated in the crucible of late modernity, from the complex fusion of technological-communicational changes with aspects of commodity capitalism and underlying shifts in the social organization of time-space.

Though it is (potentially) a global phenomenon, it seems clear that a broad cultural-imaginary principle such as immediacy cannot be properly understood in the conventional language of hegemony, cultural imperialism, cultural homogenization and so on. It helps very little in trying to take a critical grasp of the issue to think about it as the original property of any one national culture – or even as a particularly 'Western' phenomenon. Immediacy, indeed, seems to be a feature of a generalized global modernity. It is, for obvious reasons, much more commonly a feature of affluent, information-rich societies, but the point is that this circumstance does not greatly help in understanding it.

Similarly, immediacy does not seem to yield to a very fruitful analysis in terms of a straightforward political-economic reductionism. The thought that the culture of immediacy is merely an epiphenomenon of the acceleration of capitalism (the ever-increasing rate of circulation exemplified in the technologies of constant, instantaneous global market trading) is tempting, but ultimately specious. There are clearly significant connections to be made between the dynamics of capitalism and aspects of the general acceleration of cultural experience – an obvious example being the initial impetus for the development of CMC technologies in newsgathering as market intelligence rather than as general public information. However, to remain within the constraints of this line of reductive thought is surely to miss hugely important aspects of cultural experience that are critically linked to technological change, but not simply attributable to a culture of consumerism, nor in any other relevant way decisively inflected by the overall economic context of capitalism. It is these aspects of cultural experience – the ubiquity of arrival, the diminishing relevance of intervening terms and processes, the consequent decay of values of patience and deferral – that I have tried to emphasize, precisely in order to avoid too easy a resolution of the puzzle of immediacy. Time, as the saying goes, may be money; but money is by no means the key to time.

This chapter began with an expression of uneasiness, perhaps impatience, with the application of established conceptual frameworks and familiar critical agendas to the interpretation of globalization. It is easy to express such unease, of course – just as it is easy to gesture towards the iconoclastic nature of globalizing phenomena. What is more difficult is to produce sober, convincing cultural analysis without falling back on the support of existing frameworks which we know to be inadequate to the task. What is much, much more difficult is to expand the critical-cultural imagination – the partly intuitive initial sense of what is significant, what connections need to be made, what we can and cannot assume about the attribution of meaning to experience, what new moral and political agendas may be emerging in the welter of data (or, better, 'capta')[11] that the processes of globalizing modernity are relentlessly generating.

My own suggested response to this returns to the primacy of interpretation. Social and cultural analysts need first and foremost to be good innocent readers: to struggle against the constraints of pre-judgement in order to give, at least initially, *theoretically uncommitted* attention to emergent processes as they unfold before us. If we can first do this we can then make appropriate use of the conceptual, theoretical and indeed political and moral resources we already possess, without allowing these to foreclose discourse, or to constellate falsely the complex and perplexing dimensions of change that increasingly confront us.

---

11 The distinction, which stresses the inevitable selectivity of social analysis – what is taken from, rather than what is given in, the flow of experience – is from Ronald D. Laing (1967).

References

Albrow, Martin (1996), *The Global Age: State and Society Beyond Modernity*. Cambridge: Polity Press.

Auden, W.H. (1966), 'Night Mail', in *Collected Shorter Poems, 1927–1957*. London: Faber & Faber.

Bauman, Zygmunt (2000), *Liquid Modernity*. Cambridge: Polity Press.

Beck, Ulrich (1997), *The Reinvention of Politics: Rethinking Modernity in the Global Social Order*. Cambridge: Polity Press.

— (2000a), *What is Globalization?* Cambridge: Polity Press.

— (2000b), 'The Cosmopolitan Society and its Enemies'. Keynote Address to Theory, Culture and Society conference, University of Helsinki. *Cosmopolis* (June).

Blakemore, M. (1990), *The Great Railway Show*. York: The National Railway Museum.

Castoriadis, Cornelius (1987), *The Imaginary Constitution of Society*. Cambridge: Polity Press.

— (1991), *Philosophy, Politics, Autonomy*. Oxford: Oxford University Press.

García Canclini, Néstor (1995), *Hybrid Cultures: Strategies for Entering and Leaving Modernity*. Minneapolis: University of Minnesota Press.

Giddens, Anthony (1990), *The Consequences of Modernity*. Cambridge: Polity Press.

Gleich, James (1999), *Faster*. London: Little, Brown.

Hyland, A. (2000), 'Half of Britain on the Mobile'. *The Guardian* (6 July): 28.

Laing, Ronald D. (1967), *The Politics of Experience*. Harmondsworth: Penguin.

McLuhan, Marshall (1964), *Understanding Media: The Extensions of Man*. London: Routledge and Kegan Paul.

Marinetti, F.T. (1973), 'The Founding and Manifesto of Futurism 1909', in U. Apollonio (ed.), *Futurist Manifestos*. London: Thames and Hudson.

Radford, T. (2000), 'Robotic Future Rushes Towards Us'. *The Guardian* (1 May): 5.

Robertson, Roland (1992), *Globalization: Social Theory and Global Culture*. London: Sage.

Schivelbusch, Wolfgang (1980), *The Railway Journey: Trains and Travel in the Nineteenth Century*. Oxford: Basil Blackwell.

Thompson, John B. (1995), *The Media and Modernity*. Cambridge: Polity Press.

Tomlinson, John (1999), *Globalization and Culture*. Cambridge: Polity Press.

Virilio, Paul (1997), *Open Sky*. London: Verso.

PART II

NATIONAL CASE STUDIES

CHAPTER 4

Hyperpower Exceptionalism: Globalization the American Way[1]

Jan Nederveen Pieterse

We are in a unique position because of our unique assets, because of the character of our people, the strength of our ideals, the might of our military and the enormous economy that supports it. (US Vice-President Dick Cheney addressing the Council on Foreign Relations, February 2002; in Gordon 2002)

Today's era is dominated by American power, American culture, the American dollar and the American navy. (Friedman 2000: xix)

In international affairs the USA displays growing unilateralism. International development policies have been constrained by the Washington consensus. The United States fails to sign on to major greening protocols. Until recently the USA was perennially in arrears in United Nations dues. On several occasions (such as Nicaragua and Panama) the USA has not followed international legal standards and it ignores the International Court if its verdict goes against it. American policies contribute to the enduring stalemate in the Middle East. Take any global problem and the United States is both the major player and major bottleneck. It is a reasonable question to ask whether this is just a matter of current US administrations or whether more profound dynamics are at work.

If we take seriously global problems and therefore also the need for global reform (such as the provision of global public goods and the regulation of international finance) and then turn to the question of political implementation we naturally arrive at the door of the United States.[2] Progressive social forces and international institutions the world over make proposals for global reform,

---

1 I thank Jeff Powell and Joost Smiers for their comments.
2 This is how I come to the question of US politics, via work on global futures (Nederveen Pieterse 2000).

whose list is considerable and growing, but without US cooperation they stand little chance of being implemented. The world leader, then, turns out to be the global bottleneck and in this light American conditions and problems become world problems.

The thesis of 'American exceptionalism' in American social science holds that the USA is a special case. If we take this claim seriously, what does it imply for US leadership? What does it mean when a country that by its own account is the historical exception sets rules for the world? Let us revisit the arguments of American exceptionalism and then ask how this spills over into the international arena.

This exercise is not meant as another round of anti-Americanism; that would take us back decades and bring us on to conservative terrain. We may appreciate or admire American society for its many positive aspects – such as its cultural mix as an immigrant society, the vitality of its popular culture, its technological and economic achievements – and yet be concerned about the way it relates to the rest of the world. In this treatment the objective is to take a clinical look at American conditions and their consequences for global conditions. The argument under examination is that the claims and ramifications of American exceptionalism are important to understanding the politics of contemporary globalization and, accordingly, that the margins for political change in the USA hold implications for options for global change.

The first part of this exercise is easy at least in the sense that there is ample literature on American exceptionalism, mostly from American sources, and the key themes are familiar. The difficulties are to avoid mistaking American ideologies for realities, to avoid the trap of impressionism based on ignorance when everyone thinks they 'know' the USA on account of its large cultural radius, and to be concise while the data are vast. The literature on 'America', the largest and foremost developed country, is vast and multivocal. This part of the treatment is meant as a précis organized in brief vignettes. The second part probes the international ramifications of American exceptionalism. This is less widely talked about and tucked within specialist literatures on international relations and international political economy (including transnational enterprises, the Washington consensus and military affairs). Twinning the themes of American exceptionalism and global ramifications is the pioneering element in this inquiry. The terrain is large, the literatures are extensive and so this treatment is pointed, focusing on American exceptionalism and global ramifications. The closing section criticizes American exceptionalism as a self-caricature and considers possible counterpoints.

American Exceptionalism

The profile of American exceptionalism (AE) is fairly familiar. Its origins lay in 'the merger of the republican and millennial traditions that formed an ideology of American exceptionalism prominent in American historical writing' (Tyrell 1991: 1031). Another familiar line of reasoning follows Werner Sombart's question of 1906: 'Why is there no socialism in the United States?' AE is a controversial thesis also in the USA. Thus it is argued that 'because of American heterogeneity we have not had a singular mode or pattern of exceptionalism' (Kammen 1993: 3; cf. Appleby 1992). Nevertheless, it remains broadly endorsed by influential American thinkers across a wide spectrum: in political science (Lipset 1996), history (Tyrell 1991), labour studies (for example, Davis 1986) and race relations (Frederickson 2001; Jones 1998). AE of a kind has also been signalled abroad, often with admiration, from de Tocqueville to Gramsci, Dahrendorf to Baudrillard. It may be difficult to draw the line between AE as fact and as ideology, but on the premise of social constructivism it makes sense to assume that both spill over into the international arena. AE as ideology may be as significant as actual deviations from historical patterns.

There is a wider variation in the acceptance or rejection of AE, especially among American historians, than in the components of AE itself. Major strands of AE, such as laissez-faire ideology and the relative power of business, have been fairly continuous or reinforced over time. 'Prolonged post-war prosperity refurbished the classic American anti-statist, market-oriented values' (Lipset 1996: 98), which were further reinforced under the Clinton administration. With regard to working-class organization there has been an ongoing decline in trade union membership and an increase in corporate hostility to organized labour and illegal corporate tactics against organized labour (Kammen 1993; Klein 2000).

This treatment is not a critique or even a problematization of AE: the focus is not AE per se but its international ramifications. To a certain extent AE is understandable in relation to American fundamentals: a vast, resource-rich continent, without foreign wars on its territory; a history of settler colonialism and a modernity based on shallow foundations; a nation of immigrants and a huge interior market; the fourth largest population in the world and the largest among developed countries. By the same token, this serves as a warning light that the American *Sonderweg* reflects fundamentals in which others cannot follow. As a Bostonian remarked to de Tocqueville, 'those who would like to imitate us should remember that there are no precedents for our history' (quoted in Kammen 1993: 7).

The long and continuing stretch of American hegemony places its stamp on societies the world over; contemporary globalization is the latest instalment. The ongoing changes associated with contemporary globalization are partly of a structural nature – technological changes, the information society, flexibilization, individualization – and in part inflected by, among other things, American influence. Thus, to the extent that the American *Sonderweg* shapes global conditions they are being shaped by conditions in which others cannot follow. To probe the question of what kind of globalization American hyperpower produces means to re-examine US society.

There is ample reference in the literature to the exceptionalism of other countries – such as the German *Sonderweg* and Japanese uniqueness (*Nihonjiron*), the exceptionalism of Britain, France, Scandinavia, Europe, East Asia, China, Australia, and so forth. In most of these cases, however, exceptionalism is single-issue (such as British labour and French *dirigisme*) rather than multidimensional; it does not also perform as a popular ideology (except in Japan and until recent years Germany); and most importantly, these nations are not superpowers. Any country would look odd if its historical idiosyncrasies were amplified on the world stage. In the present context this is the real problem; not AE per se.

Major strands of AE are free enterprise and laissez-faire ideology, the relative power of business and limited role of government, the ideology of 'Americanism' and social inequality. To this familiar profile I add observations on the character of American modernity and the role of the military.

Free Enterprise Capitalism

Laissez-faire side by side with a weak state and weak labour organization may be taken as the cornerstones of AE. Yet none of these, except the last, is unproblematic in a factual sense.

The US federal government behaves like a minimal state but is also strongly regulatory and strong in the areas of defence and security. The USA is 'the only industrialized country which does not have a significant socialist movement or labor party' (Lipset 1996: 33). The USA has a lower rate of taxation and many fewer government-owned industries than other industrialized nations (Lipset 1996: 38–39). Yet mixed economy or John Ruggie's term 'embedded liberalism' is a more apt description than 'laissez-faire'. All along, laissez-faire has been embedded in and tempered by government interventions such as Fordism, party machines, the New Deal, military Keynesianism, export credits, local investment incentives, the 'war on poverty' and affirmative action. Unlike European social democracy, American Fordism was based more on worker productivity and pay rates than on worker rights, more on corporate designs than government policy. Johnson's Great Society was aborted by the burdens of the Vietnam War (Siegel 1984). The USA is a residual welfare state and increasingly a workfare state (Peck 1998), but still a welfare state.

The implementation of laissez-faire in the USA has been discontinuous, with many zigzags and ups and downs, and partial: some economic sectors, notably the military industries, have known government intervention all along. And it has been opportunistic: deviations occur at any time if political expedience requires. The actual deregulation of business has increased sharply since the 1980s. The Reagan era of monetarism, supply-side economics, tax cuts and government rollback helped to inaugurate a worldwide trend of liberalization and deregulation.

The Enron episode may turn out to be a watershed. This is what emerges at the end of the road of deregulation; the next chapter after casino capitalism is swindle capitalism. The turning point occurs if deregulation and no-nonsense capitalism drive the US economy down. No-nonsense capitalism has gradually removed all safeguards – accountability, transparency, legal recourse in case of malpractice by corporations, accounting firms and market analysts – leaving investors so vulnerable that eventually the stock market itself may decline.

While actual practice has been uneven and partial, the ideology of free enterprise has been virtually constant. The key features of US capitalism – free enterprise, a minimal state, an advanced degree of possessive individualism – are anomalous by international and Western standards, as Michel Albert argues in *Capitalism against Capitalism* (1993), but what is more anomalous still than American practice is American laissez-faire ideology. Yet this has been continuously upheld as the international position: 'Hardly anyone acknowledged or addressed the contradiction between practicing a mixed economy at home and promoting a laissez-faire economy globally' (Kuttner 1991: 10–11). As Paul Krugman (2001) observes, 'policymakers in Washington and bankers in New York often seem to prescribe for other countries the kind of root canal economics that they would never tolerate here in the USA ... My advice would be to stop listening to those men in suits. Do as we do, not as we say.'

Political Conservatism

> That government governs best which governs least. (Thomas Jefferson)
> Less government is better government. (Ronald Reagan)
> The era of big government is over. (Bill Clinton, 1996)

According to Seymour Martin Lipset, the enduring values of AE – in particular liberty, egalitarianism, individualism, populism and laissez-faire – have made the United States 'the most anti-statist, legalistic and rights-oriented nation'. The USA is 'the most classical liberal polity' and 'the great conservative society' (Lipset 1996: 35). If 'night watchman state' is a common description, Nettl (1968) goes further and refers to the 'relative statelessness' of the USA as a society in which only the *law* is sovereign (Lipset 1996: 40). As a result what is right-wing in most countries is the political centre in the USA.

Familiar features of the American political system include constitutionalism, checks and balances between executive and legislative powers, and the presidential system. Constitutionalism yields a law-centred polity and is the foundation of what over time has become an exceptionally litigious society.[3] The USA may be described as a 'legal-rational culture': 'In no other industrial society is legal regulation as extensive or coercive as in the United States' (Haley in Lipset 1996: 228). The 800,000 American attorneys represent one-third of the world total of practising lawyers (Lipset 1996: 227).

The American republic was designed as a weak state with a divided form of government. 'The chronic antagonism to the state derived from the American revolution' (Lipset 1996: 39); its origins lie in the American fight against a centralized (monarchical) state. It follows, according to Lipset, that there is no tradition of obedience to the state or to law. An example is the failure of the US government to impose the metric system, which is official by law but not being implemented (Lipset 1996: 93).

The American separation of powers allows and even encourages members of Congress to vote with their constituents against their president or dominant party view. American legislators, including Congressional leaders, have voted against and helped to kill bills to carry out major international agreements in response to small groups of local constituents. As former House speaker Thomas P. (Tip) O'Neill once put it, in Congress, 'all politics is local' (Lipset 1996: 42).

The country's large size, federalism and checks and balances make for a give-and-take system of spoils in Congress: cooperation at a federal level is obtained through regional and special-interest deals and redistribution. These features make it difficult to pass progressive measures in Congress, which in turn holds major implications for American world leadership.

A further consideration is the exclusion of a third party in framing American political debate. According to William Greider, 'The decayed condition of American democracy is difficult to grasp, not because the facts are secret, but because the facts are visible everywhere' (Greider 1992: 11). The facts include

---

3 'Constitutionalism, the idea that a written constitution spells out the "supreme law of the land" and sets limits on the ruling authorities – including the legislatures elected by the people – must be seen ... as one of the most important elements of American modernity... In the US, the Constitution became the locus and symbol of the "general will"' (Heideking 2000: 225).

mass voter absenteeism, campaign financing problems and sound-bite political debate (Lewis et al. 1996; Kuttner 1998).[4]

Social Inequality: Winner-Takes-All

'As the purest example of a bourgeois nation, America follows the competitive principle of the marketplace in unions, management and other relationships' (Lipset 1996: 225). Relations between management and labour are adversarial. With this comes an income spread that is the widest among industrialized nations. J.P. Morgan followed the rule that executives in his firms could not earn more than 20 times the amount that blue-collar workers earned. In 1998, CEOs at major companies earned 419 times the average pay of blue-collar workers and the trend is for this gap to widen. The pay of the average chief executive of a large company went up by 36 per cent in 1998 and that of average blue-collar workers rose only 2.7 per cent (Overholser 1999; Goodman 1999). The bottom fifth of US households receives less than 4 per cent of the national income while the top fifth takes home almost half (Henwood 1999; cf. Henderson et al. 2000). Furthermore, tying CEO remuneration to stock performance has seen CEO pay rise proportionately to the decimation of full-time jobs as downsizing increases shareholder value (Klein 2000). Frank and Cook (1995) refer to the winner-takes-all system and attribute its emergence to the competitiveness system in combination with changes in communications technologies that privilege winners – in corporations, finance, entertainment, sports and education.

Compared with other advanced countries the USA is marked by greater equality of opportunity and greater inequality of outcome. Robert Merton's (1957) classic argument suggests that the differential between opportunity and outcome accounts for the high US crime rate, as aspirations are socially shared but not the means for realizing them. The vivacity of American popular culture reflects this tension between equality of opportunity and inequality of outcome.

The USA has greater tolerance for inequality than any advanced society – materially and socially, as the most unequal among developed societies, and in terms of political culture and development philosophy. Mishra (1996: 403) notes that 'the Reagan administration replaced the war on poverty with a war on the poor ... Not poverty as such but pauperization, i.e. dysfunctional and deviant behaviour on the part of the poor was now identified as the main

---

4 During the 2000 presidential elections other features became manifest: 'Virtually alone among the industrial democracies, the United States does not have a national election commission to prescribe the do's and don'ts of voting' (Hoagland 2000).

problem of the 1980s, and the early 1990s reflected this shift in agenda from a concern with poverty to a concern with the poor.' 'From this viewpoint, then, poverty is no longer an issue. The social problems confronting Americans are now those of welfare dependency, out of wedlock births, criminality and other dysfunctional behaviour on the part of the lower strata of the population' (Mishra 1996: 404). The prevailing political discourse blames the victims, defines welfare dependency as the problem and thus views government rollback and welfare cutbacks as the main remedies. Inequality is taken as a matter of course and poverty is seen as an enemy in that it shows up failure in the culture of success. This deeply embedded strain has been reinforced in recent years.[5] Social inequality in the USA has been increasing markedly since the 1970s. Thirty million Americans live below the poverty line and 40 million are without health insurance. The life expectancy of an African-American male in Harlem is less than that of a male in Bangladesh. The fact that foundations and charities – a 'thousand points of light' and faith-based organizations included – do not make up for government failure is well documented.

Americanism

If only on account of its large size the USA, like other large countries, tends to be culturally parochial and inward-looking. The USA is in many ways a self-absorbed country engrossed in collective narcissism. One indicator is the dearth of reporting on foreign affairs. Foreign reporting has declined and foreign correspondents were cut back at a time when the US role in world affairs increased after the end of the Cold War, creating the peculiar situation that the people least informed about foreign affairs are the world's most influential.

The USA is, according to Michael Harrington, 'a country united not by common history but by *ideology* – the American Creed, or Americanism, which also serves as "substitute socialism"' (quoted in Lipset 1996: 84, 88). The ideology of 'Americanism' combined with exceptionalism yields a fervent nationalism that is exceptional among modern societies, huddled around the Constitution, the presidency, an unusual cult of the flag and a popular culture of America Number One.

The USA made early use of electronic mass media for nationwide communication – first radio and cinema, then television. American technical prowess in media and advertising sets global standards. In pioneering mass consumer culture the USA set standards in commodity fetishism, as in the

5 Further data and documentation on US and global inequality are in Nederveen Pieterse (forthcoming) (from which this paragraph is taken).

post-war 'American Dream'. Its large internal market makes the USA less dependent on and less sensitive to other countries, so there is little business incentive in foreign reporting.

Shallow Modernity

Through the centuries Europe experienced tribal and peasant culture, empire, feudalism and absolutism – an Old World indeed. In this context modernity is a stratum arising from, superimposed on and interspersed with other historical layers. Continental modernity arises out of this historical depth and so the outcome is a complex modernity. The major role of the state derives from the multiple and combined legacies of imperial history, feudalism and absolutism, and the revolutionary correction of feudalism and absolutism, which required a centralized state. 'Rhineland capitalism' (Albert 1993) and the continental welfare state hold the imprint of the moral economy and entitlements of feudal times, when lords ruled in exchange for giving economic and military protection to their bondsmen.

In contrast, American modernity is based on the experience of petty commodity production, and slave production in the South, soon followed by industrialism and Taylorism. Thus, in the USA there are 'no traditions from before the age of progress'; US society is a 'postrevolutionary new society' (Lipset 1996: 37, 228). Since American independence coincided with the Enlightenment the country was founded on the basis of rational progressivism. Scientism, along with the legacy of religious dissidence and Protestant idealism, combined to produce Manifest Destiny and the 'Angel of Progress' (Drinnon 1980). Antonio Gramsci viewed America as 'pure rationalism' (Lipset 1996: 87); according to Ralf Dahrendorf, the USA is the country of the 'applied Enlightenment'. The lack of depth of a classical tradition informs American culture which is characterized instead by the 'reconciliation of mass and class', which entails the 'deradicalization of class' (Zunz 1999). The absence of dialectics with older strata (Neolithic, feudal and absolutist) makes for unmitigated innovation unburdened by history: the unbearable lightness of America. This turns 'rupture' into religion. Immigration too makes rupture with history a part of collective experience. Key features of US capitalism may be viewed as ramifications of American thin modernity. This in turn shapes the role of the USA in the worldwide interaction of modernities.

Strength of the Military

The security apparatus plays a remarkably large role in American politics, economics and social life. The USA is a minimal state *except* when it comes to law and order, the military and intelligence. The only area in which the Reagan administration engaged in long-term planning was defence and the space missile defence shield (Albert 1993: 29).[6]

> US military expenditure has dropped by 25 per cent from its peak in 1986, somewhat less than the global average decline of 35 per cent (largely due to the break-up of the Soviet Union). The number of US military personnel has dropped even more (by 800,000 or 36 per cent) than the US defence budget, thus ensuring that the Pentagon spends more today than during the Cold War on each individual soldier. The USA alone represents approximately a third of world's military spending ... today no other country, whether friend or rival comes close to the $265 billion which the US is allocating to defence in the Fiscal Year 1998–99... furthermore, US defence spending is increasing again. (Heisbourg 1999/2000: 5–6)

The constitutional right of citizens to bear arms, the influence of the National Rifle Association and 'gun culture' on the streets and in the media, echo American historical roots as a settler colonial conquest society in which pioneer farmers acted as frontier soldiers. It finds expression in a culture in which force and coercion serve as political tools (Duclos 1998). The USA ranks first in the number of incarcerations among nations the world over; China is second (Dyer 1999). The prison population is referred to as the American 'internal gulag' (Egan 1999). The USA stands alone among wealthy countries in its extensive use of the death sentence.

The prominent role of the military enjoys broad popular and bipartisan political support. Social acceptance of the military is anchored in its serving as an avenue of social mobility for lower classes, which is one of the wheels of military Keynesianism and makes up for a weak and class-biased educational system.[7] Right after the party conventions, presidential candidates first address the Veterans' League and invariably propose expansion of resources for the military – making sure that 'the US armed forces are the best equipped and

6 'President Clinton's proposed FY 2000 discretionary budget provides in first place close to $300 billion for the Military, while education in second and health in third place are budgeted with $35 billion and $31 billion respectively! Natural resources and Environment are listed with $24 billion in fifth place' (Croose Parry 2000: 13). The 2002 military budget expansion sought by the Bush administration would bring the total to $379 billion.

7 In education, 'We rank 19th among the 29 nations of the OECD. Twenty-eight million Americans cannot identify the United States on a world map! ... The salaries of United States teachers are the lowest as a percentage of national income on earth' (Croose Parry 2000: 13).

Table 1. Dimensions of American exceptionalism

Dimensions	*Key notes*	
Free enterprise capitalism	'Business in the US has historically enjoyed an unusual degree of political power' (Kammen 1993: 5). Ideology of reliance on market forces	
Political conservatism	Institutional	Minimal state. Constitutionalism. Extreme separation of powers.
		Weak working-class organization. Unusual power of corporations
	Political process	Populism. Voluntary associations. Weak role of parties (state and local, rather than national)
	Values	Individualism. Privatized ethics. Transparency, social engineering
	Ideology	Americanism, patriotism
Minimal state	'the most anti-statist, legalistic and rights-oriented nation' (Lipset 1996)	
Weak working-class organization	'increase in the extent of illegal employer resistance to unions' (Kammen 1993)	
Race relations	Race as a substitute for working-class solidarity. Whiteness as substitute privilege (Roediger 1992). Chronic ghetto poverty, incarceration, death penalty	
Voluntary associations	De Tocqueville to Putnam. Charity. Gated communities.	
Shallow modernity	The country of the applied Enlightenment	
Americanism	Americanism as celebration of the absence of historical burdens (Howe 1979). The 'meaning of America' served as a surrogate for history (Kammen 1993).	
Culture	'in the US there is no long-standing traditional establishment of culture on the European model' (Mills 1963)	

best trained in the world'. The moral status of the US military is popularized and upheld through frequent media reiteration of its role in the Second World War (skipping over the Vietnam and Iran-Contra episodes). Military metaphors and desensitization to violence pervade the entertainment sector (Grossman 1996). A sizeable part of Hollywood production is devoted to military themes and parallels the phases of the projection of American power (Sharp 1998). To illustrate the pervasiveness of this influence, the choreography of the Broadway musical is based on military drill, going back to an American drill officer who had made his reputation in the First World War (Voeten 2000).

The role of the military-industrial complex in American industrialization is not exceptional by historical standards; building military strength has been the locomotive of industrialization in advanced countries the world over, particularly during the late nineteenth century (Sen 1995; Nederveen Pieterse 1989). What is exceptional is the *enduring* role of the military-industrial complex over time, in line with America's role of superpower. The conventional thesis of the American war economy (Melman 1974) is probably no longer tenable. The economic rationale of keeping a vast security force may now be overshadowed by political rationales, along with a regional spoils system that includes the distribution of government contracts and military facilities (details in Keller 2002). Even so the inclination towards the use of force in American political culture interacts with profit motives. Throughout the USA new prisons are the answer to local economic revival (Hallinan 2000) and privatized prisons constitute a 'correctional-industrial complex' (Reiss 1998; Dyer 1999). Gated communities and video surveillance are part of the privatization of security: 'from night watchmen and bodyguards to virtual private armies, the security services industry is booming, while the trade in firearms is breaking all records' (Albert 1993: 47).

Given the formidable role of the US military, upon the end of the Cold War, 'conversion' and the peace dividend have not paid off. Instead there has been a political and economic need, or at any rate inclination, to keep the security apparatus occupied, to upgrade equipment and weapons, and to provide opportunities for testing and military career opportunities with recurrent budget expansion and mammoth projects such as 'Plan Colombia'. This expansion pales into insignificance next to the military budget increase of $48 billion proposed by the Bush administration as part of the 'war on terrorism'. Deep tax cuts favouring the wealthy now go together with cutbacks in spending on infrastructure, social services and education.

To recapitulate this discussion of features of AE and situate it in a wider picture, Table 1 gives a brief overview of major dimensions of AE.

Globalization as Americanization?

The whole world should adopt the American system. The American system can survive in America only if it becomes a world system (President Harry Truman, 1947).

Americans who wanted to bring the blessings of democracy, capitalism, and stability to everyone meant just what they said – the whole world, in their view, should be a reflection of the United States (Ambrose 1983: 19).

There is no denying that several features of American exceptionalism shape contemporary globalization; yet developing this argument involves several hurdles. First, inherent in the notion of 'Americanization' is an element of methodological populism. To which unit of analysis does this apply – to *which* America, whose America? The USA is the fourth largest country in the world in terms of population, quite heterogeneous, and local differences play a signi-ficant part. American corporations with decentralized headquarters and off-shore tax reporting cannot be simply identified with the United States either. Besides, transnational flows do not run just one way but in multiple directions; there are also trends of Europeanization, Asianization and Latinization of America, economically and culturally (with respect to foreign ownership, management style, consumption patterns). Transnational diasporas have been changing the character of 'America' all along and this bricolage character is part of its make-up. What then is the actual unit at issue? Is it a set of 'organizing principles' that remain continuous over time, as Lipset would have it, or, at another extreme, is America a *site*, a place of transnational synthesis and bricolage? Since waves and layers of diasporas, from the Irish to the Latino, have been shaping 'America' it is not possible simply to refer back to the founding fathers in order to diagnose American fundamentals. It would not be productive either to rework the *défi Américain* type of argument (à la Servan-Schreiber 1967); that would place the argument in a setting of national comparisons and competitiveness, à la Michael Porter. This national focus is in part overtaken by the dynamics of accelerated globalization and is not appropriate to an analysis of the relationship between AE and globalization.

A second problem is to accommodate historical variation in US politics, or the relationship between structure and politics. AE does not quite match the actual profile of US administrations and is not necessarily intrinsic to American politics; to argue otherwise would be to essentialize American politics. Wilsonian internationalism was also part of US foreign policy and American contributions to world order include the establishment of the UN and Bretton Woods system, the Marshall Plan, support for European unification, and policies in favour of human rights and democracy. While these contributions are under dispute they show that there is greater variation to American foreign policy than just the profile of the past decades. While the emphasis here is on American policies in relation to contemporary globalization this serves as a note of caution. In the latter days of the Clinton administration there were some changes in the picture (mitigation of the embargo on Cuba, settlement of arrears in UN dues),[8] some of which, such as US endorsement of the permanent International Criminal Court, were reversed by the next administration.

In recent years much discussion on Americanization has focused on cultural dynamics, or what Nye calls 'soft power': the role of media, popular culture and transnational consumerism, examined in cultural studies. It is also another kind of populism for it is rarely adequately correlated with other dimensions of American influence: economic, financial, international and military.[9] This lack of articulation between soft and hard power is problematic. The question of AE and globalization differs from the conventional cultural imperialism thesis. Overall American impact is to a considerable extent a matter of what Galtung (1971) called 'structural imperialism': shaping other societies through structural leverage rather than just through direct political intervention. This includes but goes beyond popular culture, the cultural industries and the familiar litanies of Coca-colonization, McDonaldization, Disneyfication, Barbie culture and American media conglomerates. While these are high-visibility and receive overwhelming attention, the more significant impact of AE probably concerns economic policies and international politics and security. These too are 'cultural', but covertly rather than overtly so, and less visible in everyday life. They concern not just relations among advanced countries but relations across development gradients that affect the majority world. It may help to distinguish several levels of analysis:

- *Structural dynamics.* This includes scientific and technological changes pioneered by and exported from the USA. Ultimately, however, these represent an intercivilizational heritage (see, for example, Diamond 1999).
- *Fundamental dynamics which are general to industrialized countries.* Here the leading package offered by the country that pioneers these trends affects all; yet these dynamics are not necessarily peculiar to that country. This brings us to the convergence thesis of modernization theory according to which industrial societies would eventually converge (Brzezinski 1970). In this category belong trends such as mass production, mass consumption, mass media, car culture, suburbanization and information technology; that is, they are not 'American' per se but since the USA was the first comer they carry an American gloss.

---

8 The terms of this settlement bring down US compulsory UN fees from 25 to 20 per cent of the world total (while the US share of world gross domestic product stands at approximately 22 per cent; Heisbourg 1999: 5).

9 An example is the coordination between US Cold War politics and cultural policies discussed in Saunders 1999.

- American corporations and cultural industries seek to draw monopoly rents from their temporary lead 'by means fair or foul'. This is a common business practice with ample precedent in history. The British destroyed the Indian textile manufactures and trade and sabotaged incipient industrialization in Egypt, Persia and the Ottoman Empire (Stavrianos 1981).
- Through international leverage (international financial institutions and the WTO) and regional arrangements the US government seeks to consolidate its lead and institutionalize the advantage of its multinational corporations.

It follows that the *core* questions of global Americanization are the last two points: drawing monopoly rents and their institutionalization through super-power leverage.

That the line between domestic and international politics is blurring is a familiar point in international relations literature. Often the emphasis falls on the international influencing the domestic (Keohane and Milner 1996). The present query asks how the domestic influences the international domain: how does American politics influence the international domain and the politics of other countries? Table 2 gives a 'big picture' sketch of relations between AE and contemporary accelerated globalization. There is an extensive literature on virtually all of the dimensions noted. This treatment focuses on three themes as faces of AE as they appear on the world map: laissez-faire and the US role in shaping capitalism, the (post-) Washington consensus and international development politics, and world politics.

Laissez-faire

A major US export has been its brand of capitalism, as in Taylorism, Fordism, high mass-consumption, free trade, and American corporations and business practices. Since the 1980s, through the Washington consensus, monetarism, privatization, liberalization and deregulation have been added to the repertoire.

American hegemony is part of a series: the rise of US influence followed the era of British hegemony. Manchester liberalism, neo-classical economics from the 1870s and its neo-liberal resumption from the late 1970s form a historical series. This international momentum cannot be divorced from the period of approximately 170 years of Anglo-American hegemony (from approximately 1830 onwards and interrupted by periods of hegemonic rivalry).[10]

By world standards, Anglo-American free enterprise capitalism is an anomaly. Mixed economies and social market capitalism have been the majority practice throughout Europe, Asia and the developing countries, and

10 Cf. Nederveen Pieterse 1989 on 'Continuities of empire' (Ch. 12).

Table 2. American exceptionalism and international ramifications

Dimensions of AE	Contemporary international ramifications
Free enterprise capitalism	US capitalism as the norm of capitalism Washington consensus, structural adjustment, IMF and World Bank conditionalities Global model of polarizing growth: growing inequality Promotion of offshore economies Deregulation of international finance The dollar as international currency; dollarization The role of US MNCs Spread of American business standards, law and MBA
Free trade	Trade policy as foreign policy instrument; Clause 301 WTO and neo-liberal global trade rules Free trade policies in NAFTA, APEC
Minimal state and political conservatism	Permanent arrears in UN dues Government rollback in development policies Non-participation in international treaties Non-compliance with International Court Double standards in regional affairs (Middle East) Promotion of narrow form of democracy
Weak working-class organization	Conservative influence of AFL–CIO (in ICFTU) Little support for ILO (e.g. labour standards)
Residual welfare/ workfare state	Rollback of social sectors in development (health, education, social services)
Voluntary associations	'Fostering democracy by strengthening civil society' Promotion of NGOs (USAID new policy agenda)
Individualism	Promotion of NGOs along with professionalization, depoliticization and political fragmentation
Shallow modernity	Alignment of accounting systems to US standards One-way transparency (US Treasury, IMF, WB) 'Seeing like a hyperpower', panopticism
Hegemony of military	Cold War spillovers (regional intervention legacies) Policies of embargoes, sanctions Unilateralism; acting outside UNSC mandate Militarization of international affairs War metaphor in international and economic relations Promotion of enemy images (rogue states, etc.) Mammoth projects for military-industrial complex 'Humanitarian militarism': coercive approach to local conflict Refusal to serve under UN command Network of military bases and intelligence surveillance

Dimensions of AE	Contemporary international ramifications
	Redeployment of intelligence monitoring (Echelon)
	Covert operations
	Nuclear proliferation (non-ratification of NTBT 1997)
	Health and environmental hazards of military operations (Gulf War, Balkans, Afghanistan and within USA)
	Arms sales, training and fostering regional arms races
	Militarization of borders (US–Mexico model exported to Israel, South Africa)
Americanism	Promotion of the 'American way'
American culture	Automobile culture, fossil fuel dependence
	Marketing as dominant cultural style
	Star and celebrity system
	McDonaldization, Disneyfication, Barbiefication
	CNN effect and sound-bite culture
	Internet, Microsoft, dotcom
	African-American culture (jazz, hip-hop)
	Abstract expressionism, pop art

central planning prevailed in socialist countries. Further, in the British and American experience, free enterprise was part posture and programme and only part reality: the self-regulating market was implemented late, partially and intermittently and the overall reality was embedded liberalism. Differences between continental European and Anglo-American varieties of embedded liberalism are matters of degree that turn into principle at several junctures; they concern the status and role of industrial policy, labour regulation, management, banks, venture capital and stocks. Looking at the USA, the differences are significant though not quite as large as free enterprise ideology claims them to be. From a European point of view, American influence consists of the ongoing shift from the stakeholder model to the shareholder model of capitalism; or, the incorporation of the political economy of social contracts into the political economy of corporations, financial markets and stock exchanges, and an overall shift from social contracts to legal-rational contractualism. The Enron episode shows how few safeguards this system provides.

The Washington Consensus

The American role in international development goes back to Truman's declaration of the 'development era' in 1948 (Sachs 1992). Post-war American policies in the South favoured 'betting on the strong', community development that matched the American voluntary sector, nation-building and instilling achievement orientation – all strands of modernization theory in which modernization equals Westernization equals Americanization (Nederveen Pieterse 2001). Americans were looking for a middle class in the Third World as if in search of their mirror image (Baran 1973). The Alliance for Progress was a further instalment. These policies interacted with the Cold War and the 'Washington consensus'.

The Washington consensus (WC) that took shape in the 1980s matches the core profile of AE: the free market and democracy go together. The main tenets of the WC are monetarism, reduction of government spending and regulation, privatization, liberalization of trade and financial markets, and the promotion of export-led growth. The WC is a continuation of the post-war American development stance: free enterprise and the Free World, free trade and democracy. A difference is that post-war modernization was a *rival* project, a contender in the Cold War, while the WC no longer looks to national security states to withstand communist pressure or insurgency: at the 'end of history' there would be no more need for national security states. Hence, if modernization theory was state-centred and part of the post-war Keynesian consensus in development thinking, the WC turns another leaf, to deregulation and government rollback, now elevated from domestic policy to international programme. In this sense the Reagan era was a consummation of US victory in the Cold War, acknowledging no rival, no competition. This footprint shows also in the policies of the international financial institutions: 'the end of the cold war has been associated with the increasing politicization of the IMF by the USA. There is evidence that the US has been willing to reward friends and punish enemies only since 1990' (Thacker 1999: 70).

The core belief in the free market and democracy presents several general problems: unfettered market forces foster inequality while democracy presumes equality; the free market is not really being implemented in the USA; American democracy is in deep crisis. It also presents several specific problems: the kind of democracy promoted by the USA is low-intensity (Robinson 1996); dismantling government means de-institutionalization whereas development requires capable institutions. Hence the dispute over the 'East Asian Miracle' (Wade 1996) and the eventual World Bank turnaround, bringing the state back in, now under the ambiguous heading of 'good governance'.

The WC has been implemented through IMF stabilization lending and World Bank structural adjustment programmes. 'The IMF and the World Bank were agreed at Bretton Woods largely as a result of U.S. Treasury: the forms were international, the substance was dictated by a single country' (Kindleberger 1986: 10). The WC has resulted in the rollback of government and government spending and the growth of NGOs and informalization. The net outcome is that those sectors that are unprofitable and therefore weak in the USA – health, education, social services – become weak sectors in developing countries affected by structural adjustment, where these sectors are the first affected by government spending cutbacks. While many NGOs have been platforms for social change, the downside of the growth of NGOs promoted and funded by the USA has been the depoliticization and demobilization of popular forces in the South.

Amid all the criticisms of the neo-liberal turn ('the counterrevolution in development') little attention is given to the circumstance that the Washington consensus is American exceptionalism turned inside out, the outside face of AE (cf. Manzo 1999). Presenting Anglo-American capitalism as the 'norm' of capitalism, the WC represents the perspectives and interests of the Wall Street–Treasury–IMF complex (Wade and Veneroso 1998). The WC now faces mounting problems: growing worldwide inequality, financial instability and crisis management, and its counterproductive and faulty prescriptions have met widespread criticism, including criticism within Washington. The new terminology of a 'post-Washington consensus', however, papers over policies of incoherence and improvisation.

The language of international affairs tends to be framed in terms attractive enough for parties to agree and vague enough for each to attribute its own meaning and take its own course of action. International development cooperation is typically a terrain of hegemonic compromise: who can dispute the desirability of 'structural reform', 'stability', 'civil society', 'democracy' (Nederveen Pieterse 2001)?

The 1990s has been described as a time of contestation between American and Asian capitalism, and American capitalism won (Hutton and Giddens 2000). In the USA the 'Asian crisis' was hailed as an opportunity for the further Americanization of Asian economies (Bello et al. 1998: 52). The export-oriented growth path – promoted by the USA – makes emerging markets dependent on US market access, reduces their manoeuvring room and makes them vulnerable to American trade policies. While the WC proclaims free trade and export-oriented growth, the actual policies beneath the free trade banner are more complex and range from using trade as an instrument of foreign policy (for example, granting most favoured trading nation status and lifting or imposing tariffs) to introducing legalism into world trade rules via the WTO and influencing other countries' exchange rates (as in the 1985 Plaza Accord and the appreciation of the yen).

If we transpose American domestic inequality and the 'war on the poor' on to a world scale this entails a policy of slashing foreign aid, upheld by Congressional majority, in a nation that ranks as the world's stingiest foreign assistance donor (the USA transfers around 0.1 per cent of GNP to developing countries annually while the internationally agreed UN target is 0.7 per cent of GNP). As part of a relentless campaign towards corporate deregulation, conservative think-tanks rail against 'foreign welfare' on the same basis that welfare is blamed in the USA: 'economic assistance impedes economic growth'. They argue that international welfare does not work, and that Congress should eliminate aid, adopt a long-term policy for removing development assistance, and instead adopt policies to promote 'economic freedom' (read: deregulation, free trade) in developing countries (Johnson and Schaefer 1998). On similar grounds ('not enough reforms' according to the US Treasury) the IMF is prevented from bailing out Argentina.

Forty per cent of the world population lives on less than $2 a day. On the other side of the split screen, 4 per cent of the world population in the USA absorbs 27 per cent of world energy and a vast share of resources. The imbalances are so staggering that one might expect this to rank as the number one problem in American public opinion or, failing that, at least in social science. However, the issue rarely comes up, except in fringe publications, or in the guise of the 'energy crunch'.

American World Leadership

While in many terrains the USA fails to exercise world leadership, it does not permit other institutions to fulfil this role either. The USA fails to exercise world leadership in environmental, financial and economic regulation because its political institutions would not permit it to do so (in view of institutional gridlock, special interests and local politics in Congress) and presumably because its interests, as they are perceived in leading circles, would not benefit from regulation. Arguably, up to a point, American interests are a net beneficiary of lack of regulation or disarray.

The US failure to exercise world leadership then is a matter both of lack of capacity (political institutions) and lack of will (political and economic interest). For instance, the USA is the only developed country that has not ratified the UN Convention on the elimination of all forms of discrimination against women (CEDAW) because doing so would override the authority of state law in family law.[11] Similar constraints apply to several other treaties in which the USA is the only outsider among advanced countries.

The USA treats the UN as a rival for world leadership. For the USA to recognize and strengthen the UN would imply stepping down from the pedestal of world leadership and hyperpower status. In the 1980s power in the UN shifted from the General Assembly (one country one vote) to the Security Council and its permanent five members with the USA as the hegemonic force: the New World Order in brief. The USA defunded critical UN agencies such as UNESCO and the UN system generally by chronically withholding its fees, fails to empower the International Labour Organization (ILO), exercises political pressure on UNDP and other agencies, and bypasses the Security Council when convenient, as in the case of NATO operations in Kosovo. Instead of empowering the UN the USA has preferred to act through the IMF and World Bank which operate on the basis of financial voting rules. These agencies the USA can control and the outcome has been the Washington consensus.

There are multiple layers and currents to US attitudes to the UN and other multilateral institutions. Ironically the USA has been in the forefront of the creation of multilateral institutions: the International Court goes back to an American initiative in 1899; the League of Nations and then the UN and the ILO were conceived or pushed by the USA (Reisman 1999–2000: 65). Reisman distinguishes multiple US roles in its relations with multilateral international institutions (prophetic-reformist, organizational, custodial, and domestic pressure-reactive) which are repeatedly in conflict with one another. This 'puts the US among the most avid supporters of multilateral institutions, and yet, in different circumstances, pits it against the members and administration of some of those same institutions' (63). US reformism reflects 'the desire to engage in major international social engineering' (65). 'The symbol of law is extremely important. Law is to play as large a role in international politics as Americans believe it plays in their own domestic processes, and judicial institutions ... are deemed central' (65). Accordingly, the 'institutional modalities the US helped put into place' are legalistic (75). This inclination towards international social engineering centred on law shows American thin modernity and Enlightenment complex turned inside out.

To the undercurrent of American isolationism, American internationalists respond that they want international engagement but *not* under the UN. The UN is perceived as un-American in that it follows a different conception of world order; or as anti-American in view of the Third World majority in the

---

11 Cf. http://www.cwfa.org/library/nation/2000-09 and Hirsen 1999.

General Assembly and its criticisms of American hegemony. Countries in the South have been the target of stereotyping by American media and political elites who treat the world majority and its concerns as political lowlife. Henry Kissinger's comment that the world south of Paris and Bonn has no political relevance is not enabling of global multipolarity. This shows another strand in American foreign policy, the Jacksonian or 'Joe Six-Pack' approach to international affairs (Mead 2001).

As a function of American narcissism, American mainstream media tend to problematize all countries except the USA itself. In this casually homogenizing vision countries are branded as 'loony tunes' or 'rogue states', nationalist leaders are deemed 'crazy', developing countries are backward, the EU suffers from 'rigidities of the labour market' and Japan is blamed for economic nationalism. Meanwhile the USA is opportunistic when it comes to business opportunities in China or steel imports from Europe and other countries.

The US Senate has not ratified the Comprehensive Test Ban Treaty and the Bush administration plans to implement the space missile defence system. Underlying the failure to ratify the nuclear test-ban treaty is the 'desire to keep all political and military options open, and, indeed, broaden their scope' (Andréani 1999–2000: 59). The space shield programme completely rejects the architecture of arms race control built up over many years; the 2002 Congressional Nuclear Posture Review and the idea of using nuclear deterrence against up to 40 countries show what is meant by 'keeping options open'.

What is noteworthy is not AE but other countries by and large following American leadership without much question. Among OECD countries France is the major exception (Mamère and Warin 1999); other counterweights have been Russia and China. Russia has been severely weakened by Washington politics under the guise of the IMF; China has been virtually neutralized through the process of accession to WTO membership. US strength is a function of the weakness or lack of political coherence of other political constellations. In a word, European and Asian opportunism match US opportunism in international affairs: hence the global stalemate. International indignation at US withdrawal from the Kyoto protocol is an episode in which countries from Japan to the EU have converged; another major instance of this kind is states across the world coming together in setting up an International Criminal Court – without the USA.

Hegemonic stability theory, formulated by Kindleberger and elaborated by Krassner, Keohane and Ruggie, holds that 'in the absence of a world government the global economy can be stabilized when a powerful nation plays the role of flywheel', performing several stabilizing functions (Kuttner 1991: 12). This is a policy of carrots rather than sticks. Along the lines of hegemonic compromise EU countries and Japan *grosso modo* accept US policies in the context of the G7, OECD, WTO, IMF and World Bank because they share the overall benefits, such as concessions on trade and agricultural policies in the case of the EU, and find shelter under the US military umbrella. This does not rule out disputes but political differences are not great enough to upset the apple-cart. Huntington (1999) proposes instead a hybrid international system that combines unipolarity and multipolarity: a uni-multipolar system. Along similar lines Gruber (2000) explores 'go-it-alone power' along with the formation of modular coalitions, a formula that matches the Gulf War and NATO operations in Kosovo.

The problem with international relations theories is that they tend to rationalize absurdity and political improvisation. What of 'hegemonic stability' in view of recurrent economic crises (Tequila, Asian, Russian, Latin American crises, Argentina) and continuing political stalemate in the Middle East? International relations theorizing tends to privilege politics over economics and overt politics over covert politics, often underestimates questions of security and geopolitics, and puts a systemic gloss on policies that may be better described as absurd.

Coda

Anti-Americanism is so boring and old-fashioned that one response is to take American conservatism for granted, like the weather, or to appreciate it for the sake of difference and sheer American resilience. The strident conservatism in American media from CNN to the *Wall Street Journal* is so habitual that one hardly notices any more. Two counterpoints to this line of thinking are that this would mean taking the global effects of AE for granted; and that if anti-Americanism is old-fashioned, so is Americanism.

According to Lipset (1996: 267), 'the dark side of American exceptionalism' is represented by 'developments which, like many of its positive features, derive from the country's organizing principles. These include rising crime rates, increased drug use, the dissolution of the American family, sexual promiscuity, and excessive litigiousness'. This diagnosis is coined in strikingly moral terms; it overlooks more structural and troubling trends such as the persistence and rise of inequality, the decline of American democracy and the structural weakness of federal government. More important in this context, however, it is a completely inward-looking assessment that does not consider the external ramifications of AE. By world standards, the dark side of AE is that the *American way is not a replicable and sustainable model of development.* The free market and democracy made in the USA are no shining example. American consumption patterns are not replicable – they are not even replicable *within* the USA. Not everyone in this world will or can have a two-car family, a suburban home, or a college education. Of course, not everyone in the USA does either, but the standard itself is not seriously in dispute. The American ecological footprint – its excessive use of energy and other resources – is not replicable.

The second fundamental problem is social inequality. Globalization the American way and according to the Washington consensus, or what remains of it, matches this pattern; it yields winner-takes-all globalization that increasingly mirrors American conditions of glaring inequality, phoney marketing culture and a coercive approach to deviations on a world scale. This pattern of real globalization emerging over the past decades has gone into overdrive in the US reactions to the 11 September attacks.

American institutions and the US domestic balance of forces are variables in world politics. In assessing the situation we must consider not just what happens but also what does not happen. Thus an increasingly prominent discussion now concerns the deficit of global public goods (Kaul et al. 1999); yet, in fact, 'global public goods' is itself a US-enforced euphemism, for 'global governance' is a non-starter in conservative American circles.

What are possible counterpoints to the scenario of globalization the American way? The Enron episode may lead to a weakening of the stock market; it may lead to re-regulation of American corporations and, overseas, to a shift away from American accounting standards and business practices. The worldwide shift from stakeholder to shareholder capitalism, or Anglo-American capitalism, seems risky when the US model of shareholder capitalism is itself at risk. Another possible counterpoint is a re-emergence of the 'other America'. American exceptionalism after all is a caricature, a self-caricature, not unlike the old stereotypes of 'national character' in other countries. It is thoroughly old-fashioned, predates the current realities of American multiculturalism and ignores the 'other America' of the civil rights movement, 1968, social movements from the anti-Vietnam War mobilization to Seattle, and the polls that usually register majority positions on labour rights, women's rights, the environment and many other issues that are far more progressive than those held by mainstream media and the political elite; a country where Michael Moore's *Stupid White Men* (2002) goes through nine printings in a week and ends up the number one bestseller. AE refers to a non-existent fantasy land, not unlike Walt Disney's model town, misinformed by corporate Stepford media and ruled by a wealthy political elite with an agenda of its own. The emergence of a new political movement such as a green party is possible but constrained by the institutional features of the American political system discussed above.

A further possible counterpoint may be a change in policies overseas along the lines of the Kyoto protocol signed *without the USA*. A more cohesive EU and greater substantive and political rapport particularly between European and Asian countries, including Japan, would be a significant step in this direction. Newly industrialized countries in South and South-East Asia and Latin America, transitional and developing countries may find a common interest in a joint programme of multilateral regulation of international finance and a reorientation towards a social and democratic capitalism. International labour organizations and social movements that seek global reform – from Seattle to Porto Alegre – hold further potential for shaping a transnational reform coalition that could change the agenda. Such a coalition including European, Asian, American and Latin American progressive forces could redirect and reshape the course of globalization.

References

Albert, M. (1993), *Capitalism against Capitalism*. London: Whurr.

Ambrose, S.E. (1983), *Rise to Globalism: American Foreign Policy since 1938*. Harmondsworth: Pelican, 3rd rev. edn.

Andréani, G. (1999–2000), 'The Disarray of US Non-proliferation Policy', *Survival* 41(4): 42–61.

Appleby, Joyce (1992), 'Recovering America's Historic Diversity: Beyond Exceptionalism', *Journal of American History* 79: 419–31.

Baran, P. (1973), *The Political Economy of Growth*. Harmondsworth: Penguin.

Bauer, R.A. (ed.) (1975), *The United States in World Affairs: Leadership, Partnership, or Disengagement?* Charlottesville, VA: University Press of Virginia.

Bello, W., S. Cunningham and Li Kheng Po (1998), *A Siamese Tragedy: Development and Disintegration in Modern Thailand*. London and Bangkok: Zed Books and Focus on the Global South.

Brzezinski, Z. (1970), *Between Two Ages: America's Role in the Technetronic Era*. Harmondsworth, Penguin.

Campbell, D. (2000), 'Drugs in the Firing Line', *Guardian Weekly* (27 July –2 August).

Croose Parry, Renee-Marie (2000), 'Our World on the Threshold of the New Millennium', *WFSF Futures Bulletin* 26(1): 12–15.

Davis, Mike (1986), *Prisoners of the American Dream*. London: Verso.

Diamond, Jared (1999), *Guns, Germs, and Steel: The Fates of Human Societies*. New York: Norton.

Drinnon, R. (1980), *Facing West: The Metaphysics of Indian-hating and Empire-building*. New York: New American Library.

Duclos, D. (1998), *The Werewolf Complex: America's Fascination with Violence*. Oxford: Berg.

Dyer, Joel (1999), *The Perpetual Prisoner Machine: How America Profits From Crime*. Boulder, CO: Westview Press.

Egan, T. (1999), 'Hard Time: Less Crime, More Criminals, *New York Times* (7 March).

Evans, Harold (1998), *The American Century*. London: Jonathan Cape.

Frank, R.H., and P.J. Cook (1995), *The Winner-Take-All Society*. New York: Free Press.

Frederickson, Kari (2001), *The Dixiecrat Revolt and the End of the Solid South, 1932–1968*. Chapel Hill, NC: University of North Carolina Press.

Friedman, T.L. (2000), *The Lexus and the Olive Tree: Understanding Globalization*. New York: Anchor Books, 2nd edn.

Galtung, J. (1971), 'A Structural Theory of Imperialism', *Journal of Peace Research* 8: 81–117.

Goodman, Ellen (1999), 'Top Heavy on the Money Tree', *Guardian Weekly* (25 April).

Gordon, M.R. (2002), 'Cheney Rejects Criticism by Allies over Stand on Iraq', *New York Times* (16 February).

Greider, W. (1992), *Who Will Tell the People? The Betrayal of American Democracy*. New York: Simon and Schuster.

Gross, B. (1980), *Friendly Fascism: The New Face of Power in America*. New York: M. Evans.

Grossman, D. (1996), *On Killing: The Psychological Cost of Learning to Kill in War and Society*. New York: Little, Brown.

Gruber, L. (2000), *Ruling the World: Power Politics and the Rise of Supranational Institutions*. Princeton, NJ: Princeton University Press.

Guyatt, N. (2000), *Another American Century? The United States and the World After 2000*. London: Zed Books.

Hallinan, J.T. (2001), *Going Up the River: Travels in a Prison Nation*. New York: Random House.

Heideking, J. (2000), 'The Pattern of American Modernity from the Revolution to the Civil War', *Daedalus* 129(1): 219–48.

Heisbourg, François (1999/2000), 'American Hegemony? Perceptions of the US Abroad', *Survival* 41: 5–19.

Henderson, H., J. Lickerman and P. Flynn (eds) (2000), *Calvert–Henderson Quality of Life Indicators*. Bethesda, MD: Calvert Group.

Henwood, D. (1999), 'Booming, Borrowing, and Consuming: The US Economy in 1999, *Monthly Review* 51(3): 120–33.

Hirsen, J.L. (1999), *The Coming Collision: Global Law vs. US Liberties*. Lafayette, LA: Huntington House.

Hoagland, Jim (2000), 'A Civics Lesson for Americans and the Wide World', *International Herald Tribune* (17 November).

Howe, I. (ed.) (1979), *25 Years of Dissent: An American Tradition*. New York: Methuen.

Huntington, S.P. (1999), 'The Lonely Superpower', *Foreign Affairs* 78(2): 35–49.

Hutton, W., and A. Giddens (eds) (2000), *Global Capitalism*. New York: New Press.

Izquierdo, A. Javier (1999), 'Techno-scientific Culture and the Americanization of International Financial Markets', paper presented at European Sociological Association 4th European Conference of Sociology, Amsterdam.

Johnson, Bryan T. and Brett D. Schaefer (1998), 'IMF Reform? Setting the Record Straight', The Heritage Foundation, www.new.heritage.org/Research/

Jones, J. (1998), *American Work: Four Centuries of Black and White Labor*. New York: Norton.

Kammen, M. (1993), 'The Problem of American Exceptionalism: A Reconsideration', *American Quarterly* 45(1): 1–43.

Kaul, I., I. Grunberg and M.A. Stern (eds) (1999), *Global Public Goods: International Cooperation in the 21st Century*. New York: Oxford University Press.

Keller, Bill (2002), 'The Fighting Next Time', *New York Times Magazine* (10 March): 32ff.

Keohane, R.O., and H.V. Milner (eds) (1996), *International and Domestic Politics*. Cambridge: Cambridge University Press.

Kindleberger, C.P. (1986), 'International Public Goods without International Government', *American Economic Review* 76(1): 1–13.

Kirkendall, R.S. (1980), *A Global Power: America since the Age of Roosevelt*. New York: Knopf, 2nd edn.

Kissinger, H. (1985), *Observations*. London: Michael Joseph/Weidenfeld and Nicolson.

Klein, N. (2000), *No Logo*. London: Flamingo.

Kolko, G. (1969), *The Roots of American Foreign Policy*. Boston: Beacon.

Krugman, P. (2000), 'Pity the Pain of the Very Richest', *International Herald Tribune* (15 June).

— (2001), 'Do As We Do, and Not As We Say', *New York Times* (20 July).

Kuttner, R. (1991), *The End of Laissez-Faire: National Purpose and the Global Economy After the Cold War*. New York: Alfred Knopf.

— (1998), *Everything for Sale*. New York: Alfred Knopf.

Lewis, C., A. Benes and M. O'Brien (1996), *The Buying of the President*. New York: Avon Books.

Lipset, S.M. (1996), *American Exceptionalism: A Double-Edged Sword*. New York: Norton.

Mamère, Noël, and O. Warin (1999), *Non merci, Oncle Sam*. Paris: Editions Ramsay.

Manza, Jeff (2000), 'Race and the Underdevelopment of the American Welfare State', *Theory and Society* 29(6): 819–32.

Manzo, K. (1999), 'The "New" Developmentalism: Political Liberalism and the Washington Consensus', in Slater and Taylor (eds): 98–114.

Mead, W.R. (2001), *Special Providence: American Foreign Policy and How It Changed the World*. New York: Knopf.

Melman, S. (1974), *The Permanent War Economy: American Capitalism in Decline*. New York: Simon and Schuster.

Merton, R.K. (1957), *Social Theory and Social Structure*. Glencoe, IL: Free Press.

Mills, C. Wright (1963), *The Sociological Imagination*. New York: Oxford University Press.

Mishra, R. (1996), 'North America: Poverty amidst Plenty', in E. Øyen, S.M. Miller and S.A. Samad (eds), *Poverty: A Global Review. Handbook on International Poverty Research*. Oslo: Scandinavian University Press: 453–93.

Moore, M. (2002), *Stupid White Men*. New York: Harper Collins.

Nederveen Pieterse, J. (1989), *Empire and Emancipation: Power and Liberation on a World Scale*. New York: Praeger.

— (2000), 'Globalization North and South: Representations of Uneven Development and the Interaction of Modernities', *Theory, Culture and Society* 17(1): 129–37.

— (2001), *Development Theory: Deconstructions/Reconstructions*. London: Sage.

— (2002), 'Globalization, Kitsch and Conflict: Technologies of Work, War and Politics', *Review of International Political Economy* 9(1): 1–36.

— (forthcoming), 'Global Inequality: Bringing Politics Back In', in C. Calhoun, C. Rojek and B.S. Turner (eds), *Handbook of Sociology*. London: Sage.

Nederveen Pieterse, J. (ed.) (2000), *Global Futures: Shaping Globalization*. London: Zed Books.

Nettl, J.P. (1968), 'The State as a Conceptual Variable', *World Politics* 20: 559–92.

Overholser, G. (1999), 'More on the Inflated Pay of Business Titans', *International Herald Tribune* (5 November).

Peck, J. (1998), 'Workfare in the Sun: Politics, Representation, and Method in U.S. Welfare-to-Work Strategies', *Political Geography* 17(5): 535–66.

Reisman, W.M. (1999–2000), 'The United States and International Institutions', *Survival* 41(4): 62–80.

Reiss, M. (1998), 'The Correctional-Industrial Complex', *New York Times* (2 August).

Robinson, W.I. (1996), *Promoting Polyarchy: Globalization, US Intervention and Hegemony*. Cambridge: Cambridge University Press.

Roediger, D.R. (1992), *The Wages of Whiteness: Race and the Making of the American Working Class*. London: Verso.

Rogers, Mary F. (1999), *Barbie Culture*. London: Sage.

Rupert, M. (1995), *Producing Hegemony: The Politics of Mass Production and American Global Power*. Cambridge: Cambridge University Press.

Sachs, Wolfgang (1992), *Planet Dialectics: Explorations in Environment and Development*. London: Zed Books.

Saunders, F.S. (1999), *Who Paid the Piper: The CIA and the Cultural Cold War*. London: Granta Books.

Scheuerman, W.E. (2000), 'The Twilight of Legality? Globalisation and American Democracy', *Global Society* 14(1): 53–78.

Sen, G. (1995), *The Military Origins of Industrialisation and International Trade Rivalry*. London: Pinter (orig. edn 1984).

Servan-Schreiber, J.-J. (1967), *Le défi Américain*. Paris: Denoël.

Sharp, J.P. (1998), 'Reel Geographies of the New World Order: Patriotism, Masculinity, and Geopolitics in Post-Cold War American Movies', in G.O. Tuathail and S. Dalby (eds), *Rethinking Geopolitics*. London: Routledge: 152–69.

Siegel, F.F. (1984), *Troubled Journey: From Pearl Harbor to Ronald Reagan*. New York: Hill and Wang.

Slater, D., and P. Taylor (eds) (1999), *The American Century: Consensus and Coercion in the Projection of American Power*. Oxford: Blackwell.

Stavrianos, L.S. (1981), *Global Rift: The Third World Comes of Age*. New York: Morrow.

Thacker, S.C. (1999), 'The High Politics of IMF Lending', *World Politics* 52: 38–75.

Tyrell, I. (1991), 'American Exceptionalism in an Age of International History', *The American Historical Review* 96: 1031–55.

Voeten, J. (2000), 'De militaire musical-choreografie van "42nd Street"', *NRC Handelsblad* (25 August): CS4.

Wade, R. (1996), 'Japan, the World Bank and the Art of Paradigm Maintenance: The East Asian Miracle in Political Perspective', *New Left Review* 217: 3–36.

— (2002), 'The United States and the World Bank: The Fight over People and Ideas', *Review of International Political Economy* 9(2): 215–43.

Wade, Robert, and Frank Veneroso (1998), 'The Gathering World Slump and the Battle over Capital Controls', *New Left Review* I(231): 13–42.

Williamson, Anne (forthcoming), *How America Built the New Russian Oligarchy*.

Zoellick, R.B. (1999–2000), 'Congress and the Making of US Foreign Policy', *Survival* 41(4): 20–41.

Zunz, O. (1999), *Why the American Century?* Chicago: University of Chicago Press.

CHAPTER 5

Debating Americanization:
The Case of France

Richard Kuisel

The notion of a 'Global America' invites application. It asks to be tested at the national level. How might 'Global America', for example, apply to France? The question might be posed this way: has France been Americanized? There is considerable evidence, some quantifiable, that this proud nation has succumbed to Americanization.

Language is a place to begin. English, or more precisely, American-English, is the second most popular language among the French. In a recent survey, two out of three French people polled agreed with the statement that 'everyone should learn to speak English'.[1] American-English is so ubiquitous in popular music, movies, television, radio, the Internet and advertising that the government has tried to limit its use by legislative action. Since the French language is one of the prime markers of French national identity, the popularity of this Anglo-Saxon import is a telling indicator of Americanization. Fast food and soft drinks amplify this story. France now has almost 800 McDonald's restaurants and it has become the third largest overseas market for this Chicago-based multinational. Similarly Coca-Cola controls most of the cola market and about half of the French soft drinks market. In 1998 Hollywood movies earned almost 70 per cent of ticket sales in France. Of the top 20 films only three were French – the rest were American.[2] Some television channels specialize in American programming. Disneyland Paris by the late 1990s attracted more visitors than either Notre Dame or the Louvre. Sports, another form of entertainment, supply more evidence. In 1992 after an American all-star team won the basketball title at the Olympics, a poll of French teenagers voted Michael

1 *The Economist*, 24 February 2001.
2 *New York Times*, 14 December 1999.

Jordan the most popular athlete in France.[3] In 1998 the French soccer team won the World Cup and during the trophy awarding ceremony the triumphant fans heard the public address system play not the *Marseillaise*, but the theme from *Star Wars*.[4]

Business adds more data. A random walk through almost any French city will lead past the shop windows of American retailers such as Gap, Toys "Я" Us, Baskin Robbins and Ralph Lauren. American-style shopping malls and home and garden centres sit astride highways outside even small towns. Management of French multinationals, according to the business press, has become virtually indistinguishable from that of American corporations. Managers of such firms speak English, hold MBAs, and have learned how to compete successfully in the American market.[5]

Opinion polls reveal growing anxiety about America's cultural presence in France.[6] Movies and television are singled out as the most troublesome sectors. Teenagers seem indistinguishable from their American peers. French parents complain that in a cultural sense, referring to their teenagers' dress, music, speech, and eating habits, they don't recognize their own children. Prominent French politicians echo the chorus of complaints about the pervasiveness of American mass culture. The foreign minister, Hubert Védrine, criticizes the USA as a 'hyperpower' and warns about the dangers of a 'culturally uniform world'.[7] Should one conclude from this impressive list of 'facts' that Global America has conquered France? Doesn't the phenomenon need to be scrutinized more closely before we reach such a conclusion? The question itself, 'Has France (or have the French) been Americanized?' requires some clarification. What do we mean by both key terms: 'Americanized' and 'the French'? Some precision is in order before we can conclude that the answer to the inquiry is affirmative.

Definition of Americanization

The phenomenon of 'Americanization' has been intensely debated and this chapter will engage in this debate. Before examining the complexities raised by this concept, as a starting point I wish to offer a straightforward definition: Americanization is the import by non-Americans of products, images, technologies, practices and behaviour closely associated with America/Americans.

---

3 *New York Times*, 16 October 1997.
4 *Washington Post*, 14 July 1998.
5 *The Economist*, 5 June 1999.
6 *Le Monde*, 31 October 1996.
7 Védrine quoted in the *New York Times*, 7 November 1999.

Or, in more general terms, the phenomenon can be defined as the adoption of mass consumption, market capitalism, and mass culture. It is not the same phenomenon as either modernization or globalization, though there is considerable overlap. To the extent that Americanization is defined as the transfer of quantifiable units, such as products or technologies, then it can be measured (for instance, the number of movie screens devoted to Hollywood films). To the extent, however, that Americanization refers to behaviour and values, which raises the question of how 'Americanized' some group is, its magnitude is far more difficult to assess. As a historian I conceive of Americanization as a historical process that possesses its own chronology, geography and dynamics. It began in the decade or so following 1890, first in Western Europe and then expanding outwards on a global scale. For France the process was barely visible by the Second World War, in full swing by the 1950s, and far advanced by 2000.

The category of 'the French' also requires more conceptual rigour. The student of Americanization must identify who has been involved in the process in order to avoid the trap of generalizing about an entire population. Even today the process has not reached all the French. Judging solely by external appearances there are still a few villages in out-of-the-way places that remain immune. Those who have been touched have been affected in different ways and to varying degrees. Historically, for example, big business has been more receptive to American practices than small business and much of agriculture. Where possible, generalization about Americanization needs to be tailored to social groups smaller than 'the French'.

In order to decide whether France, or any other society, has been 'Americanized', the phenomenon needs to be examined in the light of recent scholarship. The general trend of this research in the last twenty years has been to make the process more complex and less potent as a force for homogeneity. The key terms in the new vocabulary are words such as 'assimilation', or 'diversity'. Doubts are raised about the very existence of a category such as 'national culture'. In some cases, Americanization surrenders to globalization. The net effect of this research is to undermine the concept. It is my task to review this scholarship and to salvage Americanization as a useful way of thinking about recent history.

The starting point of recent scholarship has been to reject the thesis of 'cultural imperialism'.[8] Before the 1980s the predominant approach heldthat Americanization could be best understood as a hegemonic America manipulating

---

8 For a review of the evolution of the debate about Americanization beginning with the theory of cultural imperialism, see Hecht 2000. This article and the subsequent commentaries contain the basic bibliographical references for my discussion. The key study is Tomlinson 1991. Another insightful review of conceptualizing Americanization is Fehrenbach and Poiger 2000. The conceptual problem is also addressed in Kroes et al. 1993; Van Eltern 1996; and Forgacs 1996.

97

and ultimately imposing its ways on passive recipients – reducing Europeans to the equivalent of the 'colonized' and bringing about a kind of global homogenization that served American interests. Americanization was thus a form of 'cultural imperialism'. This simplistic and highly tendentious perspective received its just deserts at the hands of experts who argued that the process was far more complicated and much less unilateral than the proponents of cultural imperialism assumed. Unfortunately some prominent French intellectuals, such as the late Pierre Bourdieu, ignore this scholarship and persist in propagating the notion of cultural imperialism.[9]

The new critical analysis of the last twenty years has discarded the notion of cultural imperialism and advanced our understanding of Americanization in many ways. However, it has a tendency that can lead to its own form of distortion – a tendency to deflate the phenomenon. In its extreme formulation this writing minimizes the significance of Americanization and its homogenizing effects. What this chapter proposes is the incorporation of this new, more sophisticated, apprehension of the process in a way that preserves an understanding of the disruptive and homogenizing nature of this transformation. Abandoning cultural imperialism should not drive theorizing too far in the other direction. We should not go so far in stressing processes such as assimilation or globalization that we lose sight of the significance of our subject of study. There are four perspectives in this literature on Americanization that merit examination. Each adds something to our understanding. If exaggerated, however, each can lead to a misreading of the grand narrative.

Assimilation

One school of interpretation, one that virtually dominates current writing about the subject, may be dubbed the assimilationist school. Assimilationists argue that those who import American ways and wares, the local or indigenous people, assimilate or domesticate what they receive. The exchange across the Atlantic seems closer to negotiation among equals than it is to transmission and transformation according to some American model. Europeans, from this perspective, select what they want from the American warehouse and then make it their own. A recent manifesto of the domestication thesis is the book by Richard Pells entitled *Not Like Us* (1997). The title refers to the capacity

---

9 See the collection of articles in *Le Monde diplomatique* (May 2000) under the title 'Un délicieux despotisme' that contend that America sets the agenda for political, economic and social debate by globalizing its analytical categories and its positions. Pierre Bourdieu and Loïc Wacquant contribute to this collection and further develop their attack in their article entitled 'On the Cunning of Imperialist Reason' (1999).

and the determination of Europeans to assimilate American imports. A couple of examples drawn from the Netherlands illustrates the thesis. Pells relates a famous study of how the Dutch responded to the television programme *Dallas*. Rather than being impressed by the lifestyles of wealthy Texans, Dutch viewers reinterpreted the programme's message to fit their own experiences, 'converting it from a glossy American import to a drama that illuminated their private lives' (Pells 1997: 261). Research by another proponent of the assimilationist approach points out how Dutch musicians have manipulated American popular music to create hybrid styles that are no longer American (Van Eltern 1996: 74–75). The music has become 'Dutch'. In extreme cases non-Americans have so assimilated American imports that they are no longer perceived as American. In Japan, for example, many young people think that McDonald's is a Japanese company (Watson 1997: 37).

The domestication thesis can be applied to French business. Many French companies, in order to compete, have learned to imitate the Americans. Management has borrowed practices introduced by corporations such as McDonald's. For example, French fast-food companies have replicated techniques introduced by McDonald's, including product standardization and computerized operations, which they use to market 'traditional' national dishes such as *brioches*. In the luxury goods sector the chic conglomerate LVMH has adopted American-style mergers to create a large French-based multinational that competes successfully in the American market. And the French cinema, to an extent, has followed Hollywood. Recently some French film producers have attempted to make English-language movies using Hollywood production methods to sell in global markets.

A significant variation of the assimilationist interpretation might be labelled the semiotic approach to cultural transmission. According to these experts, usually specialists in American popular culture, Americanization is essentially the reception of a cultural language, a set of symbols that the Europeans have gradually mastered.[10] They now employ them as Americans do because other Europeans readily understand them. Thus the cowboy and the American West have become global symbols of freedom and independence. Italian manufacturers use them to sell jeans to other Europeans. The American West is no longer American property.

In short, the domestication thesis celebrates the capacity of non-Americans to modify what they receive. In the case of the Old World the indigenous 'Europeanize' what crosses the Atlantic, modifying products and techniques for their consumption and use so that European ways survive and diversity

---

10 The best exponent of the semiotic approach is Kroes (see Kroes 1996; 1999).

remains. This thesis has all but buried the earlier theory of cultural imperialism, which assumes that Europeans have been weak and passive before the American intruders. This thesis can, however, be exaggerated. Stressing how Europeans have made American imports their own can lead to mistaking the subplot for the main narrative.

The experience of Coca-Cola, Disney, and McDonald's in France is instructive. These three American corporations did virtually nothing to modify their products, operations or techniques for local consumption when they arrived (Kuisel 2000). They insisted on making the French adapt to their products. There was no domestication. The Coca-Cola Company refused to countenance any modifications in its soft drink, its promotion or its operations when it launched its big expansion in the late 1980s. In fact the company employed the most aggressive American marketing practices to increase sales. The Disney Company made virtually no concessions to Europeans when it built its theme park outside Paris in the late 1980s. When faced with the choice between building an American-style theme park or bending to European tastes, Disney's management team led by Michael Eisner elected to duplicate Disneyworld in Florida. Eisner stated that he wanted to make the Paris park 'every bit as American as our domestic parks – meaning fast-food instead of smoky bistros, Coca-Cola and lemonade in preference to wine, animated movies rather than film noir' (Eisner 1998: 270). A visit to the park confirms Eisner's vision – it is a fantasized version of America (Peer 1992). Figuratively speaking these American businesses didn't want to speak French.

McDonald's behaved much like Coca-Cola and Disney, assuming that others, including Europeans, wanted what Americans wanted. Germany was a kind of testing ground for the company when it launched its business in Europe. In the 1970s McDonald's tried to give its new German restaurants a 'German look' – adding more wood panelling, dimming the lighting and serving beer. But this failed. McDonald's changed tactics and remodelled its German units to make them look like American outlets. It paid off and before long the German franchises began to show a profit. The head of McDonald's international division drew a lesson from such mistakes: 'McDonald's is an American food system. If we go into a new country and incorporate their food products into our menu, we lose our identity' (quoted in Love 1986: 437). It was better to stick to the American way and wait, if necessary for years, for foreign consumers to accept it. The French McDonald's may have made some minor adjustments in its menu, such as serving a mustard and pepper sauce with its Big Mac rather than ketchup, or in its layout by making seats movable to allow customers to reposition their chairs for conviviality, or in its marketing by adapting its advertisements for French tastes, but none of this amounts to assimilation. Nothing basic is changed about the food, the ambience, the appeal, or the operations.

The efforts by these companies to claim that they are French businesses because, for example, all the ingredients of the Big Mac or Coca-Cola come from France, ring rather hollow. They do not appear French when they try to exploit their 'Americanness', or when they vigilantly monitor their operations from corporate headquarters in suburban Chicago, Atlanta or Burbank. It should be remembered that a McDonald's french fry, whether eaten in Seattle, Paris or Munich, is exactly 9/32 of an inch in length. And what appeals about McDonald's, Coca-Cola and Disney is not their assimilation but their associations with 'America'. What the French, or at least the vast majority of them, are seeking in visiting Disneyland or eating at McDonald's is an 'American' experience. Interviews with young adults, who composed over 80 per cent of McDonald's paying customers in the late 1980s, showed that they patronized the restaurant because it was like eating in America (Fantasia 1995: 217). What they meant was the bright lights and noise, the colourful employee uniforms, the absence of adult mediators such as waiters, the self-service and open seating. One first-time customer said it was like 'visiting the United States' and adolescents found it 'relaxing' or 'cool' and 'un-French'. These corporations celebrated, and profited from, an intrinsic market advantage – offering others what Americans enjoyed. What many Gallic consumers seem to want is to consume the same products and enjoy the same entertainment as Americans. And this 'buying of America' is not confined to McDonald's, Coke and Disney. Hollywood, of course, does nothing except for some dubbing to modify its movies for French consumption. Similarly, French television networks rebroadcast American programmes. There is, in short, much that crosses the Atlantic that is not assimilated.

Assimilation theory has a second weakness. There is a logical flaw in the argument that assimilation, at least in the form of imitation, is way of sustaining diversity. That is, to the extent that the French have succeeded in competing with the Americans by adopting their ways, they have sacrificed a certain measure of 'Frenchness' and become more Americanized. For example, among French theme parks Parc Astérix was the most 'French', specializing in a comic book version of French history. To compete with the new Disneyland, Parc Astérix renovated its operations to include amusements such as a water ride called *Le Grand Splatch*, making it more Disney-like. Similarly the French fast-food industry, in learning how to compete with the Golden Arches, has been Americanized à la McDonald's.[11] One wonders about the recent effort by

11 There was widespread copying of McDonald's operations by the French fast-food business. French chains, both burger outlets such as France-Quick and *viennoiseries* such as La Brioche

French film-makers such as Luc Besson to compete with Hollywood by making English-language imitations. Might this result, as some cinema experts have argued, in depriving the French cinema of its national character and turning it into a second-rate copy of Hollywood? With respect to the semiotic thesis, if the French, like other Europeans, adopt the same symbolic language, then they have become more like Americans. Adaptation, in the form of imitation, runs the risk of advancing rather than resisting Americanization. Mimicking the Americans has made the French more like their New World cousins.

In short, the assimilation thesis, valuable as it is in pointing up the complexities of Americanization and heightening the role of the importing society, should not deflate the significance of the process.

Culture in Motion

A second approach to Americanization, which also takes as its foil the cultural imperialism/homogenization thesis, holds that it is erroneous to think of culture as stable or uniform. There is no such thing as 'American culture' to export or 'French culture' to receive. To think otherwise is to commit the sin of essentialism; that is, naïvely to ignore how varied, permeable and fluid culture is. According to this critical reading of 'national' culture then, America has never transmitted a single, coherent message. 'American culture' has many meanings for Europeans despite the stereotype that all the USA exports is vulgar mass culture. Scholars stress that American cultural exports are not monolithic. The USA exports stars from the Metropolitan Opera and rap music, and films such as *American Beauty* and *Dumb and Dumber*. Similarly, in architecture 'American culture' may mean, to the French, Pei's innovative 'Pyramid' that serves as the entrance to the Louvre, or it may evoke the banal image of the Golden Arches. It may mean fine California wine or Coca-Cola. Culture is dynamic. What was once perceived as American may have changed. In the 1960s wearing jeans carried the meaning, among French youth, of dressing like an American, but that may no longer be the case. Jeans have become so common that they have lost this symbolic reference. Similarly the receiving culture is diverse and in constant evolution. French conservatives who parade

---

Dorée borrowed directly from the Americans. What was copied ranged from restaurant layout to standardized food preparation and computerized accounting (but not the franchise system). McDonald's has also induced change in food processing and the manufacture of restaurant equipment. European food suppliers were not accustomed to high-volume, standardized output and did not produce everything needed for a McDonald's menu. The Chicago firm also changed labour practice in the fast-food business by hiring young part-time help, especially students.

'French authenticity', or 'true France', or 'French tradition' fail to recognize (from this critical perspective) that French culture is, and has been historically, diffuse, in flux, without boundaries, and constantly remade through forces such as immigration. Moreover, culture, at least today, changes so quickly that it is, at times, difficult to distinguish what is (or was) American. In a recent study of McDonald's in East Asia experts point out that cuisine evolves so quickly that it is impossible to distinguish the foreign from the local. McDonald's does not seem 'foreign' or 'American', but simply part of a rapidly developing mix of restaurants/menus (Watson 1997). If culture is in motion, then it becomes difficult even to identify what is 'American' or 'French'. In other words, culture does not necessarily come with national labels.

It also follows from this perspective that different segments of the French public, as divided for instance by class, gender, age, region and ethnicity, possess different 'cultures', and that some are more implicated in Americanization than others. We know, for example, that post-war adolescents in Western Europe were far more receptive than older generations to American music and fashion (see, for example, Wagenleitner 1994). Similarly, in France urbanites were the first to buy home appliances, often associated with the modern American kitchen, and a decade or more passed before villages such as those in Brittany acquired such amenities. Americanization has thus been unevenly distributed among the population. This argument, like the first about domestication, is a powerful reminder that Americanization is a complicated and variable process.

But the thesis of culture in motion, like that of domestication, can also be taken to such an extreme that Americanization seems to vanish. This would be an interpretive error. One can agree that cultures are difficult to define because they are diverse and porous, that it is often problematic to assign a nationality to a product or an image, and that America has never transmitted a coherent message, but this does not mean that we are dealing with an illusion. There is still substance in this cultural exchange.

There are products and images, technologies and practices that have been, and sometimes still are, closely identified with 'America'. This is evident if one looks at the process historically. In the 1920s jazz and Hollywood silent movies were unmistakably 'American' to the French. Thirty years later, if one asked a French person what was American, he or she could readily identify items such as the electric kitchen, big cars, T-shirts and chewing gum. If, in time, such identification blurred, as it did for example with cars or appliances, this does not dissolve the historical identity of such products. When they first crossed the Atlantic, they were perceived as 'American'. Today imports carrying the American label are technologies such as Microsoft, communications platforms

103

such as CNN, business practices such as downsizing, holidays such as Hallowe'en, and television programmes such as *Ally McBeal*. Some products seem permanently endowed with 'Americanness', such as Coke, Disney, the NBA (National Basketball Association), and of course the language of American-English. Similarly, there is a list of things that are commonly deemed 'French', ranging from *boeuf bourguignon* and the *baguette* to Bordeaux and the *béret*. Finally, many products are not only perceived as American, they are prized and consumed because they carry this tag. This was once true of Levi jeans and it is still true of McDonald's and Disneyland Paris. At the very least there are many in France among the political class and the gatekeepers of culture who claim that they know what is 'American' and how to defend themselves against these intruders. There has been and continues to be something identifiably 'American' about some cross-Atlantic exports. National labels have not disappeared altogether in the flux of contemporary culture.

The culture-in-motion thesis also reminds us that diversity within national societies, for example social class, accounts for the variable exposure to and receptivity towards America. If exaggerated, however, it misses the creeping uniformity caused by Americanization. Not many of the French, whatever their location, income, age, gender or ethnicity, remain completely outside the process. If as late as 1960 only small parts of the population were involved – that is, heard or spoke English, watched Hollywood movies, listened to rock and roll, or ate at McDonald's (the first outlet in France dates from 1972) – today few of the population can escape America altogether. If Americanization continues to implicate various segments of the French differently, America has become ubiquitous. Almost no one, for example, can avoid the mass media. Television brings CNN, the *X-Files* and *Bay Watch*, while the local cinema shows Hollywood films such as *Gladiator*. Meanwhile the growing numbers of Internet users rely on Microsoft and the English language. American-style suburbia, multiplexes and shopping malls are commonplace. Even small villages in rural landscapes such as Provence seem inundated. Laurence Wylie, for example, has vividly charted the evolution of Roussillon from an isolated, 'traditional' Provençal hill town that served agriculture, to an urbane centre for tourists and a hideaway for wealthy and celebrated Parisians (Wylie 1989). Now America has also come to Roussillon in the form of tourists, television programmes, and food at the local café. Of course, even today many try to remain aloof, and anti-American sentiments are popular. But the reach of Americanization encompasses far more of the population than ever before and adds a measure of cultural uniformity.

In short, I would argue that Americanization survives the notion of culture in motion because historically much of what the USA exported was perceived as 'American' and even today much of what crosses the Atlantic carries the national label. Moreover, the process has become so pervasive that it has affected almost every member of the population of France.

Globalization

Yet another way to theorize about Americanization is to take the alternative route of globalization. Those following this line ask: shouldn't we be discussing globalization rather than Americanization (see, for example, Robertson 1992; Appadurai 1996; Featherstone 1990)? This is not the place to address the entire range of conceptual issues that distinguish the two phenomena. What is possible, however, is to examine two dimensions of the globalization thesis that impinge on Americanization.

First, advocates of globalization ask: isn't it more accurate to speak of global flows of products and techniques rather than looking only at America? Aren't the French, like other Europeans, being swamped by imports from all over the world, not just by those that cross the Atlantic? Americanization, from this perspective, then shrinks to one feature of a far broader process that is contributing to diversity. American imports simply add to the growing range of alternatives, broadening the menu, so to speak, for consumers. Thus a Paris *supermarché* now offers a wide variety of choice on its shelves – feta cheese, jalapeno peppers, German beer, Indian chutney, Chinese tea, Colombian coffee, Israeli oranges, as well as American cornflakes. Why, if what we are experiencing is globalization, award priority to America?

A second contention of those who prefer globalization to Americanization is to call attention to the transnational, rather than the 'American', character of so many of these imported products, practices and behaviours. Isn't Coca-Cola, for example, a global brand? Doesn't Hollywood draw on the whole world for actors, directors, finance and locations for its movies, producing films for global audiences that are devoid of any nationality? French critics, for example, argue that the danger is less from American movies than from the hegemony of one type of film – Hollywood's expensive, violent, intellectually vapid fare. Disney executives insist that their theme parks and other forms of entertainment are not American – they are 'Disney', as though they transcend nationality. Wouldn't we do better to conceptualize these transmissions as globalization?

Globalization and Americanization have a long and complicated relationship that has yet to be examined. Nevertheless the two phenomena can, and should, be distinguished. From a historical and theoretical perspective, Americanization can be conceptualized as a stage or phase of globalization.

Globalization in the twentieth century has had (and to a considerable extent still has) an American face (see Ritzer 2000; Ellwood 1996–1997; Friedman 1999; Barber 1995). Historically the USA became the prototype of mass consumer society and the home of mass culture. The process began in America after 1890 and it developed rapidly. Even before 1914 Americans began to disseminate it. For example, as early as the First World War Hollywood gained control over much of the European film market. At the earliest stage of the Americanization process, approximately between 1900 and 1930, there was little doubt that what crossed the Atlantic was American. Whether it was the Buffalo Bill Wild West Show or the Singer sewing machine these exports carried the 'made in America' label for Europeans. After the Second World War, America was, for several decades, at the forefront in selling and promoting consumer society and mass culture to the world. A major goal of the Marshall Plan was to promote the 'American way of life' in Western Europe. By 1967 the best-selling book in France was Jean-Jacques Servan-Schreiber's *Le défi Américain*, which warned of American business winning control of the European economy. Over time, to be sure, at least for some products, the identification with the nation of origin became blurred. Equipment such as Otis Elevators, companies such as Standard Oil and, to an extent, even cultural products such as Hollywood movies began to lose their 'foreignness'. But for much of the century – though varying from one product, technique, image or value to another – the flows were from the United States and they carried the flag.

America's pre-eminent role, some think, has faded in the last years of the twentieth century, and globalized flows have become paramount. Brands such as Nike have increasingly assumed a transnational, rather than a purely American, character in the eyes of others; non-Americans have adopted the image of the cowboy as a universal symbol for freedom and adventure; and new, non-American centres of cultural production now distribute their wares around the world – for example, karate movies made in Hong Kong, television soap operas produced in Brazil, and World Music recorded in France. Nevertheless, America remains the prime producer and distributor of an identifiable mass culture as well as certain practices. Products such as the Big Mac, Coca-Cola, Disneyland Paris, rap music and the film *Titanic*, despite their transnational features, remain American in the eyes of most of the world. As English becomes the global language it too carries its associations with America. Globalization has not, at least as yet, pushed America aside as the prime producer and marketer of much of mass culture and consumerism.

Globalization also challenges the Americanization thesis by making it benign. It holds that America merely adds one dish to an ever-widening menu of choices.

One might argue, however, continuing the metaphor, that while globalization gives us a wide smorgasbord of dishes, the American dish remains the biggest and it tends often to crowd out the local cuisine. In France, American products and services often displace French offerings and come to occupy huge market shares. American food may be only one of many foreign imports on the shelves of French supermarkets, but it often takes up much of the space. Coca-Cola has come to control almost 60 per cent of the market for carbonated beverages in France and 80 per cent of cola sales. In Europe, Coca-Cola is the largest soft-drink company with almost 50 per cent of the sales of carbonated beverages.[12] The story is similar for leisure and fast food. In 1998 Disneyland Paris attracted 12.5 million customers while the 'traditional' French theme park, Parc Astérix, sold less than 2 million tickets and several small French theme parks had to close.[13] McDonald's has conquered 60 per cent of the fast-food market in France and the Golden Arches is the largest hamburger chain – almost double the size of its closest competitor, Quick.[14] The way McDonald's conducts business – everything from how it manages its suppliers to its labour policies – has changed the fast-food business in France. The situation of the cinema is much the same. One might, at least in Paris, be able to choose from an enormous variety of foreign movies, that is, a global menu. In fact in 1998 American films accounted for 63 per cent of box-office income while French films earned only 27 per cent of ticket sales; only the remainder counted as 'global'.[15] Hollywood's dominance is even more pronounced elsewhere in Europe. These American products thus not only occupy large market shares, but they have also achieved this, to some extent, at the expense of French rivals. My guess is that a similar story can be told about other American imports such as certain forms of television programmes and popular music. American products often take the lion's share of markets and displace the French. That process deserves the label 'Americanization' rather than 'globalization'.

Americanization, at the very least, has been a stage of that much older and much broader series of flows and changes that we call globalization. The response to those who wish to replace 'Americanization' with 'globalization' is that we must recognize America's historical role in the process. For most of the twentieth century, the phenomenon may be best labelled as 'American-led globalization'.

---

12 *Eurofood*, March 1992.
13 Of the 12.5 million, however, only 38 per cent were French. Data for 1998 are reported in *Le Monde*, 29 January 1999.
14 *Eurofood*, 28 February 1996 and 14 August 1997.
15 *New York Times*, 14 December 1999.

Behaviour, Meaning and Identity

The fourth, and final, line of scholarly inquiry attempts to delve behind appearances and quantities and asks whether or not Americanization has changed behaviour, meaning and identity. Has it, for example, made the French 'less French'? A sceptical answer to this question tends to deflate the significance of the phenomenon. Consumption of American imports, it can be argued, is not evidence for fundamental modification in behaviour. Even if French teenagers, for example, dress exactly like their American peers, watch the same films and listen to much of the same music, this does not make them think and act like Americans. They have not, from this more benign perspective, been truly 'Americanized'.

In contrast, a more robust view of Americanization contends that the process is not just about quantities of American goods or images consumed by Europeans, but that it extends to attitudes and beyond – to behaviour, meaning and identity. From this perspective Americanization changes not only how the French eat, dress, speak or entertain themselves, but also how they assign value. Americanization, from this perspective, extends deeply into the psyche and alters meaning – in the sense of modifying how the French attribute value or significance, for example, to activities such as shopping, or playing, or to being 'modern', or, more importantly, to defining what constitutes 'success' or 'the good life'. In contrast to the benign view, this assessment, which attributes greater historic significance to the process, holds that it may modify identities in the sense of altering the self-image of specific segments of the population or even change an idealized form of national identity – of 'Frenchness' itself.

Choosing between the benign and the robust assessment of Americanization, at least for the moment, is not easy. The choice is difficult because so little research has been directed towards finding answers; because answers to these questions involve immensely diverse populations; and because inquiries touch the private and the personal – a realm where answers are difficult to ascertain, much less to measure. We don't know how Americanization has altered meaning. Nevertheless, at this early stage of research, there is evidence that points towards an interpretation that evaluates Americanization as a profound, rather than a trivial, transformation. It is about more than appearances and quantities. It seems to have modified behaviour, identity and meaning.

The reception of America in Europe is not completely unknown territory. Scholars have, for example, examined post-war Germany and Austria, showing how America, in particular US occupation policies and American cultural presence, affected generations and gender. We know, for example, that young people used music broadcast over US Armed Forces radio and the Voice of

America to establish their separate identity and that the racial transgressions contained in such music evoked a negative response from older Germans that created a gap between generations (Poiger 2000). Similarly, Hollywood stars such as James Dean served as models of rebellion for young Germans in the 1950s (Fehrenbach 2000). In much of Western Europe in the 1960s young people donned jeans and listened to Bob Dylan in part to distinguish them-selves from their 'bourgeois' elders and to demonstrate their protest against the status quo. In Eastern Europe the same attire suggested protest against Communist regimes.

In France there are several stories that point towards confirming the robust interpretation. During the 1990s young adults have become more willing to drink a sweet drink such as Coca-Cola with meals. At the same time there has been a dramatic decline in the consumption of wine among this demographic cohort.[16] It is possible that American beverages have modified what some hold to be the quintessence of Frenchness – the drinking of wine. Similarly, eating a quick lunch or buying take-out food has supplanted the traditional midday meal at home – another marker of 'true France' (Economic Intelligence Unit 1987: 38). While fast-food outlets continue to grow, the number of cafés fell from 220,000 in 1960 to fewer than 65,000 in 1994, and they continue to disappear at the rate of 4,000 per year.[17] Causation is complicated and it would include, for example, the increase of women in the workforce, intensified urban-ization, traffic congestion, greater leisure, higher incomes among adolescents, and shorter midday breaks. Still, fast-food restaurants such as McDonald's have played some part in the change and they have been a principal beneficiary.[18]

A similar argument might be made about the new informality of dress among the French. Dress is far more casual today than it was in 1960. It is a good guess that American clothes such as sweatshirts and baseball caps retailed by stores such as Gap, which capitalize on the status conveyed by such Ameri-can imports, have had something to do with the new informality. It is possible that this sartorial informality suggests some deeper change in traditional French attitudes about hierarchy and rules.

French business may be another recipient of change induced, in this case, by the example of corporate America. French management, for example, has

---

16 Of the 14–24-year-old cohort some 70 per cent stated in 1996 that they never consumed wine compared with 48 per cent in 1980. They stated as their principal reason that they did not like the taste of wine (*New York Times*, 3 May 1996).

17 *New York Times*, 22 December 1994.

18 The consumption of fast food has grown spectacularly since the 1970s and traditional fast food, the *viennoiseries*, has lost market share to hamburger sales. *Viennoiserie* sales were down to 8 per cent of the total in 1992 from 29 per cent in 1988, while hamburgers' share of fast-food sales rose from 48 per cent to 81 per cent over the same period (*Eurofood*, April 1993).

become adept at hostile takeovers – a practice scorned by traditionalists. Entrepreneurship, which historically has not been awarded high status in France, has become highly prized. In generational terms the young, ambitious and well-educated professionals seem captivated by the style and achievements of their American peers who have succeeded in the world of high-tech business. Perhaps such activity suggests new attitudes about competitiveness and success in the business community.

Finally, there is the carrier of meaning, language itself. The French are far more conversant in English than ever before. At the very least this makes things American more available to them and it may have more profound consequences as well. Certainly, the Académie française and the French government believe that it does, which has prompted them to take actions to curb the use of English.

It would be something of a stretch to argue that the Americans also sold the French the culture of consumption. After all, the first department store was French; the roots of consumer society date back long before the twentieth century and they are as much European as they are American. But America has contributed. The USA epitomized consumerism for Europeans and preached its benefits to Europe as early as the 1920s. French automobile manufacturers such as Citroën learned marketing techniques from American manufacturers and the advertising industry borrowed from its American peers. After the Second World War the USA, as an aim of the Marshall Plan, zealously promoted the virtues of high consumption and the message found a receptive audience among certain segments of French business and labour in the 1950s. In subsequent decades the spread of new forms of retailing, from supermarkets to discount houses and shopping malls, owed something to their American prototypes. For example, the National Cash Register Company of Dayton, Ohio taught thousands of French executives the doctrine of large, self-service, rapid-turnover stores and inspired some to introduce the *supermarché* in the 1960s (Ardagh 1982: 401). Of course, the French jumped from the *supermarché* to the *hypermarché* which they, in turn, exported to the United States. American-style retailing has been so widely adopted, has become so 'natural', that many French tourists who visit New York rush off, not to the Empire State building, but to the shopping malls in New Jersey.

In brief, America has played some part in changing how the French speak, eat, dress and entertain themselves; it has modified how they shop and do business. It also seems to have altered attitudes and meaning; for example, in elevating consumption as a criterion for modernity and the good life. We do not know how to explain these changes, nor do we know to what extent America was (and still is) responsible. That is the next task for research. Given these theses, what should one conclude – has France become part of Global America?

Concluding Remarks

It would be foolish to give a categorical answer to such a question in the light of the preceding discussion. Nevertheless, if forced to choose I would say 'yes'. I am convinced that the French have been Americanized in the last half of the twentieth century. After taking into consideration the views of those who would deflate Americanization by stressing the recipients' capacity for domestication, or by emphasizing the diversity and fluidity of culture, or by conceptualizing the process as globalization, or by expressing scepticism about its power to alter behaviour and identity, Americanization, or American-led globalization, survives as a way of conceptualizing one of the principal processes of change in the contemporary world. One should not go too far, as some of this new scholarship does, towards deflating the importance of this historic transformation. Americanization has been disruptive and intrusive, rather than benign and unobtrusive. What difference these imports make in terms of French behaviour, identity and meaning has yet to be explored, but my guess is that it has been substantial. America has been the agent of change and its impact has been far greater than adding to the range of options for activities such as entertainment. Choices about values and lifestyles have been affected. If the question returns, as it usually does, to whether or not Global America has brought homogenization, I think the answer is 'yes'. It has forced some imitation. France, for example, is more like America today than it was like America in 1930. It would be a grave mistake to go too far, however, and speculate that French uniqueness has vanished into a kind of Americanized uniformity. That is absurd. In many ways the French have absorbed Americanization and remained themselves. But they have adopted much.

Let me return to where I began. When the French consume a million meals a day at McDonald's, when they queue up to see Hollywood movies, when they visit Disneyland Paris by the millions, when they consume a hundred bottles of Coke per person per year, when they speak American-English, then Americanization has occurred. Nevertheless, we still must map the breadth and depth and, above all, the meaning of this behaviour and we must learn what role America has played in these changes. The paradigm of Americanization rightly assumes that the USA has been, and in some respects still is, both an agent and a model for change – for the French, for other Europeans, and for others around the world. However, scholarship has yet to chart the making of Global America, explain its dynamism, and assess its significance.

References

Appadurai, Arjun (1996), *Modernity at Large: Cultural Dimensions of Globalization.* Minneapolis: University of Minnesota Press.

Ardagh, John (1982), *France in the 1980s.* New York: Penguin.

Barber, Benjamin (1995), *Jihad vs. McWorld.* New York: Ballantine.

Bourdieu, Pierre, and Loïc Wacquant (1999), 'On the Cunning of Imperialist Reason', *Theory Culture and Society* 16(1): 41–58.

Economic Intelligence Unit (1987), 'Fast-Food in France', *Marketing in Europe,* Special Report No. 2, Economic Intelligence Unit, No. 269 (July).

Eisner, Michael (1998), *Work in Progress.* New York: Penguin.

Ellwood, David (1996–1997), 'The American Challenge Renewed: U.S. Cultural Power and Europe's Identity Crisis', *Brown Journal of World Affairs* 4 (Winter–Spring): 271–83.

Fantasia, Rick (1995), 'Fast-Food in France', *Theory and Society* 24: 201–42.

Featherstone, Mike (ed.) (1990), *Global Culture.* London: Sage Publications.

Fehrenbach, Heide (2000), 'Persistent Myths of Americanization: German Reconstruction and the Renationalization of Postwar Cinema, 1945–1965', in Heide Fehrenbach and Uta Poiger (eds), *Transactions, Transgressions, Transformations: American Culture in Western Europe and Japan.* New York: 81–108.

Fehrenbach, Heide, and Uta Poiger (2000), 'Introduction', in Heide Fehrenbach and Uta Poiger (eds), *Transactions, Transgressions, Transformations: American Culture in Western Europe and Japan.* New York: Berghahn Books: xiii–xl.

Forgacs, David (1996), 'Americanisation: The Italian Case, 1938–1945', in Phil Melling and Jon Roper (eds), *Americanisation and the Transformation of World Cultures.* Lewiston, NY: Edwin Mellen: 81–95.

Friedman, Thomas (1999), *The Lexus and the Olive Tree.* New York: Farrar, Straus and Giroux.

Hecht, Jessica Gienow (2000), 'Shame on US? Academics, Cultural Transfer, and the Cold War – A Critical Review', *Diplomatic History* 24 (Summer): 465–94.

Kroes, Rob (1996), *If You've Seen One, You've Seen the Mall: Europeans and Mass Culture.* Urbana and Chicago: Chicago University Press.

— (1999), 'American Empire and Cultural Imperialism', *Diplomatic History* 23 (Summer): 463–77.

Kroes, Rob, R.W. Rydell and D.F.J. Bosscher (1993), *Cultural Transmissions and Receptions: American Mass Culture in Europe.* Amsterdam: VU University Press.

Kuisel, Richard (2000), 'Learning to Love McDonald's, Coca-Cola, and Disneyland Paris', *La Revue Tocqueville/The Tocqueville Review* XXI(1): 129–49.

Love, John (1986), *McDonald's: Behind the Arches.* New York: Bantam Doubleday.

Peer, Shanny (1992), 'Marketing Mickey: Disney Goes to France', *La Revue Tocqueville/The Tocqueville Review* XIII(2): 130–34.

Pells, Richard (1997), *Not Like Us: How Europeans have Loved, Hated, and Transformed American Culture since World War II.* New York: Basic Books.

Poiger, Uta (2000), 'American Music, Cold War Liberalism, and German Identities', in Heide Fehrenbach and Uta Poiger (eds), *Transactions, Transgressions, Transformations: American Culture in Western Europe and Japan.* New York: Berghahn Books: 127–47.

Ritzer, George (2000), *The McDonaldization of Society: New Century Edition.* Thousand Oaks, CA: Sage Publications.

Robertson, Roland (1992), *Globalization: Social Theory and Global Culture.* London: Sage Publications.

Tomlinson, John (1991), *Cultural Imperialism: A Critical Introduction.* London: Pinter Publishers.

Van Eltern, Mel (1996), 'Conceptualizing the Impact of U.S. Popular Culture Globally', *Journal of Popular Culture* 30 (Summer): 47–89.

Wagenleitner, Reinhold (1994), *Coca-Colonization and the Cold War: The Cultural Mission of the United States in Austria after the Second World War*. Chapel Hill, NC: University of North Carolina Press.

Watson, James L. (1997), 'Introduction: Transnationalism, Localization, and Fast-Foods in East Asia', in *Golden Arches East: McDonald's in East Asia*. Stanford, CA: Stanford University Press.

Wylie, Laurence (1989), 'Roussillon, 87: Returning to the Village in the Vaucluse', *French Politics and Society* 7 (Spring): 1–26.

CHAPTER 6

Consumption, Modernity and Japanese Cultural Identity: The Limits of Americanization?[1]

Gerard Delanty

The case of Japan suggests an intriguing alternative to the dominant conception of Americanization. With its implicit connection with a globalizing consumer culture, Americanization has become synonymous with commodification, the rationalizing and material power of modernity, and Westernization. The question is, how valid is this understanding of globalization as a project of cultural imperialism spearheaded by a Western nation state, in particular in the context of those developments that go under the rubric of postmodernity/multiple modernities/alternative modernities which have become more visible in the post-Cold War era?

Because of the non-essentialist ontology on which it is based, Japanese culture defies notions of cultural imperialism as well as conceptions of hybridity. The syncretic nature of Japanese culture rests less on a concept of overall unity or one rooted in an underlying objective reality, as in the West, than on harmony and form but in such a way that the relation between the elements is more important than a clear-cut identity. This non-synthetic sense of form – which is reflected in polytheism, a certain tolerance of contradiction and the absence of a conception of identity as equivalence – results in a strong emphasis on play, leading to a reduced level of cultural confrontation and resistance. I propose the thesis that Japanese culture, which cannot be so easily defined in terms of either the categories of Western modernity or those of late

1 This essay was written while I was a visiting professor at Doshisha University, Kyoto in 2000. I am grateful to Professor Makio Morikawa, the Department of Sociology and the Faculty of Letters, for the resources made available to me. I am also grateful to my research assistant, Atsuko Shiminzu, to Stephanie Assmann and to the graduate students who attended my social theory seminar and from whom I derived valuable knowledge about Japan. I would also like to acknowledge helpful comments on earlier drafts of this paper by Yoshida Takashi, William Outhwaite, Engin Isin and Chris Rojek.

114

Western postmodernity, has been highly subversive of Americanization. The result of this has been, to use a formulation of S.N. Eisenstadt, the primacy of the 'little tradition' over the universalistic ones of the outside – the primacy of form and play over unity and rationality (Eisenstadt 1996). This view of the ontological structures of Japanese culture has implications for understanding the appropriation of America in Japanese culture and institutions. America in Japan was an expression of something like the 'institutional imaginary' as described by Castoriadis (1987); it was important for the reinvention of Japanese cultural identity in the post-Second World War period, and the idea of America allows Japan to express the contradiction of being both victim and aggressor. However, today America is losing its symbolic, imaginary content for the Japanese, who have not only domesticated America but have brought about a certain orientalization of the West. In this pluralization of cultures, Japan re-embraces Asia, which it once rejected for the West, but in a way that is fraught with the same unacknowledged contradictions and ambivalences that have characterized its relationship to America.

In this chapter, taking Japan as an example, I shall examine some aspects of cultural resistance to Americanization, suggesting that the self is now capable of reinventing itself as otherness. America is thus to be read as an imaginary, an essentially open discourse, for one dimension of the project of modernity in Japan. For a long time, Japan was the contrary to America: based more on the particularization of the universal than on the universalization of the particular (Americanization), Japanese culture and society were characterized by their ability to adapt without assimilating the universalistic cultures of Europe and China, which were used to transform the particular. Japanism was a cultural logic of immanization and sublimation, not of universalization or of dialogue or understanding, and was capable of sustaining a powerful culture of orientalism. In Japan, more than anywhere else, the traditional culture centred on the two principal religions did not provide the resistance to consumer cultures that was the case elsewhere, and may have provided the basic cognitive structures through which modern forms of consumption developed. Never colonized in its history and suffering only one major military defeat, Japan, with a population half that of the USA and the ninth most widely spoken language worldwide, the second biggest economy in the world and a powerful and global technological culture, is the limit test of Americanization and of the presuppositions of social theory.

The Subversion of Americanization

The encounter with America has often been held to define the period of modernity in Japan. It was the sighting of American warships in 1853 that formally set off the Meiji Restoration in 1868, an encounter that culminated in the drafting of the post-Second World War liberal constitution by American leadership following military defeat. This conventional view of the epoch-shattering impact of America must be qualified in two respects. First, there can be little doubt that that Americanization was induced by factors integral to Japan and not by the compelling force of the American ideal or the threat the American warships presented in 1853 when the US Navy demanded that the Japanese open their ports. Second, the encounter with America did not really gain momentum until the twentieth century, for prior to 1945 Europe played a far greater role in shaping Japan, much of whose culture both high and low – in dress, crafts, manufacturing and technology – was borrowed from Europe, in particular from the Portuguese, the Dutch and the French in roughly that order (Keene 1969). Moreover, political modernity in 1945, while being hugely important, did not change the basic Japanese attitude to modernity and was very different from the Americanization of Germany in the aftermath of the Second World War when that country was entirely restructured as a result of an outside impetus (Willet 1989). This is not to deny the powerful symbolic resonance of Ginza, the fashionable district of central Tokyo, in twentieth-century Japan. The cosmopolitan heart of Tokyo, Ginza has been the quintessential symbol of America since the 1920s and many Japanese cities sought to imitate what in fact was an elite consumer culture. If anything, this consumerist culture was more powerful than the sighting of American warships in the fateful year of 1853. However, it must be appreciated that the Japanese were more curious about the West than overwhelmed by it. This curiosity is reflected in the eclectic nature of the response to the West, from the adoption of Western hairstyles to meat eating and the first ever translation of the complete works of Marx and Engels by Japanese scholars in the Taisho period. The Japanese were convinced that their modernity was an incomplete one, despite the fact that Japan was one of the most modern nations in the world. In this context it may be suggested, as Harootunian argues, that the very notion of incompleteness was itself the product of a relentless modernity (Harootunian 2000: 112).

The Americanization that was to come in Japan was a popular consumer culture that had little to do with old European cultural modernity or the high culture of the Edo period – and even less, as I shall argue, with America – and the disregard that Japanese post-war politicians had for the new political institutions of democracy attests to the absence of a political modernity based on a tradition of civil society (von Wolferen 1989). While displaying some similarities with organized modernity in the West, Japan was the only non-Western society to undergo modernization leading to fully fledged capitalism and a democratic polity but without experiencing colonization. As a result, and unlike post-war Germany, its basic social and cultural structures remained relatively intact and untouched by the counter-culture that spread from America to Germany in the late 1960s.[2] Defeat in 1945 was the basis of economic growth and subsequent Americanization was defined by strictly Japanese structures. The autonomy of Japan's native cultural traditions was not weakened but was considerably strengthened following the de-sacralization of the emperor and the secularization of Shintoism as a civil religion. Of course, this was considerably facilitated by the ability of the Japanese to quickly adapt the industrialized war economy, whose infrastructure was largely intact, to the national and global consumer culture that emerged soon after 1945.

Americanization can be seen as affirming and giving animus to the Japanese concept of the self as it expanded in the widening category of everyday life. The kind of mass consumer culture that developed in Japan in the 1960s and 1970s was a material one based on a democratized low culture, and it existed in a very private world. The consumers were industrial workers and most importantly the white-collar workers (the 'salarymen') who supplied the ranks for the corporate order (Vogel 1963). The process was driven by a massified society of relatively prosperous middle-class workers for whom work was participation in community, but one that had little to do with the political community of the state. Americanization was thus related to the homogeneous culture of industrial capitalism. But the Americanization of Japan was an Americanization without America, in which lost American values might be found: a work ethic, the sanctity of the family, loyalty to the community, a depoliticized kind of civic communitarianism based on cooperatism but devoid of political will. The new consumer culture was a material one and can be characterized as introducing conspicuous consumption into Japan. Previously consumption had been restricted to the traditional high culture, and self-expression and sensibility were found less in the romantic ethic, which according to Campbell (1987) accompanied capitalism from the beginning, than in self-cultivation and frugality. Americanization was a kind of consumption that affirmed group identities rather than undermined them and which allowed the individual to gain a self-identity in the group without political consciousness. Americanization thus affirmed existing identities rather than leading to the creation of new

2 For an appraisal of the Japanese left, see Asada 2000.

ones. Consumer society and civil society were always in tension even in the West, but there, especially in western and central Europe, the latter preceded the former, which never really eliminated the public sphere. In Japan, where political modernity did not lead to the formation of a civil society, it was not surprising that cultural modernity would be colonized by consumption. Once consumer capitalism emerged in the 1920s in the Taisho period (1912–1926), which can be compared culturally and politically to the Weimar period in Germany, with the emergence of a city-based consumerism and the glamour of Ginza as the new face of Japan, it did so in the context of a society whose appetite for symbolic consumption had already been whetted by the proliferation of national symbols (flags, anthems, commemorations, national holidays, a national literature and standardized schooling) from the end of the nineteenth century when nationalism became a powerful force. What happened in the twentieth century was that this space occupied by the nation became occupied by everyday life (Harootunian 2000). Ginza, once a symbol of America and consumer modernity, had now become Japanized and America quickly vanished into Japan's home-produced consumer culture.

Americanization was based on a logic of reproduction through repetition by which material objects represented symbolic meanings defined by the group rather than by the individual. A striking aspect of these symbolic meanings was their post-traditionalism. This was present in the widespread destruction of traditional Japanese culture in the 1960s and 1970s in the name of growth, modernity and Americanism. But the important point was the continued existence of essentially Japanese cognitive and normative structures which shaped the project of Americanization, a project that was easy to disguise; the Japanese remained largely indifferent to America until quite recently when foreign travel became more common. But even then the reluctance of Japanese people, especially the political elite, to learn to speak English has only recently become a matter of widespread concern. A whole series of exemptions was created for foreigners living in Japan in order to minimize their impact on Japanese traditions and the subsequent self-confrontation that this would require. Japanese social practices thus had in-built defences from outside influences, as is also very apparent from the rigid naturalization laws, which make it impossible for a foreigner to acquire Japanese citizenship and which still prevent the large numbers of those of Korean parentage from becoming Japanese nationals even though they were born and grew up in Japan.

In the massified form of McDonaldization (Ritzer 1998), Americanization was perfectly compatible with the cultural horizons of post-war Japan: individualism through materialist values, a high level of group commitment, a belief in equality, and the separation of work and leisure. Thus the Japanese assimilation of American baseball and bowling (the most popular sports activity) was possible because it could be contained within the existing cultural structures of group-oriented and rule-based behaviour. Consumption in Japan affirmed individualism within the limits of group-based choice, as is evident from the Japanese tendency to prepackage and standardize many products, for example the ubiquitous convenience store and vending machine. Equality did not extend to the rights of citizenship but to lifestyle. Americanization can be seen as extending the range of symbolic structuring by which meaning could be created but within the existing cognitive and normative structures. Americanization, for instance, led to the intensified proliferation of popular consumer cultures specific to Japan – *manga* (comics), *pachinko* (pinball games), *karaoke* – but did not create these cultural practices (see Sugimoto 1997: 225–30; Kelly 1998). Marriage, too, is one of the most commercialized of all group-based forms of collective consumption and is generally celebrated in lavish and highly expensive ceremonies, involving the consumption of Western themes but in a very non-Western manner and according to conventionalized patterns of behaviour, most of which also have no basis in Japanese tradition.

The fact that capitalism in Japan did not require a puritan work ethic may explain the apparent hedonism of much of modern Japanese culture, which has not experienced a 'cultural contradiction' between work and leisure, as Daniel Bell has claimed in the case of America (Bell 1976). As I have already argued, Japanese culture has been adept at avoiding cultural contradictions resulting in crises of identity. The diversity of Japanese popular culture and consumer behaviour can be partly explained by the role of *asobi*, or 'playfulness'. By consuming or participating in popular forms of entertainment, people can experiment with new ways of enjoying themselves and in relatively sociable contexts. This propensity for play can help us to explain the phenomenon that has often been commented on of 'frenzy consumption' in Japan.

If Americanization had a postmodern dimension to it, it was to be found in the extension of capitalism into the domain of culture through commodification as well as through the unleashing of 'desire' (Jameson 1991). In Japan this 'cultural logic' of capitalism achieves what democracy was unable to deliver: participation in society. This participation could even be extended to participation in international society, as is evidenced by the extraordinary construction of theme parks reproducing Western cities and cultural contexts from all over the world. But television is the best example of the moulding of new kinds of social integration through the radical separation of leisure and work time. Through television Japanese traditional culture is relived, possibly recreated, for urban consumption and a measure of enchantment in a work-dominated society. Many traditional festivals and performances are kept alive for consumption through television (Stronach 1989). Popular consumer cultures do not necessarily destroy tradition, as the 'post-traditionalization' thesis claims. Many traditions are sustained by popular culture, in particular by television programmes and by tourism. Indeed, many Buddhist temples have often been criticized for their consumerism (Kerr 1993). In this context, Japanese internal tourism has been an important part of the survival of tradition. We should not, then, see popular culture as necessarily leading to post-traditionalization. I would argue that in the past – the so-called pre-modern past – there was a far greater destruction of tradition than in a modernity conscious of the need for a romantic ethic and the need to feed on tradition. For instance, Kyoto is regarded as the spiritual and cultural cradle of Japan, although the city experienced near total destruction in the Middle Ages and there are few authentic relics of the pre-Edo period. Again, a recent study has documented how the Meiji state used traditional folk cultures to shape the modernizing political culture which came to rest on the incorporation of the fantastic (Figal 1999; see also Napier 1995). For these reasons, then, the Americanization of Japan is not necessarily a post-traditionalization but its reinvention. As Creighton argues in a study of the *depato*, the Japanese department store:

> The symbols and images of the West packaged by depato for domestic consumption do not necessarily reflect the reality of any part of the Western world. More often they are blurred refractions, decontextualized fragments of various Western traditions and practices that have been culled and then altered to fit the Japanese cultural context and the expectations of Japanese consumers. (Creighton 1992: 55)

This can be seen as a tendency to 'over-translate' – or, one might say, to 'sterilize' – foreign customs and products of their otherness. An example of this is the Japanese coffee-house culture: eating a miniature piece of cake, doubly wrapped in silver foil, is a deliberate exaggeration of Western customs to the point of parody. This is true too of Western marriage ceremonies that are not a part of Japanese culture (for example the large number of bridal fashion magazines and advertisements for Western marriages on public transport), or the recent phenomenon of consumption by young women of English language courses, an activity that is more about sociality and consumption than about acquiring linguistic skills.[3] McDonald's is also a good example of this. Most Japanese regard McDonald's as Japanese modern convenience culture and do not associate it with America, which if it appears at all is more likely to be

3 I am grateful to Stephanie Assmann for advice on these aspects of Japanese consumption.

miniaturized and exoticized. However, this is not to claim that Japanese consumption is entirely a process of domestication, but also of imaginary signification and playfulness. As a trope for the outside, the idea of America allowed the inside to expand symbolic production but in a way that made possible the continued transformation of both self and other. The theoretical implication of this is that Japanese cultural practices may be seen as a domestication of the radical imaginary, which has found less expression on the political level than on the cultural level. In this context it is important to note that the term 'glocalization', as used by Roland Robertson to express the local appropriation of global forces, has a Japanese origin (Robertson 1992).[4]

Although I have emphasized Japan's capacity for cultural transformation of outside influences, mention too must be made of the existence of multiple levels of experience which are to be found in Japanese everyday life and which may be seen in the context of play as a cultural category. Traditional festivities – such as the widely popular nature-viewing ceremonies, for example the cherry-blossom viewing, religious festivities and pilgrimages – can exist alongside modern consumer cultures, providing in part an enchantment destroyed by modernity. What is significant is the Japanese capacity to switch from one level of experience to another, like the paper walls that separate the traditional rooms in which interior (private) and exterior (public) are easily interchangeable.

Americanization ran parallel to Japanese economic and cultural nationalism with its proclamations of Japanese uniqueness, notions that were voiced more strongly in the 1980s in the wake of massive economic growth and in recognition of Japan's leading role in the world's economy. With the second largest economy in the world and the highest per capita income in the world, backed up by one of the highest saving rates, many Japanese social commentators sought to reinvent the myth of Japanese uniqueness. The proliferation of the *Nihonjinron* (writing on Japaneseness) literature, with considerable support from the corporate culture, was the other side to the Americanization of the society and suggests that Americanization was not perceived to be a threat to nativism (Yoshino 1992). Indeed, the Americanization of the society was hardly discernibly 'American' given the pastiche nature of Japanese consumer culture and the fact that Japanese industry was surpassing Western manufacturing, with its brand names (Sony, Honda, Hitachi, Fuji, Mitsubishi) becoming global household words. Japanese nationalism was more a celebration of cultural difference than an appeal to tradition, and ironically much of it was motivated by American nationalism which portrayed Japan and its globalizing

---

4 The term was used by Hiroyuki Itami, an academic, in 1991 to refer to Japanese management practices (*NihontekKeiei*), though the term had been commonly used in business journals since 1988.

economy as a threat to American national interests (Sugimoto 1999). Unlike many Western forms of nationalism, this was a cultural nationalism that was strongly based on the market, promoted more by business than by the state, as Yoshino has argued (Yoshino 1999). Such proclamations of superiority based on difference and uniqueness were not easily reconciled with the assimilation of Japanese products in Western societies, but, as is frequently the case, claims of difference rest on prior assimilation. In any case, it is an example of how a prosperous consumption-based society can reinvent nationalism, which can be shaped as much by the market as by the state.

There can be little doubt that Japanese consumer culture is modern, however much it is shaped by traditional Japanese culture, and that Americanization reinforces rather than undermines both modernity and tradition. After all, much of the impetus of European modernism came from Japan, for instance the famous Katsura Imperial Villa at Kyoto which inspired the Bauhaus and modernist architecture. With its concern for form and harmony of function, this is high modernism, not postmodernism. As Donald Richie has argued, the Japanese tendency to miniaturize everything is reflected in early Disneyfication, as in some of its famous gardens: 'Some Edo gardens are even more Disneyland-like – Tokyo's Rikugien for example. Here, in one place, arranged somewhat like a miniature golf-course, are most of the 88 agreed-upon canonical sites, all tiny and all with notice-boards explaining the Chinese or Japanese associations' (Richie 1999: 85). Disneyland in Tokyo is only an American version of this creative impulse within Japanese culture, the culture of the copy and the geographical microcosm. The spirit of Japan since 1945 has been modernist rather than postmodernist, as is clearly evident from its buildings and consumer culture of convenience. Shunya Yoshini has convincingly demonstrated that Disneyland in Tokyo has been diluted of its symbolic American character simply because by the time it was opened in 1983 the society had already been Disneyfied. America had ceased to be a symbol of richness and newness, becoming something that was recontextualized and consumable in everyday life and in codes that were distinctively Japanese (Yoshini 2000). This thesis is also borne out by Rojek (1995) who argues that leisure is not merely an escape from reality. In the Japanese context everyday life itself is based on the playfulness of self-seeking 'escapes'.

The alleged postmodernization of Japan then is merely a particular form that modernity took in Japan.[5] What is often called postmodernism with respect to Japanese consumer cultures is in fact merely the blending of modernity and tradition in the ever-expanding space of everyday life where enchantment

5 There is a large literature on the postmodernization of Japan, which cannot be considered due to the limits of space. See Sugimoto and Arnason 1995, and Miyoshi and Harootunian 1989.

replaces disenchantment. After all, the Japanese may be dedicated shoppers but they are also a society of savers and generally do not pay by credit. In a cash economy, their consumption, unlike that in many Western countries, is driven by savings, not by debt: behind postmodernist desire is modernist prudence. If there is a postmodern underpinning to the changing discourse of the self it is to be found more in an embracing of Asia and Europe (difference) than of America (identity). In the following section I shall discuss the significance of a nascent cosmopolitanism and how this might be an expression of a current beyond Americanization, and a further illustration of the cultural consequences of globalization in a world that is no longer exclusively dominated by America.

Cosmopolitanism and the New Consumption

To the extent to which advertising is an indicator of changing patterns in consumption, it has been noted that recent advertising tends to place less stress on differences between products and their orders of symbolic differentiation than on differences between advertisements. In this shift in the mode of advertising, there is a move from American-style persuasion to the more typically European advertising that does not use words but pictures and into which a person can read what they wish – which may not be dictated by a system of commodified needs (McCreery 2000: 174). In many of these Japanese advertisements there is also a subversion not just of meaning but of the product itself, and whatever symbolic meaning is consumed may not be 'conspicuous' in Veblen's sense. As Marilyn Ivy comments: 'While the copy of American commercials still tries to appeal to the rationality of the viewer by realistically comparing product A to product B (although recently high-tech, Japanese style ads are appearing in the United States), Japanese advertising (in particular, television commercials) appeals more directly to desire within the symbolic economy' (Ivy 1989: 38). This stress on consumption as the liberation of desire from established systems of needs breaks from the modernist limits of Americanization by bringing into the sphere of consumption the deconstructions of self and other. It is a form of consumption that does not speak in the name of an underlying self.

It has often been noted that Baudrillard has had an influence in Japanese thinking. His notion of the simulacrum has even extended into marketing, where it lends itself to ironic forms of advertising (Asada 2000: 23–24). Perhaps, as I have argued earlier, the Japanese have a unique capacity to tolerate contradiction. The Japanese word *munjun*, meaning contradiction, is often avoided and people prefer to talk about 'coexistence' rather than about contradictions, as in the seemingly inexplicable coexistence of high saving and excessive consumption. Thus in Japanese advertising, as Millie Creighton has argued, there is an avoidance of overt competition; it is widely believed that advertising should not make authoritative statements about products but should instead capture a mood. The result is the 'no-meaning ad' (Creighton 1995: 139–40).

Japanese marketing is adjusting to the changing reality of society and the diversity of its population. Instead of mass consumption of Americanized products, characterized by convenience, newness and a desire for material comforts, a new generation of Japanese are emerging who are more discriminating as well as being uncertain as to their own identity. This generation may not have the same purchasing power of the old generation, who enjoyed life-time employment in the corporate economy, and there are growing numbers of older people seeking the security of a long retirement that is becoming more and more uncertain. As a result of the increasingly differentiated nature of the Japanese population – which is about half that of the USA – it may be speculated that the changing demographic structure of contemporary Japan is leading a larger proportion of the population to approach post-material values. It is the expression less of an industrial society than of a post-industrial one. This does not indicate a decline in consumption or the replacement of one mode of behaviour by another, but the emergence of new kinds of behaviour which can be seen as in line with post-material values elsewhere (Inglehart 1977; Abramson and Inglehart 1995). Most Japanese do not aspire to purchasing American products. European designer products – such as the bag brand names Chanel, Gucci and Prada, important for a bag-conscious society – enjoy higher consumer esteem. Europe is also a more popular tourist destination, rivalling Hawaii and Hong Kong. European cars, clothes and food are preferred to American products – hardly anyone buys American cars, for instance. The cultural content of the media is also relatively low on American products; Japan is one of the few countries where virtually all media content is home-produced.

While the older forms of consumption affirmed existing identities and established only the identity of the individual within the parameters of the group, the new kinds of consumption are based on a growing critical space between the individual and the group, a space that is also to be found between the individual and the product. The new consumption is based less on making choices defined by a particular lifestyle shaped around a lifelong career, as was the case with the baby-boom generation who found security in the post-war corporate economy. As John McCreery remarks:

> As consumers they enjoyed novelty. But instead of personal creativity, they preferred the stance of connoisseurs. They would cultivate personal taste and skillfully choose the products and lifestyles that suited them best from

the cornucopia that industry provided them. An education built around the multiple-choice test legitimated the correct choice as an ultimate value toward which to strive. (McCreery 2000: 248)

The new post-industrial consumers live in a more fragmented context than these corporate warriors and their choices are shaped by identities that are not underpinned by roles and participation in established structures. We are dealing here with a more individuated kind of consumption than is suggested by lifestyle consumption and one shaped by more temporary kinds of networks. Rosenberger argues that while rationality and efficiency are still highly valued, style and fulfilment are increasingly the focus of consumer values (Rosenberger 1992). It may be suggested that a kind of consumption is emerging in which individuation is more apparent than commodification.

New technologies in communication have been crucial in shaping the new Japanese consumer. Information is more central to consumption than previously and the older separation of high and low cultures that characterized Americanization is less prevalent. Knowledge is itself an object of consumption, as is apparent from the way the Japanese regard education as a commodity to be consumed (though not always critically appropriated). Advertising for private schools for 'cramming', language schools, colleges and universities suggests that education and knowledge more broadly is an object to be consumed not unlike the consumption of any other object. The consumption of knowledge is also linked to easy communication. The existence of mobile phones, which in Japan are more or less universally used by young people, has increased the extent of personal networks, especially among women who are almost invariably to be seen with their personally decorated, nail-varnished phone, which may also have 'traditional' accessories.

As the peer group expands numerically, the commitment to the group is weakened, providing a wider space for personal individuation. These groups are temporary networks and it is less important to demonstrate social status in them than in the more pronounced conspicuous consumption of class. According to Maffesoli (1996), the age of the masses is giving way to new social relationships akin to 'tribes', as expressed through the constant flow of images and situations, a kind of 'cute-consumption' (Kinsella 1995). Unlike the consumer cultures of the past, which were spatial and fixed, these new 'tribes' are unstable and open, a product of the fragmentation of the social and the disintegration of mass culture. People are increasingly finding themselves in temporary networks, or 'tribes', organized around temporary affiliations and images. The new products are being sold in this space, which is not always the space of the home or of class.

Internet use will also play a role in this. Access to the Internet among Japanese women jumped from 1 per cent in 1997 to 36 per cent in 1999.[6] At the time of writing (2000) there is an explosion in e-commerce in Japan, and the theme of informational economy and technology that was central to the G-8 summit at Okinawa in 2000 has reinforced the perception that Japan – lagging some two years behind the Western world in its information technology – must make a rapid if late entry into the informational technological world.[7] Clearly this will have implications for modes of consumption, which will be less likely to be contained within the existing structures of national consumption. What is characteristic of the new modes of consumption – the Internet, mobile phones, friendship networks, fashion, foreign travel – is the social role of information. John Clammer argues that friendships often involve the sharing of information: 'in some cases to the degree that "friends" can sometimes be defined as the network of those with whom one regularly exchanges such consumption information' (Clammer 1997: 5). Shopping is often about the sharing of information and Japanese consumers, especially women, are highly informed about all kinds of consumer affairs. Group shopping is still a feature of Japanese consumption practised by women, but it is being transformed by the changing nature of the group, which is becoming more diffuse and less capable of defining the identity of the person. The group is also the site in which play is expressed, and which can be seen more fundamentally as what Asada has called 'infantile capitalism' (Asada 1989).

This new kind of post-industrial consumption cannot be so easily called 'conspicuous' in Veblen's (or in Bourdieu's) sense, since the objective of consumption is not always to demonstrate to which group the self belongs – relations between self and other have become too diffuse for this to be possible. The group is being reshaped as a network of acquaintances. It is no longer easily definable in class terms, or in any terms (as is the case in Bourdieu's [unacknowledged] reappropriation of Veblen). Rather than being about belonging, it is a question of a withdrawal of the self, and frequently, as in the case of many Japanese women, of a withdrawal from the world of work. For many others who have entered professional life consumption is located outside the space of everyday life in a highly personalized context and in a world that is largely devoid of meaning (see Kelsky 1996). The unity of the self and the exteriority of the other taken for granted in Veblen and Bourdieu are no longer adequate for an understanding of contemporary cultural identity for which

6 *The Japan Times*, 5 June 2000: 18.
7 The irony is that, according to Castells, the concept of the 'information society' – *Johoka Shakai* – was invented by the Japanese in 1963 and exported to the West in 1978 in the title of a report to the French government (Castells 1998: 236).

neither self nor other is fixed. For example, Japanese gift-giving is not designed to establish a harmony based on a shared reciprocity between self and other but to reproduce, through established and complex rules, the distance as measured by relations of obligation and status between giver and receiver. Because of the way this distance is measured – with lists of presents being kept and etiquette manuals consulted in case of doubt on the rules of exchange – a form of reciprocity is created that lends itself as much to commercialization as to group solidarity. In this sense, then, the gift, so much a part of Japanese consumption (accounting for as much as 10 per cent of the income of a middle-class family), separates the self from the other while at the same time expressing a social relationship based on the exchange of a carefully chosen commodity (Clammer 1997: 18–19).

I have characterized the contemporary kinds of consumption associated with post-industrialism and postmodern culture as more related to a nascent cosmopolitanism than to Americanization. This does not mean that the latter is in decline but that a new logic of consumption is emerging, which cannot be understood solely in terms of Americanization and in the conventional terms of social theory. Symbolic consumption of a fantasized America is relatively insignificant in relation to the consumption of the self, albeit a self that has been exteriorized and even made exotic to itself.

Globalization is also having an effect on the internal structure of Japanese society. As Sassen has shown, Tokyo is a global city, linked more into global finance capitalism and information systems than into Japanese society (Sassen 1992). The European Union is also becoming more present in Japanese external relations (Abe 1999). As Japan enters the melting pot of globalization, many logics of consumption emerge and old ones return in new forms. One dimension to this is the reinvention of *Japonisme*, the primarily European reception of Japanese traditional culture, ranging from fashion to gardens, since the Enlightenment (Wichmann 1981). In the 1980s *Japonisme* was revived when Japanese fashion designers became world famous and Tokyo became one of the fashion capitals along with Paris, Milan, New York and London. According to Skov, in an insightful article, Japanese fashion blended in well with European consumer cultures because of its stylistic and technological anonymity (Skov 1996: 144). However, the penchant for *Japonisme* in Europe is based on simplistic ideas of Japanese culture as an 'Otherness' devoid of individualism except when it enters Western contexts, where it becomes a design capable of expressing Western individualism, as the explosion in sushi in Western countries demonstrates. But, despite this Eurocentricism behind *Japonisme*, there are also movements in the opposite direction, Skov argues, for as Tokyo becomes a cosmopolitan fashion capital, Japanese women for their part are buying the products of Parisian fashion houses and thus becoming part of a transnational community (Skov 1996: 136). Undoubtedly developments of this kind have led to a reduction in the stereotypes that have shaped perceptions of Japan in the past, such as the image of the 'yellow peril', the samurai economy, or a nation of group zealots, though these images still influence Western advertising using Japanese motifs (Moeran 1996; Raz and Raz 1996). But the real developments are to be found in the transformation of popular cultures in Japan, as well as in Asia more widely,where Japan's cultural influence is growing – and in a way that fundamentally challenges the notion of Americanization.

While Europe and Japan may be self-consciously penetrating each other's cultures more and more, we also have the growing importance of the diffusion of Japanese popular culture, especially popular music, in Asia. Japanese culture is very popular in Asia, rivalling American consumer culture. Much of what is often called American culture in Asia is in fact Japanese culture, which is now a creative culture with innovating designs, as opposed to being the culture of the copy, as has often been thought. Indeed, since the late 1990s, with its growth rate slowing down, it is evident that Japan is settling on being a major Asian power. No longer seen as a challenge to the USA, in 2000 a major survey of US elites in business, media, academic and politics reported positive images of Japan. Japan's embracing of Asia is one of the great changes in its history and may be the basis of a new cultural identity (Iwabuchi 1999).

With modernization reaching its limits and Americanization giving way to more pluralized forms of consumption, Japanese culture is finding a new embodiment in the consumption of the culture of the other. If America symbolized identity, Europe – which is becoming present in the society – stands for difference, and it is this turn to the other, including the 'self as other', that has more resonances in contemporary consumer cultures, which are capable of transforming all cultures, including the native one, into otherness. Americanization in Japan allowed the individual to express a personal identity within the limits of group affiliations. Consumption was conspicuous in the sense of making public the inner self. Contemporary forms of consumption are less organized around the expression of self-identity within a publicly visible lifestyle. Lacking this security and guarantee of meaning, the self today finds itself in a much more fragmented situation and has itself become fragmented. To use postmodernist language, it is a question of desire escaping the bounds of need. The problem is that this has not been accompanied by a significant degree of self-confrontation.

Conclusion: The Triumph of Expressiveness?

Since 1945 Japan has moved slowly towards globalization. But this was always a contained globalization. The growth of the Japanese economy depended on highly protected internal markets, and the entry of Americanization into consumer culture tended to affirm rather than undermine the relative autonomy of Japanese society. For instance, 60 per cent of the Japanese economy depends on domestic consumption.[8] Since the 1990s the nationalistic ethos of the previous two decades has given way to a new concern with a soft cultural kind of internationalism, known as *Kokusaika*, in the sense of a strengthening of cultural exchange and openness. The end of the bubble economy, the earthquake in Kobe in 1995 which led to the deaths of over 6,000 people, intimations of the risk society with a serious nuclear accident in 1999, the crisis of the dual economy and the end of lifetime employment are all reminders that Japan is no longer a fundamentally different place, and its increasing international role (in particular in Asia), the desire to have a place on the UN Security Council, the need for dialogue with China and Korea, the need to secure natural resources and energy, and the need to import labour in order to maintain industrial productivity require it to become more open. In this chapter I have emphasized how these developments are reflected in the growing pluralization of cultural identity, as exemplified in the changing kinds of consumer culture and the growing presence of subcultures and alternative lifestyles as well as a recognition of the internal cultural diversity within the Japanese population (reflected also in the increase in transnational marriages).

As cultural identity comes to rest on more and more expressiveness, developments in the opposite direction can also be observed, leading to forms of expressiveness that are not accompanied by self-confrontation. The same expressiveness that lies at the root of the new consumerism is also present in other avenues of escape, for example in Japanese new religions such as the *Aum Shinrikyo*, the sect responsible for the poison gas bomb attack in a Tokyo subway in 1995 (Metraux 1999; Reader 2000). In general, books related to religion sell well.[9] In a culture that has historically been past- rather than salvation-oriented, seeking in the past a source of generation, the new religions of authoritarian occultism and mysticism are offering people alternative kinds of consumerism and expressions of personal identity. This is not unconnected to a subterranean discourse of violence in much of Japanese popular culture, such as the *Mangas*. However, the violence is largely imaginative and may be seen, following Elias, as a pacification of violence, since there is relatively little overt

8 Reported on Japanese news programme, 9 June 2000.
9 This and other statistical information is taken from Asahi Shimbun 1999.

or visible violence in the society. *Manga* can also be a means of articulating a political consciouness and cultural identity (Kinsella 2000). In it one can find all kinds of political critique, generally in the form of parody. It is an example of how the aesthetic public sphere is also constituted by reflexivity and critique. My earlier emphasis on play (*asobi*) might help to understand this uniquely Japanese phenomenon.

As far as religion is concerned, there is not only the emergence of new religions but the growing discourse of re-sacralization of the public sphere and a more explicit kind of political nationalism. In April 2000 the newly appointed prime minister Mori created widespread controversy over remarks in a speech to a Shintoist convention that Japan was 'a divine nation centred on the emperor'. While there are clear signs of a more pronounced nationalism coming from some Japanese politicians as well as more expressions of anti-Americanism, there is much to suggest that the society is sceptical of nationalism. The death of the dowager empress[10] in June 2000 was not an occasion for nationalist sentiment but a cautious reminder of the final passing of the Showa period. While the critical response to the prime minister's remarks made clear that re-sacralization and the significance of the imperial institution will be limited as far as political culture is concerned, there is growing anxiety in the society that social change is undermining social relations. Crime and violence, though negligible in comparison to most other countries, are on the rise and Japan has one of the highest rates of suicide in the world (in 1999 reaching 31,000).

The state institutions in particular have not changed to match other developments, despite a considerable loss in the electoral power of the Liberal Democratic Party after some four decades of government. In particular, education is rigid, ineffective and stifles creativity. The bureaucratic political culture does not encourage democratic participation or debate on issues such as ecological sustainability, corruption or the improvement of the situation of women, who earn 60 per cent of male salaries. The work culture is still rigid and extremely hierarchical. As a result, popular consumer cultures, including the new religions, are offering people alternative fantasies from those of work, education and politics. The Japanese self is not equipped to resist the negative aspects of modernity that have been intensified by globalization. The re-enchantment that is offered by popular consumer cultures is powerful and does not come up against the resistance that civil society presents. Most Japanese consumption takes place in an expanding space of everyday life and has very little impact on the world of work and institutions. Consumption gives to the individual a freedom denied in other parts of the society. Everyday life is

10 The widow of the Showa Emperor Hirohito who died in 1989.

more anarchic than in other societies as a result of its relative separation from the formal institutions of the society. But it is from there that citizenship will emerge, for, fragmented though it is, everyday life offers more possibilities for change than the official public culture. Some case can be made for consumer markets taking the lead in cultural citizenship in Japan; for example, the Japanese opposition to genetically modified foods derives from consumer markets. However, there is relatively little sign of something like a flexible citizenship emerging in Japan, as is the case in other parts of South-East Asia (Ong 1999).

It is in consumption, as John Clammer has argued following Bourdieu, that most cultural differences are expressed (Clammer 1997: 102–03). In Japan, where the income divide is low and where ethnic differences are minimal, group differences are more likely to be expressed in forms of consumption. The institutions of education, the state and work may eventually be forced to adapt to the utopian currents of everyday life, where there are no limits to consumption. But until these currents take a political form, the capacity for social change will be limited. While displaying a remarkable capacity for symbolic production, Japan's cultural capacity for social change is limited. Consumption is being contained with the depoliticized structures of privatized individualism, which, while radically reshaping Japanese cultural identity, has not had any significant impact on political identity. Political identity has not fully come to terms with some of the contradictions inherent in Japanese modernity. It is not surprising, then, that we find cosmopolitan identity only fully expressed in the identities of the marginalized. Tessa Morris-Suzuki (2000: 79) discusses, for instance, how the minority group, the Ainu, have the consciousness of belonging to a world community of indigenous peoples. The motif of modernity and the idea of America allow the Japanese to express their national identity as victims of America and as oppressors (of Asia) at the same time.

While consumption continues to diffuse identities, Japan is unable to escape from modernity: the symbolic presence of the Rape of Nanking and the atomic bombing of Hiroshima remain striking reminders of the contradictions of Japanese modernity and of the contradictory role of both America and Asia in its modern consciousness.

References

Abe, A. (1999), *Japan and the European Union*. London: Athlone Press.

Abramson, P., and R. Inglehart (1995), *Value Change in Global Perspective*. Ann Arbor, MI: Michigan University Press.

Asada, A. (1989), 'Infantile Capitalism and Japan's Postmodernism: A Fairy Tale', in Miyoshi and Harootunian (eds).

— (2000), 'A Left within the Place of Nothingness', *New Left Review* 5: 15–40.

Asahi Shimbun (1999), *Japan Almanac 2000*. Tokyo: Asahi Shimbun.

Bell, D. (1976), *The Cultural Contradictions of Capitalism*. London: Heinemann.

Beng-Huat, C. (ed.) (2000), *Consumption in Asia: Lifestyles and Identities*. London: Sage.

Campbell, C. (1987), *The Romantic Ethic and the Spirit of Modern Consumerism*. Oxford: Basil Blackwell.

Castells, M. (1998), *End of Millennium*. Oxford: Blackwell.

Castoriadis, C. (1987), *The Imaginary Institution of Society*. Cambridge: Polity.

Clammer, J. (1995), *Difference and Modernity: Social Theory and Contemporary Japanese Society*. London: Kegan Paul.

— (1997), *Contemporary Urban Japan: A Sociology of Consumption*. Oxford: Blackwell.

— (1999), 'Transcending Modernity? Individualism, Ethics and Japanese Discourses of Difference in the Post-War World', *Thesis Eleven* 57: 65–80.

Creighton, M. (1992), 'The Depato Merchandising the West While Selling Japaneseness', in Tobin (ed.).

— (1995), 'Imagining the Other in Japanese Advertising Campaigns', in J. Carrier (ed.), *Occidentalism: Images of the West*. Oxford: Oxford University Press.

Dale, P. (1995), *The Myth of Japanese Uniqueness*. London: Routledge.

Eisenstadt, S.N. (1996), *Japanese Civilization: A Comparative View*. Chicago: Chicago University Press.

Figal, G. (1999), *Civilization and Monsters: Spirits of Modernity in Meiji Japan*. Durham, NC: Duke University Press.

Harootunian, H. (2000), *History's Disquiet: Modernity, Cultural Practice and the Question of Everyday Life*. New York: Columbia University Press.

Heidegger, M. (1971), 'A Dialogue on Language between a Japanese and an Inquirer', in M. Heidegger, *On the Way to Language*. New York: Harper & Row.

Inglehart, R. (1977), *The Silent Revolution: Changing Values and Political Styles Among Western Publics*. Princeton, NJ: Princeton University Press.

Ivy, Marilyn (1993), 'Formation of Mass Culture', in Andrew Gordon (ed.), *Postwar Japan as History*. Berkeley: University of California Press: 239–58.

Iwabuchi, K. (1999), 'Return to Asia? Japanese Audiovisual Markets' in K. Yoshino (ed.), *Consuming Ethics and Nationalism: Asian Explorations*. Richmond, Surrey: Curzon.

Jameson, F. (1991), *Postmodernism; or, the Cultural Logic of Late Capitalism*. London: Verso.

Keene, D. (1969), *The Japanese Discovery of Europe, 1720–1830*. Stanford, CA: Stanford University Press, rev. edn.

Kelly, B. (1998), 'The Empty Orchestra: Echoes of Japanese Traditional Culture in the Performance of Karaoke', in D. Martinez (ed.), *The Worlds of Japanese Popular Culture: Gender, Shifting Boundaries and Global Culltures*. Cambridge: Cambridge University Press.

Kelsky, K. (1996), 'Flirting with the Foreign: Interracial Sex in Japan's "International" Age', in R. Wilson and W. Dissanayake (eds), *Global/Local: Cultural Production and the Transnational Imaginary*. Durham, NC: Duke University Press.

Kerr, A. (1993), *Lost Japan*. Hawthorn, Victoria: Lonely Planet Publications.

Kinsella, S. (1995), 'Cuties in Japan', in L. Skov and B. Moeran (eds), *Women, Media and Consumption in Japan*. Richmond, Surrey: Curzon.

— (2000), *Adult Manga: Culture and Politics in Contemporary Japanese Society*. Richmond, Surrey: Curzon.

McCreery, J.J. (2000), *Japanese Consumer Behaviour*. London: Curzon.

Maffesoli, M. (1996), *Time of the Tribes: The Decline of Individualism in Mass Society*. London: Sage.

Metraux, D. (1999), *Aum Shinrikyo and Japanese Youth*. Lanham, MD: University Press of America.

Miyoshi, M., and H. Harootunian (eds) (1989), *Postmodernism and Japan*. Durham,

NC: Duke University Press.

— (1993), *Japan in the World*. Durham, NC: Duke University Press.

Moeran, B. (1996), 'The Orient Strikes Back: Advertising and Imagining Japan', *Theory, Culture and Society* 13(3): 77–112.

Morris-Suzuki, T. (2000), 'For and Against NGOs: The Politics of the Lived World', *New Left Review* 2: 63–84.

Napier, S. (1995), *The Fantastic in Modern Japanese Literature: The Subversion of Modernity*. London: Routledge.

Ohnuki-Tierney, E. (1993), *Rice as Self: Japanese Identities Through Time*. Princeton, NJ: Princeton University Press.

— (1997), 'McDonald's in Japan: Changing Manners and Etiquette', in Watson (ed.).

Ong, A. (1999), *Flexible Citizenship: The Cultural Logics of Transnationality*. Durham, NC: Duke University Press.

Raz, J., and A. Raz (1996), '"America" Meets "Japan": A Journey for Real between Two Imaginaries', *Theory, Culture and Society* 13(3): 153–78.

Reader, I. (2000), *Religious Violence in Contemporary Japan: The Case of the Aum Shinrikyo*. London: Curzon.

Richie, D. (1999), *Tokyo*. London: Reaktion Books.

Ritzer, G. (1993), *The McDonaldization of Society*. London: Sage.

— (1998), *The McDonaldization Thesis: Explorations and Extensions*. London: Sage.

Robertson, R. (1992), *Social Theory and Globalization*. London: Sage.

Rojek, C. (1995), *Decentring Leisure: Rethinking Leisure Theory*. London: Sage.

Rosenberger, N. (1992), 'Images of the West', in Tobin (ed.).

Sassen, S. (1992), *The Global City: New York, London, Tokyo*. Princeton, NJ: Princeton University Press.

Skov, L. (1996), 'Fashion Trends, *Japonisme* and Postmodernism', *Theory Culture and Society* 13(3): 129–51.

Stronach, B. (1989), 'Japanese Television', in R. G. Powers and H. Kato (eds), *Handbook of Japanese Popular Culture*. Westport, CT: Greenwood Press.

Sugimoto, Y. (1997), *An Introduction to Japanese Society*. Cambridge: Cambridge University Press.

— (1999), 'Making Sense of *Nihonjinron*', *Thesis Eleven* 57: 81–96.

Sugimoto, Y., and J. Arnason (eds) (1995), *Japanese Encounters with Postmodernity*. London: Kegan Paul International.

Tobin, J. (ed.) (1992), *Re-Made in Japan: Everyday Life and Consumer Taste in a Changing Society*. New Haven: Yale University Press.

Vogel, E. (1963), *Japan's New Middle Class: The Salaryman and His Family in a Tokyo Suburb*. Berkeley: University of California Press.

— (1989), Japan as Number 1. Cambridge, MA: Harvard University Press.

Watson, J. (ed.) (1997), *Golden Arches East: McDonald's in East Asia*. Stanford, CA: Stanford University Press.

Wichmann, S. (1981), *Japonisme: The Japanese Influence on Western Art in the 19th and 20th Centuries*. New York: Harmony.

Willet, R. (1989), *The Americanization of Germany, 1945–1949*. London: Routledge.

Wolferen, H. von (1989), *The Enigma of Japanese Power*. London: Macmillan.

Yoshini, S. (2000), 'Consuming "America": From Symbol to System', in C. Beng-Huat (ed.), *Consumption in Asia: Lifestyles and Identities*. London: Sage.

Yoshino, K. (1992), *Cultural Nationalism in Contemporary Japan: A Sociological Inquiry*. London: Routledge.

— (1999), 'Rethinking Theories of Nationalism: Market Place Perspectives', in K. Yoshino (ed.), *Consuming Ethics and Nationalism: Asian Explorations*. Richmond, Surrey: Curzon.

CHAPTER 7

Americanization, Westernization, Sinification: Modernization or Globalization in China?

Yu Keping

China has long embraced the golden mean of the Middle Way, yet, since the beginning of the twentieth century, extremism has prevailed. The Cultural Revolution is a typical example of extremism that was a catastrophe for China. The reform promoted by Deng Xiaoping as of the early 1980s was not only significant on the socio-economic level, but also for politics and ideology, since his attempt to stress both the anti-left and the anti-right was a way of avoiding both extremes. Twenty years of reform have shown that Deng basically succeeded, in the sense that extremist ideology no longer dominates Chinese politics. Yet, as the old extremisms faded, new forms were taking their place. Currently the two most popular extremes in China's ideological spectrum are Westernization and its inverse anti-Westernization, or more concretely, Americanization and its contrary anti-Americanization. In fact, these new extremes have affected politics, economy, academia, education, literature, arts, publishing and even people's habits and daily lives.

I would like to highlight a few examples of this Westernization or Americanization that I personally experienced. In 1999, I was invited to deliver a lecture entitled 'Globalization and its Impacts on China' for local executives of the Chuyong government, a Minority Autonomous Regional Authority. It was striking in itself to be asked to discuss globalization in an area where the economy is underdeveloped and most people live below the poverty line defined by the state. What was even more telling was that my lecture on globalization was warmly welcomed by the audience and I was asked to present another. One of the topics this audience focused on in particular was the relationship between China and the USA, and China's attempts to become a member of the World Trade Organization. Chuyong is located in a subtropical region that is very good for agriculture. Flowers are one of the major sources of income for the local peasants. There is a wide range of colourful flowers at the market at extraordinarily low prices. I was surprised at the price and was told by my hosts that it was equally low all the year round except February. I asked why and was told that prices rise because of Valentine's Day. Chinese people, for the most part, do not even know what Valentine's Day is, yet it has now become a key market hotspot in this marginal underdeveloped area. This only hints at how Western marketing, and in particular the American economy, have influenced this poor minority region.

Americanization does not stop with flowers. Something I do not like doing in Beijing is taking my young daughter to McDonald's. This is not primarily because I have not adapted to Western food, since I am used to waiting in line and even the discomfort of eating standing up. Going to McDonald's is my daughter's favourite reward for her excellent marks; so her enjoyment is the exact counterweight to my unhappiness. Over 70 McDonald's outlets have opened in Beijing alone during the last ten years. McDonald's is perceived as a symbol of American culinary culture, which the Chinese used to sneer at. Today American food has been launched in China and represents a challenge to classic Chinese food because it has captured Chinese children's taste buds before their parents have been able to inculcate the enjoyment of delicious traditional foods.

The signs of Westernization or Americanization are apparent to anyone living in China. Language is a prime example. Learning English is a major task for students at universities, colleges, high schools, middle schools and even some primary schools. An English test is required not only for the equivalent of SSATs, for job promotions and even to be hired for some jobs. English terms and names used to be transcribed with Chinese characters; today the trend has been reversed. Western and American advertisements decorate the main streets in China's major metropolitan areas. The operating system we use is the Chinese version of Windows and the word processor we use is Word. Both are authorized by Microsoft. American novels, movies, music, painting, cartoons and so on are quickly translated into Chinese and become as popular as they are in the USA. Some blockbusters like *Titanic* were screened in China at the same time as they were showing in Western countries and got the same type of enthusiastic welcome. American public figures such as Bill Clinton, Hillary Clinton, Alan Greenspan, Monica Lewinsky, Madonna and Michael Jordan are people that ordinary Chinese talk about. Many Chinese publishers are interested in buying American copyrights of books and publishing them in Chinese since these translations make a lot more money than other books. The academic bestseller list includes many American scholars, such as Samuel Huntington, Milton Friedman, Alvin Toffler and Paul Samuelson. Any self-

respecting Chinese scholar has them on his or her bookshelves. Most textbooks in management and economics currently touted at Harvard have been translated into Chinese and published in Chinese, and almost all students in economics or management at colleges or universities find them on their required reading lists.

These are the superficial examples. What is more important is that American values have become the ones that the Chinese and in particular young people adopt, such that there is what can be termed an Americanized mindset. The American lifestyle, political system, economics, management system, ideology and liberal arts have become 'objects' sought after and imitated by many Chinese. The USA is perceived as a paradise, making the American Dream the greatest aspiration of the generation that came of age after the reforms. Everything in the USA, including the American people, institutions, economy, culture and land, is viewed as so perfect, so lovely and so attractive for many young Chinese that the American moon may just be rounder than in China. Attending American colleges and universities is the fondest hope of many Chinese students and their parents. Study abroad programmes have multiplied since the reforms in China, above all to the USA. Many young students long to be American citizens or permanent residents. Even the powerful and rich worship America and send their children on expensive trips to the USA. It is ironic that some former revolutionary cadres – the self-declared enemies of the USA – have sought opportunities for themselves or their children to go to the USA to gain first-hand knowledge of 'capitalist evil and adversity'.

One author depicts China's Americanization as follows:

> Since the 1980s, more and more commodities, movies, videos, country music, rock-and-roll, Donald Duck, Mickey Mouse and American brand toys, value and culture have hit the Chinese market. Even purely entertainment products with little ideological bent demonstrate and advocate something of the Western life style that exerts enormous impact on people, especially young people in developing countries. In particularly, the rapid growth of the Internet has resulted in an information explosion. Information is very different from other industrial products because a great deal of information flowing on the information highway necessarily contains obvious political and cultural value. The US and other Western countries control most of the soft and hard ware on which the circulation of information depends. For instance, the US has over 70% of the databanks in the world. Moreover, the US instills its laws, human rights and technology into its international label and imposes these on developing countries. Thus, the 'Americanization' of the Internet has begun to threaten some countries' social, political, legal and cultural values. (Qi 1999)

A few writers have gone further and argued that many Chinese intellectuals and senior officials have been Americanized due to powerful American pressure and policies and that the culture of the Chinese elite has in fact become American. In their view, there is a deep-seated conflict between 'the Americanized elite' and the masses with Chinese spirit. An article written under a pseudonym recently published in the on-line edition of *The People's Daily* stresses that the US (government)

> has paid off some Chinese to sing the praises of the multi-party system on behalf of the US, in order to divide China. The US has been successful to some extent in the sense that many Chinese intellectuals and officials have been Americanized. The US can pay off a few members of the social elite but is not able to buy off all the 1.3 billion Chinese people. What emerges is that the lower classes are nationalists while the 'elite' is exerting its utmost efforts to destroy the people's nationalism.[1]

Anxiety over Americanization not only comes from Chinese intellectuals and officials, but from ordinary people as well. I occasionally read an article dealing specifically with the dangers of Americanization and the concomitant eclipse of our national identity in an informally published newsletter issued by a local government, which mainly reports on the political activities of local leaders. This type of article typically puts forward data and facts to explain the dangers of Americanization: the US controls 75 per cent of all TV programmes, such that many TV stations in developing countries act as US retransmission stations; 90 per cent of the news is manipulated by the US and Western countries; US movies account for over half of all screening times the world over. A survey conducted by a Beijing institute indicates that in people's minds American culture reflects the following: romantic Hollywood movies, barbaric American cowboys, convenient McDonald's, technologically excellent Windows and Intel. Today's Chinese children eat McDonald's, drink Coca-Cola, play American games, watch American and European movies, listen to Western music and speak English. There is nothing of the traditional Chinese culture in their minds, only cultural symbols such as Donald Duck, action toys, Jurassic Park and the Lion King. This Americanization is true not only for Chinese intellectuals but also for ordinary Chinese people who don't even know where the USA is. They capitulate to the American cultural hegemony because of its might and predominance in state power, academia, culture and information.[2]

This evidence suggests that it would be hard to disprove the claim that China is being Americanized. Yet it would be a mistake to ignore the other side

1 Mathematics, 'The US Has no Good Way to Deal with China', *www.peopledaily.com*
2 Newsletter of Zhuji, published by the Office of Zhuji Government, No. 8 (2000): 38–39.

of the ideological coin: namely anti-Americanization, anti-Westernization and Sinification. Since the inception of modern China, there has been a permanent national complex against Westernization and Americanization, and generally a resistance to the USA. Modern Chinese history, in particular the revolutionary history of Chinese communism, is basically a history of anti-West and anti-US dogma. This attitude was partially responsible for Mao Zedong's closed-door policies. Anti-US emotions have been greatly mitigated since the reforms at the end of the 1970s, but a new wave of anti-US feeling has resurfaced since the 1990s, especially since the US-led NATO bombing of the Chinese embassy in Yugoslavia in 1999. Huge numbers of critical articles and essays were written against the USA and a casual glance at newspapers and periodicals will easily produce such commentary in the fields of international relations, national culture and globalization. Some Chinese intellectuals have attempted to 'reveal' American intentions to 'Westernize and divide China'; some excoriate the USA as a world policeman; some exhibit their disdain for American arrogance; and some scorn those Chinese whose US cultism has made them 'the slaves of a foreign master'.

Many Chinese insist that for years the USA has been developing a vast conspiracy to 'Westernize and divide China'. In their view, US foreign policy can be reduced to hegemony or imperialism. The USA regards not the former Soviet Union but rather China as its strategic enemy since the Cold War ended after the collapse of communist regimes in Eastern Europe. As a result,

> keeping China within limits, trampling upon China and removing socialist China from the world political map has become US policy. Fighting between China and the US could begin with such thorny issues as Taiwan, Tibet, Sinkiang and the Korean Peninsula. Tactically, the US is likely to 'destroy China politically' by means of military force; and strategically, the US is likely to use the by-pass policy with carrot and stick tactics. (Jiaxi 1999: 18)

For some Chinese intellectuals, this is not only a theoretical issue but also a concrete one since the end of the Cold War, in that the USA is seen as having struck China and as holding China back strategically. In their view, the USA has begun to put China under siege militarily and each strategic step that the USA takes in Pacific Asia is aimed at China, directly or indirectly. One writer listed and analysed all the US military activities in Pacific Asia in 2000 in an article entitled 'Look Out, the US is Besieging China!' (Xin 2000): 'The US is firmly grasping the Taiwan card to threaten China strategically on the one hand, and is eagerly developing a quasi-military coalition in Pacific Asia while tightening the strategic siege of China on the other hand'. The author calls on the Chinese never to forget the American 'insidious conspiracy':

In recent years, the US has been working hard not only to develop relationships with former allies, but to penetrate other Asian countries. In Northeast Asia, the US is strengthening US–Japan and US–South Korea military alliances while adjusting its policies to North Korea and attempting to throw a wrench into the relationship between China and North Korea. In Northeast Asia, the US has increased its political influence on Northeast Asian countries by renewing its military relations with the Philippines while cottoning up to Vietnam. In South Asia, the US has begun to carry out its new policies of 'looking upon India while looking down on Pakistan' and wants to make India one of the powers to counterbalance China in Asia by actively conducting military and other exchanges with India. In Central Asia, the US wants to strengthen its relationships with the five Central Asian countries for two reasons. The first is to checkmate China, and the second is to use them as a bridge to penetrate China's western borders. Meanwhile, the US is extending its hand to Northern China by improving its relationship with Mongolia. Furthermore, the US supports Taiwan's separation from the Mainland under the table by selling weapons and bringing it into the US regional defence missile system. (Xin 2000)

Many scholars believe that the USA has devised new strategies to divide and block China but that its purpose remains the same. One new US tactic to 'divide and Westernize' China since the 1990s is to increase heavily the pressure of globalization. Globalization is hence seen as the newest tool to establish US hegemony, and as an American trap. Globalization is simply Westernization or Americanization:

> The US combines 'soft' and 'hard' tactics through its control over the dissemination of information, so as to place the Pacific Asian region firmly in its grip. There are strange and popular indications that globalization in the information age stands for Americanization. This originates from the American concept that the US economic and military power derives from its social system and cultural values, rather than from its high technology. Globalization in this sense is neither gospel nor inevitable. The true face of such a globalization was fully exposed in the US-led NATO invasion of Yugoslavia. (Chu et al. 2000: 43–44)

Chinese intellectuals are thus loudly proclaiming that 'globalization is Americanization'. Many globalization theorists do not stop at the emotional anti-US level. A young professor specializing in globalization studies states:

> Many people thought globalization was purely an economic process. However, it is not as simple as that. Clearly there is a powerful political and

economic hegemony lurking behind globalization. This is not only true for developing countries but also for developed ones. In a nutshell, globalization is essentially global homogenization in terms of American values and standards. (Nin 1999: 32)

One writer provides a detailed illustration of the 'globalization trap' laid jointly by the USA and the UK, the principal institutions used to manipulate the trap, the elements and major tricks of the trap, the mass media and scholars advocating globalization, and so on. People who read these articles can only be convinced that globalization is a swindle initiated by the USA. 'It is vital to see that the essence of globalization is its evil underhanded purpose, rather than its American brand name on the surface' (Fangshi 1999: 15).

For some theorists, not only globalization but also almost all American cultural products contain an 'evil intent' to Americanize China and the world. One author describes how the USA is carrying out the CIA's policies through movies and how movies are used as tools of Americanization. The author begins by quoting from a CIA programme stating that '[we] must do everything possible to propagandize, including movies, publications, TV programs, radio and so on... [We] will be successful in part only if foreigners are longing for our clothing, foods, houses, entertainment and education'. He then points out that

the stars of American movies, whether they are playing ordinary people or soldiers, are characterized as individuals coping with disaster and saving all other people from their sufferings. Many American movies propagandize 'the American spirit' and 'Pan-Americanism'... What is the image of China in American movies? The Chinese or China town as depicted in American movies are usually demonized. Hollywood exerts its 'magic power' in that few Chinese are employed as actors, who in fact denigrate their own people.[3]

Like Americanization, anti-Americanization is reflected in Chinese literature and arts and people can find anti-US satire everywhere. A cartoon of the Olympic women's football game between China and the USA was aired on Beijing television's evening news on 19 September 2000, with the comment: 'Four years ago, the US women's football team defeated China by an obvious foul and the Chinese women's football team lost the gold medal. One year ago, the US women team's goalkeeper broke the rule by blocking our penalty shot while the judge ignored it. Chinese-US women's football teams met again in the Sydney Olympic Games and it was very clear what the referee did. Thanks to Ms. Gao Hong and Sun Wen, their excellent performance accounted for the results'.

3 Anonymous, 'Inclement Purpose hiding behind American Movies', *www.netsh.com* (14 August 2000).

Anti-Americanization is manifested not only by hatred of the USA and exposing the 'Conspiracy of Americanization', but also through forms of slander and attempts to convince the Chinese that the USA itself is in a disastrous state and unworthy of being an example for China. For instance, many articles have been written to expose the corruption in American education in spite of the fact that there are estimated to be 200,000 Chinese students studying abroad. Many intellectuals try systematically to shed light on the shortcomings and evils of the modern-day USA in terms of culture, politics and the economy. Politically, it is claimed that 'democracy' is enjoyed only by a minority of the powerful and rich rather than being a true people's democracy. Rather, the elections are rigged, and there are political scandals and quarrels between various in-groups. Economically, a crisis is imminent and there is an even greater gulf between the rich and the poor. Culturally, consumerism prevails as morals decline. Some Americans are said to be aware of these shortcomings and crises although some pessimists even believe that the USA is too sick to be saved (Zhikun 1994).

For many Chinese, the USA does not deserve to be viewed as a role model for China. China has been able to contend with the USA and should take uncompromising diplomatic stances against it. In 1996 three young journalists published a book entitled *China Can Say 'No'* (Qiang et al. 1996*)*, which became one of the bestsellers of that year. Several other publishing houses quickly realized that this type of literature was a money-maker and came out with several similar books such as *Holding China Back* (Keqing et al. 1996), *Behind Monsterizing China* (Xiguang et al. 1996), and *Why China Can Say 'No'* (Peng et al. 1996). Regardless of title, the purpose was basically the same: it allowed Chinese intellectuals to let off steam against the USA. In fact there would have been more books like these if the authorities had not stepped in to stop them. These books cater to the tide of anti-US feeling among young nationalists, whose reasoning is that China's power derives from its huge population, its nuclear capacity and its rapid economic growth, which can outstrip the USA. Meanwhile, the USA is still a paper tiger, outwardly strong but inwardly weak, as Chairman Mao Zedong pointed out, and it will collapse earlier than expected. The USA lost to the Chinese Communist Party (CCP) during the CCP–Kuomintang War and the Korean War. This prompted a few young intellectuals to make an appeal to the Chinese people to 'stop buying American commodities, watching American movies and eating American food, and reject the US most-favored-nation clause'. People should 'burn down Hollywood and prepare to fight against the US'.

At first glance, anti-Americanization and Americanization appear to be at either extreme of the spectrum. A closer look, however, shows that they are in some ways bound together. Anti-Americanization is a reaction to the process of Americanization now ongoing in China. In present-day China, the real forms of non-Americanization are the all-pervasive signs of Sinification. Deng Xiaoping's theory is a holistic one, including domestic reform and opening up to the world. Opening up simply means introducing advanced Western, and above all American science, technology, products, management, market systems, culture and knowledge. Since this reform and the implementation of the open-door policy, Western politics, economy and culture have exerted such a profound impact on Chinese society that Westernization, Americanization and anti-Americanization have taken root in China. On the other hand, however, in order to integrate advanced Western technological and cultural civilization, China experienced a renaissance of its traditional culture after the CCP came to power in 1949. Mao Zedong launched two battles. One was to lock China's door to the West, while the other was to root out traditional Chinese culture (the so-called 'Movement of Destroying Four Olds', in other words, destroying old ideas, old cultures, old customs and old habits). Taking a radically opposed stance, Deng Xiaoping advocated opening up to the West and reviving traditional Chinese culture. The process of reform and openness in China is both a process of accepting Western civilization and a process of systematically reviving Chinese traditional culture, in what can be termed a Sinification of Western civilization.

For instance, politically and ideologically, Deng Xiaoping terms his theory and practice of reforms 'socialism with a Chinese face', which is fundamentally different from traditional socialism in Mao's era. It affects the whole list of 'Chinese traits' such as Chinese politics, economy, culture, academia, education, literature and so on. The 'fervour of traditional Chinese culture', which reached its peak in the 1990s, canonizes traditional Chinese civilization. It is striking that Confucianism, which used to be viewed as opposed to a market economy, is now interpreted as the basis of economic success in East Asia and China. In the eyes of partisans of traditional Chinese culture, all good things originate in traditional Chinese civilization. Chinese civilization can overcome the shortcomings of Western civilization and the twenty-first century will be a century of Chinese civilization.

The renaissance of Chinese traditions has also emerged. Traditional Chinese literature, opera, folk art, gymnastics, crafts, rituals, customs and habits which vanished after 1949 have resurfaced and become popular again since the reforms. Ordinary people have been deeply affected by traditional culture now that such popular events as the Spring Festival, First Lunar Month Festival, Dragon Boat Festival, Double Nine Festival, Mid-Autumn Festival, Wine Festival, Foods Festival and Tea Festival have been reinstated. Since the

1980s, Chinese people have been so eager to revive the traditions that disappeared during the Cultural Revolution that they made little distinction between positive and negative. Thus many negative traditional customs have also returned. For example, the deeply rooted traditional concept of 'getting a promotion and striking it rich' can doubtless account for the terrible rise in corruption; and the vigour of traditional superstitions challenges modern science. It is a ridiculous misunderstanding to attribute the widely existing phenomenon of executive mistresses to 'Western corrupt capitalist notions',[4] when it is the exact revival of the degenerate Chinese traditional notion that every official should have his concubines or female slaves.

What best accounts for the fact that Americanization, anti-Americanization and Sinification coexist in contemporary China? What does this imply for Chinese society? What should be the attitudes of Chinese intellectuals and politicians? The answers can be found in modern Chinese history and the impact of globalization on China today. China is an ancient civilized country and for centuries was one of the most highly developed. Traditional Chinese society existed for thousands of years on the basis of political absolutism, a feudal peasant economy and cultural Confucianism, which snuffed out Chinese creativity and the ability to innovate. China has made social progress very slowly and has scarcely contributed to the world since the South Song Dynasty (1127–1279). Meanwhile, Western countries experienced the Industrial Revolution and its resulting progress. Consequently, China has lagged behind Western countries since the start of modern times. Some Chinese intellectuals identified the gulf between China and Western countries as early as the middle of the nineteenth century when the Western powers forced open ancient China's door through superior weapons and commodities. They came to the conclusion that if China were to regain its former splendour, the only way was to learn from Western industrial countries and introduce Western civilization into China. The Qing Dynasty had no other choice than to accept the intellectuals' demands to initiate the 'Westernization Movement'.

The 'Westernization Movement' was the first step on China's path to modernization and the inception of its modern history. Two features underscore modern Chinese history as a whole. The first is that China wanted to put an end to underdevelopment and catch up with the West; and the second is that China wanted to avoid being dominated by the Western powers. In other words, modernization and national independence were the two major tasks for modern China (Danian 1996). Fundamentally, the contradiction between Westernization and Sinification can be explained in this context.

---

4 Li Jun, 'Don't Neglect the Fact that some Party Members are being "Westernized" and "Separated"', *www.netsh.com*

Objectively, modern civilization is an industrial one that originated in Western industrial countries. All modern industries, including machines, the energy industry, the chemical industry, engineering, communication, the drug industry and so on have arisen in Western developed countries. Modernization is a process of learning from and approaching Western countries, if we define modernization as industrialization. There is no doubt that some intellectuals simply defined modernization as Westernization in this narrow sense, reasoning that an underdeveloped country must approach and learn from Western developed nations, and that the result would be a more modernized country. Axiomatically, the less learned from Western countries, and the greater preservation of tradition, the greater the lag. The debate between radicals and conservatives, which typified the clash between Westernization and Sinification, is due to the fact that Western civilization was synonymous with progress while the traditional Chinese culture was equated with underdevelopment. As a well-known CCP thinker pointed out, one of the conservatives' most subtle arguments on behalf of the class with vested interests was to refuse advanced Western civilization by overemphasizing Chinese characteristics, the preponderance of Chinese traditional culture and the corruption of Western civilization (Shiqi 1990).

However, China's second aim, of national independence, runs somewhat counter to the methods espoused to achieve its first goal. One of the dilemmas facing modern Chinese intellectuals and politicians is how to deal with Westernization and Sinification, or more precisely how to learn effectively from Western countries while at the same time preserving China's independence. Western powers were the cause of China's semi-colonization. Thus China's independence is defined as freeing itself from Western control and influence. Yet China's modernization depends on learning from Western powers. Therefore, modern Chinese intellectuals and politicians have had to deal with both facets of Westernization; namely, China should never become a colony in the process of learning from Western countries. This is why most Chinese scholars and politicians have stressed ways in which to Sinify all things Western while being concerned at the same time about Westernizing Chinese society. Strikingly enough, an identical relation between Sinification and Westernization has held under three different regimes – the Qing Dynasty, the Kuomintang Republic of China and the CCP People's Republic of China. The modus operandi has been to Sinify Western industrial civilization to ensure China's modernization. This goal has been known respectively as the 'Chinese body with Western functions' under the Qing Dynasty, as 'Chinese nativeness' under the Kuomintang and as 'Chinese characteristics' under the CCP.

There is a general consensus that China did indeed accomplish one of these two tasks while failing to achieve the other. The CCP established the People's Republic of China after it came to power in 1949. That is, China obtained complete independence but was not modernized. Mao Zedong and his comrades took on this unaccomplished task, expecting that China could catch up economically to the Western developed countries in the short term. It would be a mistake to believe that Mao Zedong did not want a wealthy and powerful China. Mao actively sought a way for China to modernize by advocating such movements as 'Catching up with the UK while overtaking the US', 'Steel-making across the country' and 'The Great Leap Forward', which in retrospect were so disastrous for China. Mao indeed never wanted China to follow in the footsteps of Western modernization. He neither wanted to introduce capitalism to China nor to open up to Western developed countries. Among the many reasons why Mao refused the Western road to modernization was his concern that China would lose its independence once opened up to the West. Therefore, there was no Westernization or Americanization during the Maoist period, since Mao was too afraid of dependency on the West to open the door.

Mao's development strategy succeeded in securing China's independence while it failed in its modernization. As a matter of fact, towards the end of Mao's reign, the economic gap between China and the West widened. Many intellectuals and the Party elite came to recognize that China remained far behind the developed countries in economy and culture after Mao had been in power for 30 years and that China had to learn from Western developed countries to achieve modernization. This was the basis for Deng Xiaoping's reform of Mao's traditional socialism, and why he opened China up to the Western capitalist countries. This once again brought the debate on Westernization and Sinification in modern China centre-stage. On the one hand, China has to learn from Western developed countries, but on the other hand, it must maintain its independence. Thus the Chinese are once again facing the same dilemma: how to introduce Western civilization into China while keeping China independent of the West.

All Chinese intellectuals who are concerned about China's modernization need to address this issue. Two very different, even conflicting attitudes have arisen. Some prefer to focus on development for the sake of national independence and put their emphasis on the introduction of Western civilization rather than the revival of traditional values. Others prefer to focus on national independence for the sake of national development and put their emphasis on a revival of traditional culture rather than the introduction of foreign civilization. Both are likely to go to opposite extremes: for the former, the latter's thoughts are too conservative; while for the latter, the former's are too Westernized.

145

Deng Xiaoping launched reforms and opened up China at the end of the 1970s and the beginning of the 1980s when Western countries in general were much further developed than other countries. The process of modernization of developing countries, including China, remains to some extent a process of approaching Western developed countries. Relatively speaking, the USA has been at the forefront among developed countries and is leading Western civilization and culture. Doubtless, the USA has exerted much more impact on developing countries than have other Western nations. In a sense, not only developing countries but also other Western nations have been more or less Americanized. It is understandable that the Westernization of the past has turned into Americanization to a significant degree. It follows that the 'Sino-West' debate has now become the 'Sino-US' debate, while Westernization and anti-Westernization have become Americanization and anti-Americanization in China.

Humanity has entered into a new age of globalization since the end of the twentieth century. Globalization based on Westernization, Americanization and Sinification needs to change, and a new context in which different civilizations can learn from one another should be inaugurated. Globalization is sometimes viewed as a process of homogenization, and it is argued that globalization is a process of world capitalism, Westernization or Americanization. This is not true. Globalization is not a process of mere homogenization but rather a unification of plurality. In essence, globalization is a contradictory form of unity and antinomy. The process of globalization is intrinsically contradictory: it has tendencies towards both homogenization and fragmentation; it combines unification with plurality; it includes both centralization and division; and it embodies internationalization and nationalization.

First, globalization is a unit combining universalization and particularization. On the one hand, globalization is a process of homogenization characterized by a convergence of lifestyles, modes of production and values among various civilizations. For instance, the market economy is becoming a worldwide feature beyond its European origins; people everywhere are seeking democracy and human dignity while totalitarianism is on the decline. On the other hand, universalization is always accompanied by particularization. Although the market economy has become international, market systems in various countries are quite different. Furthermore, the differences among the market systems in various countries have remained as sharp despite the expansion of the market economy as a whole. For example, the market economy in Germany, known as 'social market economy', differs considerably from the laissez-faire market economy in the USA or the UK; the market economy in East Asia is different from other market systems because of greater government intervention. The same is true of democracy. People all over the world are longing for democracy, which, however, has many diverse versions in different countries. For instance, Japan and South Korea have adopted representative democracy, which is quite different from the forms of democracy found in the USA or the UK.

Second, globalization combines integration and fragmentation. Integration and homogenization are highlighted by the rapid growth of international organizations such as the United Nations, the World Bank, the IMF and the WTO, whose roles are much more important than before. A greater degree of integration among nations leads to a breakdown of traditional national sover-eignty and barriers. A cosmopolitan ideal has begun to materialize in the sense that there is a growing movement towards the integration of nations (such as in the European Union), global floating of capital and global sharing of increas-ingly common information. At the same time, however, there has been a growing trend towards particularity and independence for both nations and regions. Movements of national independence or autonomy provide a good example. The trend towards individuation has developed steadily as global integration increases. More and more small ethnic groups are demanding independence. The wave of regional, local and communal autonomy is not disappearing, but rising along with globalization. Community movements and communitarianism are key political issues in developed countries. The term 'global localism' was coined to reflect the fact that local autonomy is develop-ing rapidly against the backdrop of globalization.

Third, globalization combines centralization and decentralization. One of the major features of globalization is the enormous centralization of capital, information, power and wealth, especially in transnational corporations. Big companies have increasingly merged since the 1990s, accelerating the centralization of power and wealth. A good example is the recent merger of McDonnell-Douglas and Boeing, two large firms in the aviation industry. On the other hand, there have been major trends to decentralize capital, inform-ation, power and wealth. Small capital is still very active and developing and is apparently not affected by the centralization of capital. This shows that the higher the degree of centralization of information, the more difficult it is to monopolize. The best example is the Internet. So far it has become the prime medium through which information is exchanged and innumerable amounts of information flow from all parts of the world, all sectors and all walks of life. No one has the monopoly on this discursive information, since anyone whose computer has been connected to the Internet can share information.

Lastly, globalization unites internationalization and nationalization. As I mentioned above, globalization has broken down traditional national barriers. As a result, more and more international conventions, covenants, agreements and standards have been signed and implemented by nations all over the world; 'bringing into line with international practice' is becoming a typical phrase and many international principles have authentic international meaning for the first time. On the other hand, no nation will ever forget its own traditions and characteristics while accepting international conventions, agreements and principles. Each nation tries to deal with international principles in the light of its own specific national conditions, so as to nationalize these international principles and norms. For instance, most countries in the world accept international agreements on the protection of human rights and the environment, while imbuing them with their own national characteristics when explaining or applying them.

Thus globalization is an objective reality and is an inescapable trend in human development. When a country opens up to the outside world, it will enter into the process of globalization, and China is no exception in this global age. Globalization is initiated and dominated by the US-led, Western developed countries. However, no country, including the USA, can completely control the process of globalization; developing countries, including China, also impact on the process. Globalization is a double-edged sword for both developed and developing countries. Both can either benefit or lose out from globalization. Globalization changes modern civilizations into a cosmopolitan unit, regardless of whether the civilization originated in the East or the West. Therefore, learning from Western civilization never simply results in Westernization, just as learning from Eastern civilizations will never mean Easternization. China's membership of the WTO and the introduction of a market economy will never mean 'Westernizing' or 'Americanizing' China. Internationalization, nationalization and localization complement one another. China must participate actively in globalization if it wants to preserve its own unique civilization; just as China must enhance its national resources if it wants to participate in globalization effectively. Globalization in an authentic sense is by no means Westernization or Americanization. Those who express their anxiety that China will be Westernized or Americanized once it participates in the process of globalization will be shown to lack foresight.

References

Chu, Zhao (2000), 'Is Globalization a Good Fortune or Misfortune?', *Guide To Opening Up* 9: 43–44.

Danian, Liu (1996), 'The Subjects of China's Modern History', *Studies in Modern Chinese History* 6.

Fangshi, Lin (1999), 'Behind Globalization – An Analysis on the US and the UK's Strategic Trap', *Zhongliu (The Central Stream)* 2: 13–17.

Jiaxi, Chen (1999), 'History of American Hegemony', *Journal of Technology University in Central China* 3: 17–32.

Keqing, Sun and others (eds) (1996), *Holding China Back*. China Yanshi Publishing House.

Nin, Wang (1999), 'The Cultural Debates and Discourses in the Age of Globalization', *Eastern Culture* 3: 31–36.

Peng, Qian and others (eds) (1996), *Why China Can Say 'No'*. New World Press.

Qi, Bian (1999), 'Reflection on the Cultural Homogenization', *Aspects of Social Sciences*.

Qiang, Song and others (eds) (1996), *China Can Say 'No'*. China Industrial and Commercial Press.

Shiqi, Ai (1990), 'On the Chinese Characteristics', in Luo Rongqu (ed.), *From Westernization to Modernization*. Beijing University Press: 592–93.

Xiguang, Li and others (eds) (1996), *Behind Monsterizing China*. Chinese Social Sciences Press.

Xin, Zhang (2000), 'Look Out, the US is Besieging China!', *Technologies China online* (6 July).

Zhikun, Guang (1994), 'A Mistake of Complete Westernization', *Journal of Teacher's College of Qingdao University* 2: 23–27.

PART III

TRANSNATIONAL PROCESSES

CHAPTER 8

Techno-Migrants in the
Network Economy

Aihwa Ong

Every autumn, wealthy Chinese resident-aliens of Vancouver leave for Hong Kong, like Canada geese departing for warmer climes. Thousands of Indian techno-migrants employed in Silicon Valley firms also make many trips across the Pacific, some of them to set up high-tech businesses in Bangalore. Less well-heeled migrants – Chinese waiters, Hispanic janitors and Cambodian electronic homeworkers – supply the open labour markets that service the feverish centres of the new economy driving the American West. What can these new mobile figures tell us about citizenship, its cosmopolitan and local dimensions, and the political implications of neo-liberal governance?

'Liberalism' is fundamentally concerned with an economy of government. Colin Gordon, paraphrasing Foucault, defines liberalism as a government 'that economizes on the use of resources and effort to achieve its ends, and more particularly accepts that to govern well is to govern less' (Gordon 2000: xxiii). It should not be supposed, however, that liberalism means hostility to or the reduction of regulation. On the contrary, liberal initiatives foster conditions for the emergence of a variety of regulatory practices that create markets and particular kinds of modern subjects. In liberal economies, the state relies on a multiplicity of regulatory bodies to shape an objective economic and social reality that is distinct from the state apparatus. The study of sovereignty and citizenship in liberal formations thus requires us to shift from the level of political institutions to the study of government as a set of practices of regulation and normalization (Foucault 2000). In recent decades, *neo*-liberalism, an ethos that would permit no barrier to market forces, has spread unevenly across the world as market criteria come to shape regulatory processes that directly affect the meaning and practice of citizenship.

I have thus explored citizenship not simply as a juridical status, but as rationalities of government that have conditioned the flexible strategies of managerial migrants who seek residence and opportunity in different countries (Ong 1999). I also argued that neo-liberal policies introduced in South-East Asia have transformed political sovereignty, bringing about new social spaces that are defined by different rationalities of disciplining or caring (Ong 2000). In this chapter, my attention shifts to the implications of the new migrant flows and new landscapes of governmentality in North America.

The new spaces of globalization go beyond global cities such as New York, London and Tokyo. Suburban techno-citadels in North America – Silicon Valley, Route 128, the North Carolina Science Park – have spawned many high-tech spin-offs from Berlin to Beijing, Oxford to Osaka, as the sites of new capital accumulation. Observers argue that such nodes of the information economy capitalize on a 'regional advantage' drawn from a network-based synergy – between electronics firms, universities, venture capitalists and city governments – that is very open to change and experimentation (Saxenian 1996). What, one may also ask, are the strategic networks of governmental rationalities that have drawn particular populations and defined specific social norms of rights and citizenship?[1] Indeed, Silicon Valley may be ground zero of what Ulrich Beck (1994) calls reflexive modernization, a second modernization in which the old structures are superseded, and the new ones are highly provisional, risky and unpredictable. What are the connections between the extreme radicalization of the market and experimentations in neo-liberal governance? How has a new spatialized world of regulation come about without the state?

This chapter will argue that the governmental rationalities of neo-liberalism have extremely variable, contingent and local constructions, with differential effects on different categories of immigrants, and transforming the everyday practice of citizenship in North America. First, I will consider how different migratory regimes have brought about divergent spaces of governance on the West Coast. The influx of Asian business investors and high-tech professionals has made ethnicity a part of cosmopolitanism, and the universalization of the particular – Indians as international high-tech professionals, Chinese as global businessmen, or Filipinos as global nannies – is central to the constitution of flexible transnational economies. Second, I will explore how such spaces of flows are linked to specific spaces of governance. Neo-liberal regimes that privilege cosmopolitan migrants – defined by mobility and professional exper-tise – have contributed to a fragmentation of rights in the local practices of

---

1 There is a single ethnographic study of the effects of the upheavals wrought by Silicon Valley culture on family forms and gender relations (Stacey 1998). Other aspects of the societal transformation represented by the open-ended network industrial system have not been seriously examined.

governance. Third, I explore the splintering effects of cosmopolitan citizenship based on human capital and residence, so that intensified competition for entitlements between migrant and long-term residents has transformed people's understanding of community.

Globalizing and Localizing Processes

In considering how global migrations have affected national sovereignty and citizenship, it seems helpful to talk about globalizing and localizing trends. Thus, we can say that the flexible transnational economies have depended on globalizing processes of production and labour markets, as well as on their localization in particular sites of capital accumulation and growth. Global theorists have identified two kinds of globalizing trends: the rise of city-networks and managerial spaces of flows. Saskia Sassen argues that global cities, as sites of international financial activity and specialized services, are the nodes in the 'new geography of power' (Sassen 1991: 1–30). Manuel Castells argues that the emerging 'space(s) of flows' have enabled dominant managerial and entrepreneurial elites to create new segregating spaces spanning cities and continents, giving rise to network society (Castells 1999: 416). Scholars combining the insights of Sassen and Castells have suggested that we think of 'the world city network' as the new metageography (Taylor 2000). The focus on city-networks and managerial flows has not been accompanied by serious attention to the localizing processes that embed and regulate workers, knowledge and practices in particular places. Indeed, Castells has claimed that in the informational economy, the spatial logic of flows in the new economy dominates what he calls 'the space of places' (Castells 1996: 416).

On the contrary, I would argue, we need a fuller ethnographic description of the divergent processes that link transnational practices of managerial elites in the space of flows with the localizing practices in the space of places. While the world city-network concept has been concerned about the spatiality of information, capital and markets, it does not pay enough attention to the spatiality of governmentality, where formal and substantive rationalities vie for supremacy. In local spaces of governance, what strategic networks of rationality shape the deployment of capital, labour, resources, norms and force? Specifically, what regulatory conditions promote investment flows and business talents, while penalizing and managing illegal migrant workers?

The Image of America and Conditions of Mobility

I would consider the vision of the good life as a force driving global migrations. This vision of freedom and the good life has driven generations of migrants from Asia to North America, to gain access to certain economic, cultural and informational resources. People's sense of their destinies apparently can only take shape in these transnational spaces of mobility and possibility. After decades of rejecting and discouraging migrants from Asia, North America since the 1980s has sought to capitalize on the economies and middle classes in the Asia-Pacific. The growth of trade with Asia, and the demands of a new knowledge economy, have stimulated Canadian and US governments actively to attract Pacific Rim investors and professionals. For many Asian migrants, North America as a paradise of middle-class comfort and security is now enhanced by its allure as the high-tech frontier of the world. Only with the experience of localization, of being embedded in the spaces of accelerated market civilization, will the new-comers find that the apparently limitless conditions of possibility also harbour dark promises. But as Zygmunt Bauman (1998) reminds us, there is a polari-zation between those free to move and those forced to move, namely between tourists and vagabonds, or travellers and refugees.[2] Such a 'global hierarchy of mobility' is part of a worldwide and local redistribution of privileges and deprivations; a restratification of humanity (Bauman 1998: 70). In other words, some migrants can take advantage of flexible citizenship more than others, and migrants belong to flows that can be differently managed and controlled.

Since the early 1980s, the USA, Canada and Australia have introduced new visa categories in order to re-regulate the influx of people, increasingly from Asian countries. Such immigrant regulations respond strategically to the demands of the new economy for the influx of capital and professional talent. Thus, while Asian managerial, professional elites can arrive with legal papers, poor and unskilled rural folk who cannot qualify for the same must take a more arduous and expensive route. I will contrast the migratory flows to Canada, which seems to have focused mainly on attracting Asian investors to build up property markets in cities, and the migratory regimes to the United States, which recruits business investors and knowledge workers to California. At the same time, neither country has been able to control the intensified influx of illegal, low-skilled migrants. The clash between the formal regulations and the substantive rationalities in the American destinations conditions the differential access of migrants to entitlements and cultural citizenship.

Resident Expatriates and Floating Coffins Bound for Vancouver

On a per capita basis, Canada receives more immigrants than any other country in the world. In the early 1980s, the Canadian Business Immigration Program

---

2 Bauman seems to locate the tension between the mobile and the localized outside this hierarchy of mobility. For ethnographic renderings of this other dimension of polarity and power imbalance among ethnic Chinese migrants and their families, see Ong and Nonini 1997.

sought to attract business migrants from Hong Kong and Taiwan, specifying categories such as 'self-employed', 'entrepreneurial' and 'investor'. Most of the flows of Asian capital and business migrants have been to Vancouver, where the state government has established a minimum investment of C$150,000 for each entrepreneurial migrant business (which are expected to employ some workers), while investor migrants must invest at least C$350,000 in a business in other parts of British Columbia (Business Immigration Office, 1998). During the 1980s and 1990s, Hong Kong Chinese bought over two billion dollars' worth of real estate in Vancouver, and effectively transformed a sleepy British port into a Pacific Rim megalopolis, complete with Chinese McMansions (Mitchell 1997). The city of almost two million is one-third Asian, with ethnic Chinese making up 20 per cent of the total. A joke about the city's Pacific Rim character goes like this: The Japanese want to buy Vancouver, but the Chinese won't sell it. The accelerating family and business networks linking Vancouver and Hong Kong are producing a new globalized space in which Vancouver is more linked to Asia-Pacific sites than it is to the rest of British Columbia or to other parts of the Canadian nation.

The use of the visa as an instrument to admit Asian business people and students has worked to keep out the poor and the unskilled. However, Canadian laws have a loophole for the uninvited, in the generous programmes for granting asylum status to refugees, and in the provision of generous welfare services to the poor. Thus thousands of unskilled Chinese migrants have managed to enter the country without visas. It is estimated that each year about 5,000 people flying into Canada tear up their papers and seek asylum. Others take a less direct route. In April 1999 two boatloads of undocumented Chinese from Fujian were deposited near Vancouver. When apprehended by coastguards, these migrants pleaded refugee status (citing China's one-child policy or religious persecution, since many Fujianese are Christian) and sought asylum. More recent arrivals have been equally dramatic. Some Chinese migrants from the same province paid US$30,000 to $50,000 to be smuggled in container ships – called floating coffins because some migrants do not survive the trip. In January 2000, another floating coffin containing 18 survivors docked in Seattle. There is strong cross-border traffic with Vancouver, and the refugees probably hope to escape into Vancouver since stowaways arriving in the USA are more likely to be deported.[3] Altogether, in 1998–2000, more than 200 people were caught while being smuggled in container ships bound for Canadian and US ports.[4] Other illegal

3 Stowaways must be able to establish well-grounded fears of persecution if returned to their home country. In January, the United States deported some 250 stowaways back to China. See *The New York Times*, 'Deadly Choice of Stowaways: Ship Containers', 12 January 2000.
4 *San Francisco Chronicle*, 'Three Weeks in a Floating Coffin', 12 January 2000.

migrants who manage to escape detention slip underground, bound for indentured servitude to pay off their debts to their 'snakeheads' or smuggling syndicates.

The waves of illegal Chinese migrants arriving in Vancouver introduce an unwelcome spectre, an unexpected status risk, for the jet-setting business migrants. For the affluent Hong Kongers, who had helped to develop the former world trade fair site into a centre of commercial and residential skyscrapers, their image as the new entrepreneurs of Canada is being undermined by impoverished Chinese migrants, many of whom do not come from the same place in Asia, and represent the backwardness from which the former wish to be dissociated. This tension between legal and illegal migrants, welcomed business investors and unwelcome illegal labourers, intensifies fears of an anti-Chinese backlash. In a recent public debate, a Chinese Canadian activist remarked: 'These are working class, peasant farmers. We have well-heeled Hong Kong Chinese, Canadian-Chinese and Taiwan Chinese looking down their noses at them. They feel these people water down their community.'[5] A lawyer from Taiwan notes that the government has raised the cash amount required for business immigrants to obtain a visa. He continued: 'There is a feeling we are kicking out the business people and taking in the boat people. The immigration system is not smart. We are pushing out the good quality people who can help Canada – and we are taking in the freeloaders.' While Hong Kong business elites have taken seminars on British Columbian social and aesthetic mores regarding neighbourliness and multiculturalism, and abided by the regulations of commercial and property markets (Mitchell 1997; Mitchell and Olds 2000), they felt that the illegal Chinese newcomers must submit to the regulations of the scaled down welfare state. Thus the clash between the two sets of governing rationalities – the neo-liberal migratory regime on the one hand, and the liberal democratic values of human rights on the other – highlights the new instability in Canadian notions of who deserves citizenship.

The insistence that 'good-quality' ethnic Chinese should properly represent Canadian citizenship is somewhat undercut by their long absences for much of the winter. Hong Kongers take off in the autumn for Asia, a re-migration that empties out the apartment towers lining the Vancouver shoreline. Curtains uniformly drawn across hundreds of apartment windows present a blind visage to the harbourscape. Such 'resident expatriates' have come to symbolize the new cosmopolitan citizenship: one that is fuelled by globalizing processes, but

---

5 The following account of conflicts among different categories of Chinese immigrants is drawn from James Brooke, 'Vancouver is Astir over Chinese Abuse of Immigrant Law', *The New York Times*, 29 August 1999, A6.

mediated by ethnicity and lifestyle.[6] Thus, while citizenship has always been based on legal status and property ownership, today the element of hypermobile cosmopolitanism has gained as much currency. The Hong Kong business elites have come to embody the forms of correspondence between economic, social and cultural capital, so that there is a new fusion between ethnicity and class which qualifies them as 'good quality' Canadians. The outcome seems to be a reverse Hongkongization, a Chinese-Anglo cosmopolitanism that is a reimagining of Hong Kong through trans-Pacific entrepreneurial dynamism, with an unstoppable undertow of illegal entries so reminiscent of colonial days on both sides of the Pacific.

The Networks of Astronauts, Techno-Migrants and Illegals in the High-Tech Borderland

While British Columbia is rebounding on the basis of geo-colonial networks, Silicon Valley is a slice of high-tech globalization that is experimenting, at a feverish rate, with novel combinations of peoples, industries and urban planning. The high-tech borderland is the opposite of the old-line industrial insularity (Saxenian 1996). It is a site of extremely liberal conditions for entrepreneurialism, networking and flexibility, and thus a rich source of opportunities for new regulatory activities that distribute benefits unevenly. Here, I can only mention three sets of regulations that have favoured the influx of Asian elite migrations from Hong Kong, Taiwan, China and India. The paths of 'astronaut families', the high-tech professionals and the high-tech contract workers may converge in high-tech industries and the surrounding suburbs, but they represent different migratory regimes within the transnational network economies linking Asia to North America.

The Astronaut Families

The astronaut family phenomenon is a late modern set of transnational practices that – through the acquisition of multiple passports – both utilizes and subverts the rationalities of the politic-spatiality of governmentality. As I have argued elsewhere, Hong Kong émigrés have excelled at what started off as a need to balance the risks of communist rule with opportunities to make money in China's booming economy, but then became a normalized part of trans-Pacific commuting. From the perspective of Hong Kong, they are astronauts shuttling between livelihood and family on opposite sides of the Pacific. From the view of North America, they are resident expatriates who

---

6 The term 'resident expatriate' was coined by Kaplan (1998: 101). For a discussion of cosmopolitan citizenship as based on residence rather than on membership in a nation state, see Delanty 2000: 51-67.

bring Pacific Rim investments, and are sometimes the butt of resentment for American minorities worried about opportunities in the changing economy. While some have misread my image of astronauts as agents of instrumental rationality, I see them more as reflexive modern subjects in a world where the pluralization of risks conditions people to make calculations that take into account the unseen and the unintended by spreading their chances across national spaces.[7] Thus the family and business networks linking Hong Kong and California create a space of flows where the immigration rules of different countries are manipulated with a dexterity informed by the dialectic of risk and insurance.

The unintended effects of such flexible citizenship manoeuvres include the proliferation of divided loyalties – to the family in California, to the company in China, to the ethnic nationality (localized Chinese-ness) and to the new locality (multicultural California). The dispersal of family and the fragmenting of domestic and work activities across many sites have engendered a sense of cultural dislocation. Hong Kong women with children who live in fancy sub-urbs, acquiring educational capital and gaining time for residency rights, are often unable to identify with Chinese Americans who are descended from earlier migrations into California. Some have thrown themselves into fighting Ameri-can educational systems in order to ensure that their children acquire the mix of cultural capital – high scholastic norms, music and sports activities, but also Mandarin classes and Chinese cuisine in the cafeteria – that will continue to ethnicize and index their cosmopolitan citizenship. Others have been motiva-ted to create mini-Hong Kong cultures in upscale restaurants, old-boys' school clubs, tennis courts and mah-jong parties. Business migrants and families frequently return to Hong Kong where life is considered more exciting and sophisticated, and takes on a more real quality than life in a complacent Cali-fornian suburb. The managerial elites experience Hong Kong and California in real time, and yet as places with different temporal qualities, differently weighted in terms of cultural resonance and belonging. Shuttling across the Pacific is never merely for business reasons; such circulations have become an imperative to activate the dialectic of dissolution and reintegration of ethnic identity between the two poles of their existence. The imperative of the flexible family regime, interacting with the rationality of market flexibility, steadily whittles away a notion of citizenship defined by membership in a nation state. Instead, in the space of flows, different juridical status and the possession of

7 Beck observes that in late modernization the 'self-endangerment' of society includes the immanent pluralization of risks, a historical loss of certainties that calls the rationality of risk calculation into question. The unseen and the unintended, not instrumental rationality, 'is becoming the motor of social history' (Beck 1994: 181).

social and cultural capitals enable these cosmopolitan migrants to construct an ethnicized cosmopolitan citizenship linked to a space of flows, a citizenship that is by no means uniformly available to others of the same ethnicity or living in the same locality.

Ethnicized Professional Networks

Besides the Hong Kong business immigrants largely concerned about residential and commercial property, other Asian resident expatriates have become a significant socio-cultural force because of their centrality to the growth of the computer industry that has come to dominate Northern California's economy. In the 1980s, the early years of the high-tech industry, companies hired Taiwanese and Indian citizens already in the country and trained in American universities. Many US-trained Asian engineers, programmers and venture capitalists have contributed to the growth of the industry as a whole. But as the demand for professionals grew to keep pace with the booming economy, the computer industry put pressure on the federal government to increase the intake of skilled foreign workers to 65,000. Under the H-1B visa programmes, elite skilled workers were admitted to the country for six years, but they were now free to pursue permanent residency, or 'the green card', while working for an American company. Many of the computer migrants came from Asian and European countries and China, but in most technology firms such as Hewlett Packard and Intel, one-third of the engineering workforce is composed of skilled immigrants from Taiwan and India (Saxenian 1999). Taiwanese professionals and capitalists now form a major presence in Silicon Valley communities such as Sunnyvale, which boasts a Taiwanese Cultural Center funded by the Taipei government. Indian engineers and programmers have also spread across middle- and upper-middle-class suburban cities such as Fremont, which are served by Hindu temples, Indian shops and entertainment centres.

During the 1990s, foreign-born entrepreneurs have also started up dozens of public technology companies, and over 300 private companies have been founded by Taiwanese immigrants. Ethnic Chinese ones are predominantly focused on computer and electronic hardware manufacturing and trade, while Indian immigrant-operated firms specialize in software and business products (Saxenian 1999). Many Taiwanese-owned companies use ethnic and professional networks to form partnerships with firms in the Hsinchu Industrial Park in Taiwan, creating a process of reciprocal industrial upgrading across the Pacific. Furthermore, thousands of Taiwanese expatriates have returned to Taiwan, but maintain daily contact with partners in Silicon Valley, and some visit the USA almost monthly. These North American expatriates are returnees in their homeland, and yet family and business connections keep

California an alternative home site. Indian high-tech professionals are less likely to engage in the astronaut circulations of the Taiwanese entrepreneurs.

Thus the growth of the computer and information industry has spawned the inflows of skilled Asian workers and entrepreneurs who, by their presence, networks and cultural interest, have effectively ethnicized a new kind of corporate citizenship. But all resident expatriates, whether ethnic Chinese or South Asian, enjoy the opportunity of earning citizenship entitlements through local investments or employment with an American company, and can afford to purchase homes in the stratospheric real estate market. Their companies help them settle in, and get their children into the good schools in expensive suburbs. An upbeat report commissioned by a pro-immigration advocacy group notes that new immigrants mainly from Asia, Latin America and the Caribbean are embracing the American lifestyle, according to four indexes: mastering English, home-ownership, becoming citizens, and marriage across ethnic lines, especially in California.[8]

Body shopping for Silicon Valley

In contrast to these privileged corporate classes, there are now new streams of contract skilled workers who do not enjoy the same protections in their work conditions or in acquiring legal citizenship. So-called body shops have sprung up to form employment chains linking Silicon Valley firms to Bangalore and other sites of software expertise in India. By the end of the 1990s, more than half of the contract (H-1B) visas issued to foreign employees in the high-tech industry were to professionals from India.[9] Body shops are operated by Indian resident expatriates, and have become a key mechanism for supplying the high-tech industry with foreign hired hands who are cheaper than equally qualified American nationals. Taiwanese and mainland Chinese entrepreneurs have also more informally recruited skilled computer workers from China, and the expectation is that their numbers will increase. In other words, the body-shop migratory regime regulates a secondary skilled labour force that does not enjoy the citizenship entitlements of the resident expatriates.

★　★　★

Nikolas Rose (1999) uses the term 'the capitalization of citizenship' to describe the ways in which neo-liberal criteria have come to dominate our norms of citizenship. American visa instruments have directly and indirectly regulated

8 'Immigrants Quickly Becoming Assimilated, Report Concludes', *San Francisco Chronicle*, 7 July 1999.
9 'Ambiguity Remains Despite Changes in H-1 Program', *San Francisco Chronicle*, 21 September 2000.

the status of business and professional resident expatriates, as well as of legal and illegal uneducated labour. We have the ethnic Chinese astronauts who rely on multiple passports to manage family life and economic holdings located on opposite sides of the Pacific. Their networks facilitate capital and commercial flows. Taiwanese immigrant entrepreneurs in Silicon Valley represent another kind of astronaut, forging transnational technological-industrial-business networks with Taiwan. The high-tech industry also benefits from temporary contract workers whose status as a temporary secondary skilled labour market is vulnerable to exploitation and unprotected by citizenship entitlements. The influx of legal and illegal unskilled migrants from Asia (and Latin America) continues unabated. While not directly sought by the computer industries, less skilled workers are critical to the growth of the overall economy. Migrant subjects – transnational entrepreneurs, resident expatriates, temporary skilled workers, unskilled workers, asylum seekers and undocumented illegals – enact different forms of citizenship. I turn now to the effects of flexible rationalities of work, communities and politics on the formation of differently capitalized citizen-subjects. Does differential access to political, information and cultural resources inform their reflection on conditions of possibility for the further development of American neo-liberalism?

The Spatialization of Power: Strategic Networks of Rationalities

Manuel Castells has briefly discussed the *interactions of spaces of flows with spaces of places*, focusing on the ways in which the urban landscape channels and integrates physical elements in shaping social interactions (Castells 1996: 424). He recognizes that 'people do still live in places', but 'because function and power in our societies are organized in the space of flows, the structural domination of its logic essentially alters the meaning and dynamic of places' (Castells 1996: 428). However, Castells puts analytical weight on the spatiality of built urban forms, while ignoring the spatiality of rationalities that shape conditions of livelihood and of sociality. If we are to capture what reflexive modernization means for the emergence of new social forms, we need to ask how rationalities governing the biopower of migrant workers, the social norms of employment, and the administration of needs set the stage for the creation and contestation of different kinds of entitlement.

The new landscapes of globalized America are very evident in California, a state characterized by political fragmentation and regional autonomy, and an international cast of migrants, rich and poor, skilled and unskilled – a potent mix exacerbated by rapid technological industrial growth. A shake of this kaleidoscope discloses the flexible patterning of power shaping labour markets, residential communities and the idea and practice of citizenship itself.

Below I will discuss three sets of rationalities in the strategic apparatus that spatializes power in a number of localities: first, the interpenetrations of class, nationality and race in the restratification of skilled workers; second, the proliferation of subcontracted labour controls and ethnic enclaves; and third, the new suburban-oriented governance informed by lifestyle entitlements.

The New Techno-Migrant Market

Scott Lash has argued that in reflexive modernization, an expanding proportion of the workforce will be active in the advanced services, and linked to the information and communication structures as users, consumers and producers of informational goods and services (Lash 1994: 128–29). The expanded middle class work inside such informational and communication structures and 'they do so largely as the *"experts" inside the expert-systems*, which themselves are "nodes" of accumulation information and accumulated information-processing capacities' (129). However, I disagree with Lash that the middle class in such informational industries 'becomes more a "served" than a service class, as its mainly information-processing labor is no longer subsumed under the needs of manufacturing accumulation' (129). Indeed, the high-tech demands for overseas talents are precisely to attract a cheaper expert class who can provide the service necessary to the processing of information, a demand so great that no immigration barriers are tolerated.

As the Silicon Valley has grown by leaps and bounds, high-tech firms have annually lobbied the US government to raise the numbers for contract skilled migrants, especially from Asia. Companies claim that American universities are not producing enough qualified engineers to keep up with the numbers needed to sustain the growth of the technology industry. An Asian American maker of circuit chips protests that if visas for contract high-tech workers were not readily available, businesses like his would fail: 'We have been hiring people from Canada, from France and from Yugoslavia. We have engineers from Taiwan, and Vietnam. It's like a small United Nations.'[10] Such computer industry demands are shaping a kind of market rationality whereby the status of elite technology workers becomes mediated by nationality and ethnicity, leading to a restratification of skilled workers in California and beyond.

The body-shopping role has created a more exploitable category of skilled foreign workers, providing opportunities for a kind of illegal immigration of skilled workers. Body shops operate as agencies for admitting a secondary

10 'A New California', *San Francisco Examiner*, 20 February 2000.

skilled labour force, relying on recruiters in India to find technical workers. Some body shops have been suspected of exploiting these foreign workers from the moment of recruitment to the possible outcome of eventual expulsion from the USA. Recruitment practices may include receiving bribes from would-be contract workers in India, who may be able to buy false papers and qualifications. Once contract workers arrive in the USA, many are vulnerable to exploitation by the body shops and corporate firms. Body shops hold their visas and find them employment, often taking a cut of their salaries (from 25 to 50 per cent).

Furthermore, by keeping the workers' visas and holding out the promise of eventually getting them green cards, the body shop makes it risky for the migrant workers to change employers, complain about illegal conditions, or undertake unionizing activities without jeopardizing their green card prospects.[11] Constrained by their fear of losing jobs and also their immigrant status, body-shop workers are thus reduced to a kind of glamorized indentured servitude. An Indian engineer complains that a body shop 'threatened to send some [workers] back to India if they did not get contracts [to work with high-tech firms]. These workers were in tears. They were nervous wrecks, ashamed to ask for money or help from their families back home.'[12] The prospect of getting citizenship is used as a weapon to deny these elite workers citizenship rights.

Despite the reported abuses of the system, Silicon Valley executives have kept up their demand for foreign experts. According to labour organizers, the real issue is not the lack of qualified Americans, including those of African-American and Latino ancestry, but that companies have had trouble finding engineers and programmers willing to accept the salaries offered. As thousands of computer programmers are recruited from overseas, the class identity of computer workers is thus thoroughly infused with South Indian ethnicity, and with the insecurity of transient residents employed on the basis of temporary work permits. Compared with the resident expatriates, many of whom share the same nationality and ethnicity, and enjoy access to legal and cultural power, these experts on temporary visas enjoy no such protection. Meanwhile, qualified native-born Americans of minority status are marginalized by the presence of these temporary foreign professionals in the technology industry. Silicon Valley firms depend on Latino and African-American labour, but do not integrate them at the level of skilled workers. Clearly, the imperatives of neo-liberalism do not including investing in or training native-born American

11 'Question of Fraud: Silicon Valley Pushes for More Foreign Workers Despite Federal Probes', *San Francisco Chronicle*, 21 September 2000.
12 David Bacon and Judy Goff, 'Law Shouldn't Allow High-Tech Industry to Indenture Immigrants', *San Francisco Chronicle*, 9 September 2000.

minorities, preferring to use a regime of foreign circulating indentured expert labour as a way to 'remanagerize' the risks of the volatile computer industry.

What are the substantive demands of contract workers in the face of the temporary permit as a state mechanism for regulating migrant labour? Some American labour organizers would like to end body shopping altogether, and have the technology industry invest in training Americans, especially minorities. Others argue that a first step in controlling the exploitation of migrant workers would be to allow them to work for different employers. A contract worker who changes employer or loses his job forfeits the chance of gaining immigrant status. By removing this control, contract workers can fight for their rights without fear of losing their entitlement to citizenship.[13] But contract high-tech workers are at the upper end of an ethnicized hierarchy that has been intensified by the regulation and management of the variety of migrants to California.

The Ethnic Enclave: Subcontracting Work and Social Control

Fables about techno-industrialists and immigrant superheroes in the Silicon Valley only reinforce the plight of poor or illegal low-skilled workers who are employed in a multiplicity of low-paid jobs – as electronics factory labour, garment workers, office cleaners, hotel maids and janitors, restaurant and supermarket workers, farm hands and house maids, all critical to sustaining 'the quality of life in California'. Scott Lash has argued that the exclusions of African-American inner-city populations from information and communication structures doom the ghetto young to downward mobility from the working class (Lash 1994: 132–33). For low-skilled migrants in the restructured flexible economy, such isolations are further intensified because of lack of access to the institutions of civil society. Few African-American workers, for instance, realize that there are good jobs in Internet companies that do not require a college degree. This is often the effect of a deep dependence on ethnic networks for jobs, and a tight social control wielded by ethnic power brokers to localize unskilled newcomers as a cheap and highly exploitable labour force. As a cost-cutting measure, American businesses subcontract work to smaller US-based companies – electronics assembly plants, garment sweatshops, food-processing centres – where operations are more flexible because they employ unregulated workers. Tapping into ethnic networks, Asian-owned electronics companies take advantage of the ignorance, isolation and poverty of unskilled immigrants.

In Southern California, ethnic Chinese garment sweatshops have been exposed for hiring illegal immigrants (Asians and Latinos) at $3 an hour for 10-hour days (the legal minimum in California is $5.75), with no overtime,

13 Before he stepped down as president of the USA, Bill Clinton signed a law allowing contract workers to change jobs without risk of damaging their chances of acquiring citizenship.

sewing designer clothes. In an infamous case uncovered in 1995, an El Monte sweatshop forced Thai and Latino immigrants to work for 70 cents per hour. The Department of Labor estimates that at least 60 per cent of the approximately 150,000 garment workers in the Los Angeles area are routinely underpaid, but language barriers between the workers have obstructed union organizing.[14] Labour violations' akin to those in the garment sweatshops have emerged in Silicon Valley. An Asian-American-owned electronics factory and its subcontractor were charged with underpaying South-East Asian immigrants, who worked in the factories as well as taking work home. The high demand for computer parts has spurred many computer firms to outsource work to poor South-East Asian immigrants at home, where women are paid at piece rate. This practice violates state laws on two counts: the home workers' total earnings did not meet the state minimum wage, and electronic assembly is not permitted as industrial home work in California.[15] Altogether, an estimated 45,000 of Silicon Valley's 120,000 Vietnamese-American population are employed as temporary workers assembling printed wire boards, with no legal protection.

In extreme cases, ethnic employment networks and ethnic enclaves can exert overwhelming power over co-ethnics desperate for jobs in familiar situations where a good command of English is not a necessity. Peter Kwong has described New York Chinatown enclaves that exploit undocumented immigrants from Fujian, who, burdened with debts to the snakeheads, must work punishing hours in substandard jobs for years on end just to repay their debt. Kwong goes on to note: 'The ethnic enclave, however, is a trap. Not only are the immigrants doomed to perpetual subcontracted employment, but the social and political control of these enclaves is also sub-contracted to ethnic elites, who are free to set their own legal and labor standards for the entire community without ever coming under the scrutiny of U.S. authorities' (Kwong 1997: 10–11). In other words, the ethnic enclave model has allowed new affluent immigrants to create conditions of indentured servitude for illegal co-ethnics, which, unlike the ethnic enclaves of earlier generations of immigrants, are not necessarily a stepping-stone to upward mobility. Many unskilled ethnic immigrants are easily exploited by co-ethnic bosses, hampered by language barriers, and, fearing deportation, have difficulty breaking into the wider, unskilled secondary labour markets. The workers have no benefits, and may as well be working in China or Brazil.

The most vivid kinds of ethnic enclave exploitation in California are in the restaurant and supermarket trade, which has greatly expanded to serve an

14 'BCBG Names in Sweatshop Suit', *Asianweek*, August 1999.
15 'High Tech's Low Wages: Two Silicon Valley Firms Sued over Alleged Labor Violations', *Asianweek*, 23 December 1999.

affluent Asian expatriate community. Mega-supermarket chains have used kinship, language and cultural authority to control and exploit Asian immigrant workers. The United Food and Commercial Workers Union's effort to organize underpaid workers in ethnicized supermarket chains have been unsuccessful because the owners employ relatives and friends, and invoke kinship as a way to inculcate worker loyalty. A Cantonese-speaking union organizer said: 'In Chinese culture, employers have the same kind of authority as teachers and parents. If that's the case, you can't get workers to challenge them. And I think, partly, confrontation and conflict are not highly valued. I talked to one worker who said, "We're in a new country. We don't want to start problems."'[16]

The interweaving of personal relationships and formulaic invoking of tradition disguise the lack of honour and the diversity of Asian migrant subjects who are not bound by the same sets of collective memory. Instead, the compulsions of normative expectations (Giddens 1994) are intertwined with market rationality in disciplining unskilled immigrants as indentured servants. As Nikolas Rose has argued, in advanced liberalism: 'Individuals are to be governed through their freedom, neither as isolated atoms of classical political economy, nor as citizens of society, but as members of heterogeneous communities of allegiance, as "community" emerges as a new way of conceptualizing and administering relations among persons' (Rose 1996: 41).

The labour market in Silicon Valley is shaped like an hour-glass, drawing workers at both ends from the immigrant streams, subjected to different systems of regulation. Foreign knowledge workers on temporary visas constitute one community, but they have the expertise and support of labour organizers which they can use in fighting for their rights as workers and would-be citizens. The humbler unskilled migrants are integrated into ethnic enclaves which form virtually self-governing communities largely unregulated by the law. Such diverse communities of migrant workers have re-naturalized and re-segmented labour markets, giving a strong ethnic cast to occupational status and creating communities with different registers of entitlement. In this process of political fragmentation, what kinds of claims do the affluent make in their new homeland?

Lifestyle Entitlements and Suburban-Level Government

Perhaps the elite business and professional newcomers are the migrants most able to make the kinds of choices that simultaneously pursue the good life and express their continual dissatisfaction. Unsurprisingly, a business calculus informs the way they shape debates about civic life. Wherever they relocate

16 'When Unions Attempt to Organize Silicon Valley's Growing Vietnamese Workforce, They Find Custom, Language and History Stand in the Way', *Metro, Silicon Valley's Weekly Newspaper*, 16–22 September 1999.

168

their families – in Australia, New Zealand, Canada or the USA – astronaut entrepreneurs have been obsessed with what they call 'good education, good environment, and political stability'. As migrants who 'maximize their quality of life through acts of choice, and their life meaning and value to the extent that it can be rationalized as an outcome of choices made or choices to be made' (Rose 1996: 57), they are the ideal consumer-subjects of advanced liberalism. While family and economic rationalities underpinned their decisions to migrate as a strategy to reduce wide-ranging insecurities and concerns about safety, the consumer choice approach to citizenship reduced it to single-issue 'lifestyle' concerns. In the Silicon Valley, business migrants are mainly concerned about buying nice houses and enrolling their children in good schools, while highly paid high-tech workers seem to put more emphasis on other lifestyle issues such as taxes and good environments. As business people, many Asian immigrants are ideologically conservative, and supported Republican candidate George Bush in the 2000 presidential elections because of his promise to cut taxes, but they were also worried about his lack of interest in higher education. A Chinese-American mother, the president of a student-teacher association in an affluent suburb, said, 'It would be nice if we could cut taxes, but I don't think it would be feasible because of the state of our highways and our education system. I think the voters are willing to pay a bit more for a quality education system and good quality roads.' Asian-American leaders came up with an initiative to persuade Asian-Americans to throw their support behind 'information highway' presidential candidate Al Gore.[17] Nevertheless, there was substantial support for the Republican hands-off approach of government towards private business, and its limits on class-action suits against corporations. Whatever their partisan choices, there was a widespread attitude that citizenship issues are specific to locality. The Asian-American councilman of Cupertino, an important centre of high-tech corporations, said, 'The candidates who take notice and pay attention to our concerns are going to be the ones who deserve our votes.'[18] In other words, the fierce entrepreneurship of Silicon Valley expresses worries about threats to business, personal property and the body. Home-ownership associations have sprung up as a localized form of sovereignty, around which these single issues about safety of person, family and personal possession are paramount in an age of free-floating insecurity.[19] But their flexibility in gaining access to the good life and in defending them-

17 'A New California', *San Francisco Examiner*, 20 February 2000.
18 'A New California', *San Francisco Examiner*, 20 February 2000.
19 'On the way, concerns with "safety", more often than not trimmed down to the single-issue worry about the safety of the body and personal possessions, are "overloaded", by being charged with anxieties generated by other, crucial dimensions of present-day existence – insecurity and uncertainty' (Bauman 1998: 5).

selves against uncertainty has been bought at the expense of an impoverishing life and increased insecurity for others.

For instance, in contrast to the gated communities and privatized values of the affluent newcomers and high-tech elites of the Silicon Valley, ordinary working people, many of them new migrants as well, have to contend with a situation of reduced public support and increased uncertainty. There is an acute housing shortage in San José, the heart of Silicon Valley. Millions have been spent on civic renovations and redevelopment projects to lure middle-class professionals and high-tech business to the city, while the growing plight of the working people has been overlooked.[20] Thousands of ordinary workers have to make long commutes because they cannot afford housing in the Valley. There is an urban folktale about people making $45,000 having to sleep in their cars. An increasing number of working people are homeless, and some spend the night in buses or local shelters. The intensified gap between affluent young professionals (both migrants and citizens) and working families has rippled across Northern California. Thus families in long-term immigrant neighbourhoods in San Francisco are being displaced by skyrocketing real estate prices, and the city itself has become 'a combination bedroom, office and den for Silicon Valley'.[21]

The diverse localities that have developed in response to corporate globalization and intensified migration constitute a terrain of competing entitlements, where migrants with capital and talent seek to maximize their personal and corporate security, while reducing social protection for the temporary, underpaid, migrant workers on whom their industry depends. We have the emergence of 'a supplementary citizenship based on residence' that is creating islands of security in the midst of demographic, social and economic upheavals and even disenfranchisement for ordinary people and poor migrants.[22]

Splintering Cosmopolitanism

In this chapter, I have approached the subject of a global America by looking closely at the migratory regimes that govern the space of flows, and at how the

---

20 A 2000 report estimated a housing shortage of about 46,000 homes in Silicon Valley by the year 2010. San José authorities are planning to build affordable housing for low-waged workers and the homeless, and to double the number of shelter beds in the city. 'San José Mayor Forms Housing Crisis Group', *San Francisco Chronicle*, 14 September 2000.

21 'Misson District Fights Case of Dot-com Fever', *The New York Times*, 5 November 2000.

22 Gerard Delanty argues that the formation of the European Union has brought about the codification of a post-nationalist citizenship based on residence, giving citizenship an existence independent of the nation state (Delanty 2000: 120). Here, I borrow his concept of citizenship based on residence to highlight the power and sociality of transnational elites, which is almost entirely market-driven.

diverse rationalities that govern the space of places have led to the splintering of cosmopolitanism. A variety of privileged migrants – investors, managers and professionals – have introduced a splintering effect to our notion of cosmopolitanism. These mobile high-tech figures are cosmopolitan in several ways: they possess the human capital in demand regardless of borders between rich and poor countries, and they also enjoy the perks that come with being first-class corporate employees, regardless of their technical status as citizens of the USA. Such bundling of cosmopolitan capital and privileges in specific high-tech zones has induced a cellular patterning that unevenly distributes citizenship rights and obligations across the national territory. The splintering of cosmopolitan privilege in neo-liberal America challenges the uncritical acceptance of a cosmopolitan project that some consider a positive answer to globalization and its discontents. Scholars such as David Held are guardedly optimistic about the proliferation of democratic forms that can come with the stretching and deepening of connections across spaces, and the growing awareness of 'communities of fate' (Held et al. 1999). However, we need to qualify unwarranted optimism that sees such 'a new civics for a global world of difference' as a first step towards 'global governance'.

However, when we look at the high-tech figures as agents in the thickening of transnational connections, the question remains whether the privileges of flexible citizenship can be linked to the obligations of substantive citizenship. There is as yet no systematic empirical evidence that the crisscrossing webs of multilateral agencies or the fostering of civic education will bring about more effective accountability from governments or business. Proponents of a positive cosmopolitanism have not looked at the layering of governance and the splintering of cosmopolitanism below the global or national levels. They have not paid attention to how migratory regimes, and the spatializing technologies of power shape the norms and possibilities for different kinds of belonging and claims on entitlements. The empirical evidence has demonstrated that contemporary market activities and regimes of regulation intensify the fragmentation of political space, and attenuate relations between citizens and their wider society and between different kinds of mobile figures (professional and low-skilled) who become embedded in different axes of citizenship.

A cosmopolitan citizenship based on residence and market criteria exacerbates democratic shortcomings in representing conflicting interests and uneven political participation of all citizens. As Gerard Delanty has argued, the response to the globalizing fragmentation of citizenship requires responses at different levels of the polity and society (Delanty 2000: 136). At the local level, cosmopolitan citizenship can only nurture democracy by re-establishing a connection to community. Globalization has returned citizenship to the city.

Instead of seeing the promise of cosmopolitan citizenship exclusively in the multilateral modes of governance, what seems necessary for democracy is a reinvention of new forms of sociality and civic society in a limited cosmopolitan public sphere, in one of the many nodes linking our globalized world.

References

Appadurai, Arjun (1995), *Modernity at Large*. Minneapolis: University of Minnesota Press.

Bauman, Zygmunt (1998), *Globalization: The Human Consequence*. New York: Columbia University Press.

Beck, Ulrich (1994), 'Self-Dissolution and Self-Endangerment of Industrial Society: What Does this Mean?', in Ulrich Beck, Anthony Giddens and Scott Lash (eds), *Reflexive Modernization*. Stanford, CA: Stanford University Press: 174–83.

Business Immigration Office (1998), *Entrepreneurial Immigration http//www/ei/gov.bc.ca/ immigration*

Castells, Manuel (1996), *The Rise of the Network Society*. Oxford: Blackwell.

Castles, Stephen, and Alastair Davidson (2000), *Citizenship and Migration: Globalization and the Politics of Belonging*. New York: Routledge.

Delanty, Gerard (2000), *Citizenship in a Global Age*. Milton Keynes: Open University Press.

Dicken, Peter (1998), *Global Shift: Transforming the World Economy*. New York: Guilford Press.

Foucault, Michel (2000), *Power*. Ed. James D. Faubion. Trans. Robert Hurley et al. *Essential Works of Foucault, 1954–1984*. New York: The New Press.

Giddens, Anthony (1994), 'Living in a Post-Traditional Society', in Ulrich Beck, Anthony Giddens and Scott Lash (eds), *Reflexive Modernization*. Stanford, CA: Stanford University Press: 56–109.

Gordon, Colin (2000), 'Introduction', in Foucault (2000): xi–xli.

Held, David, Anthony McGrew, David Goldblatt and Jonathan Perraton (1999), *Global Transformations: Politics, Economics and Culture*. Oxford: Blackwell.

Holston, James (ed.) (1999), *Cities and Citizenship*. Durham, NC: Duke University Press.

Kaplan, Robert D. (1998), *An Empire Wilderness: Travels into America's Future*. New York: Vintage.

Kwong, Peter (1997), *Forbidden Workers: Illegal Chinese Immigrants and American Labor*. New York: The New Press.

Lash, Scott (1994), 'Replies and Critiques', in Ulrich Beck, Anthony Giddens and Scott Lash (eds), *Reflexive Modernization*. Stanford, CA: Stanford University Press: 198–215.

Mitchell, Kathryn (1997), 'Transnational Subjects: Constituting the Cultural Citizens in the Era of Pacific Rim Capital', in Ong and Nonini (eds): 228–58.

Mitchell, Kathryn, and Kris Olds (2000), 'Chinese Business Networks and the Globalization of Property Markets in the Pacific Rim', in H. Yeung and K. Olds (eds), *Globalization of Chinese Business Firms*. New York: St Martin's Press.

Ong, Aihwa (1999), *Flexible Citizenship: The Cultural Logics of Transnationality*. Durham, NC: Duke University Press.

— (2000), 'Graduated Sovereignty in Southeast Asia', *Theory, Culture, and Society* 17(4) (August): 55–75.

Ong, Aihwa, and D. Nonini (eds) (1997), *Ungrounded Empires*. New York: Routledge.

Rose, Nikolas (1996), 'Governing 'Advanced' Liberal Democracies', in A. Barry, T.

Osborne and N. Rose (eds), *Foucault and Political Reason*. Chicago: The University of Chicago Press.

— (1999), 'Inventiveness in Politics', *Economy and Society* 28(3): 467–93.

Sassen, Saskia (1991), *The Global City: New York, London, Tokyo*. Princeton, NJ: Princeton University Press.

— (1996), *Losing Control? Sovereignty in an Age of Globalization*. New York: Columbia University Press.

— (2000), 'Theoretical and Empirical Elements in the Study of Globalization', paper presented at the American Anthropological Meetings, 18 November 2000.

Saxenian, Anna Lee (1996), *Regional Advantage: Culture and Competition in Silicon Valley and Route 128*. Cambridge, MA: Harvard University Press.

— (1999), *Silicon Valley's New Immigrant Entrepreneurs*. San Francisco: Public Policy Institute of California.

Soysal, Yasmine N. (1997), *Limits of Citizenship: Migrants and Postnational Membership in Europe*. Minneapolis: University of Minnesota Press.

Stacey, Judith (1998), *Brave New Families, 1990*. Berkeley: University of California Press.

Taylor, P. J. (2000), 'Embedded Statism and the Social Sciences II: Geographies (and Metageographies) in Globalization', Research Bulletin 15, *Environment and Planning A* 32(6): 1105–14.

CHAPTER 9

The Americanization of Memory: The Case of the Holocaust

Natan Sznaider

Almost 300 years ago, John Locke began his political investigation into the nature of modernity with the statement, 'Once, all the world was America'. At the turn of the millennium, I would like to ask if we are returning to the point at which all the world is becoming America again. The purpose of this chapter is to present the distinctive form that collective memories take in the age of globalization. My focus will be on the American case and the particular significance of Holocaust memory, or what is often called 'the Americanization of the Holocaust'.

Over the 1990s the concept of 'globalization' and with it, of course, 'Americanization' has caught the attention of public discourse regarding the prevalence of consumption and popular culture. Anxieties over the global in our time replay similar anxieties regarding Americanization just a century ago. Then and now, the theme of a 'global culture' has become the subject of political, ideological and academic controversies. Many of these debates are framed in dichotomous terms, juxtaposing national and post-national models: the former perceives globalization as a shallow replacement for national values. These so-called 'national values' are often called 'authentic' in times of post-nationality. The emergence of mass consumption has played a major role, since the existence of transnational modes of identification is often equated with the imminent end of the nation. Consumption patterns across nations are interpreted as leading to global homogenization. Thus, in the anti-modernist mind, America stands for everything evil: soullessness, alienation, loneliness, a hell of egoism. Something more than the consumption of food, clothes and other goods is at stake here, however. One of the dramas of this process is played out in the relationship between globalizing processes and the political-cultural foundations for new forms of collective memory – the consumption of memory, so to speak. What has emerged is a distinctive type of collective memory that transcends the confines of the nation state without necessarily replacing national memories. This form of memory is *global*, because it refers to memories that are shared and disseminated by a particular group of people whose claims for collective identities are no longer articulated in particularistic national terms but rather universalistic global terms. Here again the role of America is crucial. It is my contention that *global memory* is the product, among other things, of an encounter between different spatial modes of identification and changing apprehensions of time. I will approach these issues in regard to the so-called 'Americanization of the Holocaust'.

The Americanization of the Holocaust

When it comes to the 'Americanization of the Holocaust', misunderstandings abound. The phrase is well integrated into anti-American discourse; critics use such terms as 'banalization', 'trivialization', 'Disneyfication', even 'McDonald-ization' of the Holocaust (Cole 1999; Flanzbaum 1999; Junker 2000; Novick 1999; Rosenfeld 1997; Shandler 1999). This criticism, which can also be heard in Jewish circles in America, resonates with Frankfurt School criticism of America and what it perceives as mass culture. The 'instrumentalization' of the Holocaust has become a code word. Clearly, this is connected to a broad critique of 'sentiment', unmasking – so to speak – the economic or symbolic class interests of those who attempt to convey memory through different means of communication (Finkelstein 2000; Novick 1999).

In my opinion, all these thinkers believe in the existence of pure, perfect and transcendental memory, which, of course, cannot be represented by what are perceived as American consumer products, such as the soap opera *Holocaust*, the film *Schindler's List*, or even the 'US Holocaust Museum'. However, memory, especially in times like ours, depends on mass-mediated forms of communication. These forms, at times, transcend the boundaries of the state; at other times they are in tune with it. This is particularly true for the memory of the Holocaust, which cannot be restricted to place or space (Hansen 1996).

Thus, my view of the 'Americanization of the Holocaust' will take a different turn. I will try to show that concepts such as 'banalization' or 'trivialization' are connected to a greater extent to a classical European critique of mass culture, but do not contribute much to a deeper understanding of the phenomenon at hand. Furthermore, I would like to argue that if we look more closely at the so-called narrow-minded insistence on Jewish singularity and its concomitant particularism, we will find that it yields an unintentional universal message and, furthermore, that those who high-mindedly fear the Holocaust's

'Disneyfication' or 'Spielbergization' are missing the function of this process as a gateway to the increasing universalization of the Holocaust. Therefore, a sociological rather than a normative look at Americanization can perceive it as a mode of dissemination. As such, it leads neither to homogenization nor to trivialization. Instead, through its penetration on the global and local/national level, it challenges the particularistic frameworks that were established, mostly through the interaction between American Jewish groups' efforts to establish a clear-cut ethnic identity between the 1960s and the 1990s, and US foreign policy objectives.

Globalization and Collective Memory

First, however, let me share a few conceptual thoughts on the relationships between globalization and collective memory. Up to now, most scholars of collective memory – Anthony Smith (1995; 1998), for example – have considered it exclusively as a national phenomenon. Globalization has been viewed as something that dissolves collective memory and sets up inauthentic and rootless substitutes in its stead. This position on global culture as memory-less is predicated on a homogenized conception of this culture. This brings us to the first problem, namely that global culture as it exists today is not really homogeneous. A better provisional starting point would be that global culture *hybridizes* (Albrow 1996; Cheah and Robbins 1998; Gillespie 1995; Nederveen Pieterse 1995; Robertson 1995; Tomlinson 1999).

The same is true for time. Global culture does not erase local memories, but rather mixes in with them. To say that nations are the only possible repositories of true history is a breathtakingly unhistorical assertion. There is now a vast literature on national traditions, and it is clear that every single national tradition has gone through a moment of 'invention'. What heightens the ironical twist is that when national cultures were being invented, the same arguments that are being aimed at global culture today were used to oppose them: that they were superficial and inauthentic substitutes for rich local culture, and that no one would ever identify with such large and impersonal representations. This leads me to a fundamental point. In both transitions, to the national and to the global, the imagined plays a key role. In his classic book *Imagined Communities*, Benedict Anderson (1983) described how communities – and especially nations – are unities that are fundamentally imagined. The very belief that there is something fundamental that lies at their core is always the result of a conscious myth-building process. The emergence of the nation state, at the turn of the twentieth century, relied on a process by which the existing societies used representations to turn themselves into a new entity, which would impact immediately on people's feelings and on which they could build their identities – in short, a group individuals could identify *with*. This nation-building process fully parallels what is happening through globalization at the turn of the twenty-first century. The nation *was* the global when compared with the local communities that preceded it. But the nation was not for that reason inauthentic. The ability of representations to give a sense to life and shared community is not ontologically but rather sociologically determined.

Anderson makes it clear that it was precisely the now-lambasted media (in the case of the nation, the printing press) that produced the requisite solidarity through a constant repetition of images and words. In the era of globalization, an analogous role is played by the electronic media. The speed and imagery of the new global communications are what make possible a shared consciousness, and hence a collective memory that spans territorial and linguistic borders. The new identity is produced not instead of the old, but by transforming it – just as in the building of nations. Today this is done through global media events. Thus, if the nation is the basis for authentic feelings and authentic collective memory – as the critics of global culture are almost unanimous in maintaining – then it cannot be maintained that representations are a superficial substitute for authentic experience. On the contrary, representations are the basis of this authenticity. This holds true for both the national and the global, as both require an imagined community.

Memories of the Holocaust

The history of the memory of the Holocaust – or rather of its various representations – provides an ideal opportunity to bring into focus both the creative powers of globalized culture and the central role of its social carriers, the cosmopolitans. The Holocaust has been the leading example of the attempt to internationalize collective memory throughout the post-war period, and I argue that it is now the paradigm of collective memory in the global age. The ongoing discussion about the Holocaust thematizes the problem of remembrance and forgetting, and the changing relations of universal and particularistic self-understandings.

Universalism and Particularism: Cosmopolitanism and the Jewish Experience

What group is most suited to be the carrier of such global memories? I will look at a group that supports global memories not through their physical presence but rather through their representation as the Universal Other. Furthermore, this Universal Other is defined as the 'innocent victim'. Here I am concerned with the representation of Jews as cosmopolitans. Part of the reason is that

Jewish experience can be considered the original, paradigmatic case of cosmo-politanism during the times of nationalism. Jewish existence before the Holo-caust, and before the founding of the state of Israel, mixed longing for territorial independence with attraction to and enmeshment in other cultures. This condition of diaspora did not grow out of Judaism per se, but out of tensions among citizenship, civil society and cultural identity. Jewish culture was not only mixed with other cultures, it was itself a mixture of cultures. In a certain sense, it was a culture that 'Judaized' the cosmopolitan mixture of cultures it absorbed – it gave them a unifying cast without negating them. This is part of the reason why Jewish culture is so well adapted to being the background model of global modernity. The experience of diaspora, of life in exile, is the clearest example modernity can put forward of sustained community life that did not need a territorial container to preserve its history. In Jewish experience, similar to the Black experience, life outside the nation state is nothing new. Thus, not only the memory of the Holocaust, but the Holocaust itself, as the event that sought to destroy this culture, is becoming central to moral concerns in our age. It is no coincidence that this process moved from Europe to the USA and from there back to Europe.

What can be seen from the example of the USA is that group membership does not have to be connected to allegiance to the state. Ambiguity is built into such relations. Jews in America can be everything: Jewish, Americans, loyal to Israel or none of the above. Whatever they choose to be, it does not contradict their being Americans. Part of the emergence of multiculturalism means that each ethnic group asserts its own unique history and tries constantly to univer-salize this uniqueness. As allegiance to the state diminishes, group identity plays itself out through a heritage of suffering. In the USA this began notably with Blacks and women in the 1960s and 1970s who tried to define themselves through a moral identity of suffering. The Americanization of memory, I would like to argue, liberates memory of its parochial and particularistic stronghold, even though often carried by particular Jewish interests and politics.

The former research director of the US Holocaust Memorial Museum, Michael Berenbaum, defined the Americanization of the Holocaust as follows: 'to tell the story of the Holocaust in such a way that it would resonate not only with the survivor in New York and his children in San Francisco, but with a black leader from Atlanta, a Midwestern farmer, or a Northeastern indus-trialist' (Berenbaum 1990: 19). This remark clearly demonstrates to what extent the museum is an example of the desire of Jews in America to be part of the majority culture, by linking the Jewish history of suffering to the present and future institutions of America. Yet at the same time there is a thrust to be different, by claiming and insisting on the uniqueness and particularity of their history as a minority. Like the global and the local, universalism and particularism do not need to be mutually exclusive. These issues were, of course, the topic of heated debate among all those involved in the project (Linenthal 1995).

These developments are even more astonishing when we take into account the fact that the Holocaust, as we understand it today, did not actually play a large role in American public life prior to the 1960s. Before then, there was no 'Holocaust'. There was simply a holocaust that encompassed all the mass killings of the Second World War, and included the mass murder of the Jews. In other words, the six million were originally subsumed in the 60 million. This was not because observers were indifferent towards the Jews, but because they perceived these events against the background of a global war that killed between 50 and 60 million people. Nazi atrocities were originally interpreted in a universalistic fashion. Jews were considered one group among the many victims of Nazism. This position was well anchored even in the indictment of the Nuremberg trials (Marrus 1998). This was also why the trials were supported by a small number of cosmopolitan intellectuals on both sides of the Atlantic, such as Hannah Arendt, Karl Jaspers and Dwight MacDonald. This was a small cosmopolitan moment in history and it was attached to America's moment as victor in the Second World War, ignoring the atrocities of the Soviet Union, as well as ignoring Hiroshima and Nagasaki. It was also the time of the Cold War.

All this began to change in the 1960s. Campaigns by Jewish organizations were very much the driving force of these changes. All these campaigns were vitally connected to the changing status of victimhood – to its transformation from something to be ashamed of to a sign of grace and moral righteousness. This was connected to the rise of 'identity politics' in America, which shifted the focus of political rhetoric from universal concerns to the particularistic claims of groups and subcultures. It was during these decades, when the 'voicing of pain' replaced the voicing of interests in American politics, that the Second World War made the transition from a holocaust to 'the Holocaust'. This represented the successful assertion by the American Jewish establishment that it represented an ethnic group that had a special moral claim based on having suffered the ultimate victimization. The story of Jews and the Holocaust steadily took predominance in the public's eye over all other aspects of the war. Pivotal points in this narrative are the Eichmann trial of 1961, and the Israeli wars of 1967 and 1973, during which the Holocaust became an effective weapon for defending Israel in American political forums. While Israel might have been the initial mover of Holocaust consciousness, it was the emergence of Jewish particularistic identity that moved the Holocaust to centre stage in American consciousness. Here, the notion of 'uniqueness' is central. There is an irony that 'absolute' and 'unique' victimization became the main marker of Jewish identity at just the time that American anti-Semitism was entering into decline and the last barriers to Jewish advancement were being lifted. The Holocaust became the central Jewish American narrative at precisely the time when the Jews were becoming the most successful minority group in the USA. However, and critically, the Holocaust moved centre stage in other countries as well, and not just in terms of local Jewish identity politics. Nor should its meaning for non-Jewish Americans – that is, for 97 per cent of the US population – be overlooked. This development has maintained or increased the universalization of the terms in which America understands the Holocaust – a universalism that is striking in a comparative perspective, when the American discourse is compared with the German or the Israeli discourse.

There are two reasons why the particularization of the Holocaust among the Jewish elite contributed to the universalization of the Holocaust among Americans as a whole. The first reason is that the campaign to make the Holocaust a central element in American life was such a success. Yes, it gave the Jews a privileged role as victims. However, it also gave America a much odder role as privileged witness. Since the politics of victimization are also the politics of identification, non-Jewish Americans have come to identify en masse with the Holocaust in a way that strikes Israelis, Germans and even American Jews as unsettling. Non-Jewish Americans have come to count themselves among the primary keepers of the flame of remembrance. This is why they have a Holocaust museum in a country where there were no concentration camps and where Jews are a tiny minority.

Can we look at the US Holocaust Memorial Museum as the 'Christianization' of the Holocaust, comparing it even to the 'Stations of the Cross?' Does this not mean the 'de-Judaization' of the Holocaust? This was one of the frequent arguments against the museum in Washington, seen as 'Americanizing the Holocaust'. However, 'Christianization' is what universalization means in the 'Western' context. Further, secular Christianity, by and large, is what the West means by secularism. Remove religion from the Holocaust, invite non-Jews – namely, secular Christians – to consider it vitally their own, and this is what you get. It is hard to see how you could get anything else. Hence it is fitting that the establishment of the US Holocaust Memorial Museum is at the centre of America's symbolic life – the Washington Mall – and it demonstrates that the Holocaust has become part of the American secular religion. Since most of America is not Jewish, this is in itself a massive act of universalization.

Such sacralization is an unavoidable by-product of collective memory. If something becomes indelibly inscribed in the identity of a group, ethnic or national, then it is necessarily ringed round with taboos – and that is the simplest definition of the sacred. There are drawbacks to sacralization. The same passions that preserve memory against forgetfulness also defend it against desacralization. These same passions will be turned against any investigator who tries to examine the phenomenon in question dispassionately. Any such investigation will be taken as an offence against memory and the group. Nevertheless, something cannot become part of the civic religion without taking on an air of the sacred. If it is sacralization that is distasteful, the only alternative is collective forgetfulness. In the 1950s, we had universalization without sacralization – and without collective memory. Instead we had individual memory, and collective silence. One can argue about relative proportions – about *how* important this or that event ought to be in the collective memory of the Jews, or in the collective memory of the world's only superpower. If you think it ought to be part of the collective memory, then you must allow it to be sacralized. The second and related way in which this sacralization of the Holocaust has led to the universalization of the terms in which America understood it stems from the end of the Cold War.

The Universalization of Holocaust Memories

In the remainder of this chapter I will focus on the emergence of an increasingly global and universalized discourse about the Holocaust during the 1990s. The role of the USA and what is commonly referred to as the 'Americanization of the Holocaust' are decisive factors in this development. I am referring here to the particular American treatment of the Holocaust as an event that has come to this 'world' as a crime upon humanity, the worst of all crimes. This is also the universal meaning of the Holocaust – the beginning of a pervasive human rights discourse and the foundation for globalized memories. In other words, the Americanization of the Holocaust is synonymous with its universalization.

The Holocaust as Genocide: Kosovo and the Americanization of Memory

A key reason that propelled the universalization of Holocaust memory stems from the end of the Cold War and growing awareness of genocidal acts. This is because genocide *is* the universalization of the Holocaust. It is essential to the concept that the Holocaust is but one instance of a class of (by definition comparable) phenomena. The UN Declaration against Genocide in 1948, where the idea first took shape, was the product of precisely that period when the universal understanding of the Holocaust was as yet unchallenged. The Kosovo conflict was a turning point for the memory of the Holocaust. Kosovo was a globally televised morality play. The war was repeatedly justified with metaphors articulated in reference to the 'lessons of the Holocaust'.

References to the Holocaust featured prominently in articulating a moral and political response to Kosovo. In contrast to genocidal activities in Rwanda, inter-ethnic warfare in Kosovo with its European setting and its televised images resonated with Holocaust iconography. America's involvement in Kosovo was primarily framed as a moral obligation, largely in response to previous failures to intervene on behalf of innocent civilians. The slogan of 'Never Again' was simultaneously a reminder of the Second World War and the delayed involvement of the USA in Bosnia. Kosovo provided an opportunity to reconfirm the lessons of 'Never Again' revealing the full extent of the Americanization (and universalization) of Holocaust memory. If we take these UN conventions seriously in all their clauses, then the danger of a 'new Holocaust' is ever-present, and it is the duty of the USA and others not to sit by, but to do something about it. In the USA, this is what is widely considered the 'lesson of the Holocaust'. This 'lesson' represents a completely universalized understanding of the Holocaust.

The frequent invocation of the Holocaust raised public awareness around questions of uniqueness and comparability, and the use of the past in general. As such, Kosovo and its connection to the Holocaust greatly contributed to an increasingly self-reflexive form of globalized memory drawing on its universal message. Nevertheless, the full extent of the Americanization of Holocaust memory was evident in the pervasiveness of the moral imperative to assist innocent victims threatened by genocide. It was not so much the Holocaust per se, but rather the universal lessons derived from the bystander syndrome that mattered. Holocaust memory was no longer confined to Jewish groups or historians, nor was it simply a metaphor for good and evil. Instead, it was reconceptualized as a matter of civic responsibility for those suffering at a distance. A particular obligation to remember was complemented with a universal demand to act. All victims have turned into Jews. These kinds of 'Americanized' versions of memory, which need to be understood as a particular mixture of ideal and material interests, have been further read and interpreted outside the USA as well. Israel and Germany provide very good examples.

Compared with Germany or Israel, where the uniqueness of the Holocaust has much deeper roots in national experience, America was originally, and is now once again, the land of the universalized Holocaust. How could it be otherwise, in a country that was neither the victim nor the perpetrator? It is not only that the thirty years between 1960 and 1990 were an exception, and it is not only that the exception has lasted almost as long as the rule. Through America, the Holocaust has become central to the discourse of the world. Both of these outcomes are the unintended but world-historical effects of the in-group jockeying of Jewish ethnic politics in the USA. Second, this thirty-year period has put a peculiar stamp on the specifically American understanding of the Holocaust. What the Jewish American establishment has succeeded in accomplishing is that the Holocaust is never universalized for the past. The overwhelmingly dominant narrative in America is that the Holocaust was a crime perpetrated against the Jews. Even when other groups, such as homosexuals and gypsies, are included in the litany of Holocaust victims, their presence does not dilute the Jewishness of the catastrophe; they are simply unfortunates dragged into its wake. For the immediate future, the Holocaust is universalized. Almost anyone might be the victim of the 'next' Holocaust. This stands out in stark contrast to Germany, where the comparisons that cause public debate have all been about the past – attempts to relativize the guilt of the Nazis by asserting that their actions were comparable to similar regimes. This explains why during the Cold War the 'comparability of the Holocaust' in Germany was the cause of the Nazi-sympathizing right, where in America it was the cause of the human rights left.

The US Holocaust Memorial Museum perfectly embodies the American split perspective. The permanent exhibit of the museum is about the past suffering of the Jews. But the special exhibits – which, like all special exhibits, draw special attention – are about non-Jewish victims suffering somewhere in the world today. Like a huge camera obscura superimposing the image of the past onto the screen of the present, the museum is a universalization machine. When Elie Wiesel stood next to President Clinton in front of the museum exhibit on Bosnia and said he could not sleep at night thinking about the Bosnians' suffering, the two sides of the narrative merged. It was a perfect demonstration of how the particularist discourse of 1961–1991 had been transformed into the universalist discourse of the post-Cold War era while still preserving a privileged place for the original Jewish victims. Here the ultimate victim wielded his unique moral authority to attempt to shame the country that considers its foreign policy uniquely moral to stop the new holocaust of non-Jews. Here the chief representative of the American Jewish Holocaust could confirm himself as the world's true moral authority by setting high moral standards for real world action. He could preserve this authority by always setting them slightly higher than 'mere realpolitik' could ever meet. On the other hand the Americans, having erected a monument to this moral authority, now had someone to vouch for their chosenness, for the fact that their actions, unlike those of all other countries in history, were motivated first and foremost by moral concerns. If the two groups – the Jewish organizational elite and the American foreign policy elite – needed each other during the Cold War, they may need each other now even more. Their moral claims are if anything even more ambitious, and their need for mutual reinforcement and support even greater.

There are four ways in which the Holocaust can be universalized: victims in the past (was it the Jews plus a supporting cast, or many different peoples who suffered?); victims in the future (is the lesson Never Again for the Jews, or Never Again for anyone?); perpetrators in the past (were the Nazis uniquely evil, or were they only different in degree or quantity from other mass murderers?); and subjects in the present (who remembers? in other words, who has the right to pronounce the truth of the Holocaust?) What has happened in America due to thirty years of Jewish ethnic politics is that the Holocaust past is now considered entirely in particularistic terms: the Nazis were uniquely bad, the Jews uniquely innocent victims, and everyone else in the story played a secondary role. But the Holocaust future is now considered in absolutely universal terms: it can happen to anyone, at any time, and everyone is responsible. Nevertheless, this universality is considered a form of fealty to the Holocaust, a way of magnifying its importance rather than diminishing it – a way of making it a moral touchstone, a call to action, and a sign of liberal and patriotic virtue. This definitely distinguishes the meaning of the Holocaust in America over the last fifty-five years from the meaning it has had in Israel or Germany.

Elie Wiesel Meets Oprah Winfrey

Eva Illouz shows in her article in this volume how the *Oprah Winfrey Show* is a good example of a genre that documents, discusses and gives voice to suffering. This is also connected to the present topic. Oprah Winfrey has her own wildly successful magazine called *O*. In the November 2000 issue, Oprah talked to Elie Wiesel, the American icon of the Holocaust. The article starts like this:

> He's a man who's lived through hell without ever hating. Who's been exposed to the most depraved aspects of human nature but still manages to find love, to believe in God, to experience joy. (*O* magazine, November 2000: 232)

The cover banner headline reads 'Elie Wiesel and the Holocaust: How He Saved Himself – And His Heart'. The interview is about Wiesel's recovery, his being a victim and becoming a fully human being. All this can be seen as the most eloquent example of the trivialization, or the Americanization, of the Holocaust, but as Illouz claims in her reading of the *Oprah Winfrey Show*, 'a therapeutic narrative is a story about the self, which connects a present suffering to a past event, often called a trauma'. Could this be true for the case of the Holocaust as well? This raises the question of the 'true' meaning of the Holocaust. If one takes as a given that the meaning of the Holocaust is fundamentally collective and political, then this kind of 'Wieselized' reading is trivial and superficial. An alternative reading, however – the modern, Protestant, individualized (Americanized) point of view – is one-to-one, responding in an individual way to the question: 'What is the Holocaust for me?' Wiesel's story appeals to the reader/viewer in such a way as to ask, 'What does it make me think, how does it make me feel, how can I possibly comprehend the enormity that seems beyond words?' To make an analogy to the church, this represents a desire for a one-to-one relationship to the Holocaust, unmediated by priests.

In other words, it is possible to relate to the Holocaust individually and psychologically rather than collectively and politically (defining the 'political' as collective undertakings). If one believes that depoliticization is in essence wrong, then, of course, one will argue that this is wrong as well. This partly accounts for the anger that the US Holocaust Memorial Museum or Spielberg often provoke. The depoliticization of the Holocaust is simply a reflection of the depoliticization of America – or, viewed from another standpoint, the individualization and decollectivization of its culture. The Holocaust is primarily an identity issue in America because everything is primarily an identity issue once individuality replaces collectivity as the ultimate reality of reference. What, of course, troubles so many intellectuals when they relate to the vocabulary of victimization (of 'survivors', for example, who survive alcoholism, child abuse, being an orphan or living in a poor neighbourhood – the typical topics of the *Oprah Winfrey Show*) is the democratization of psychology – a psychology that anyone can apply, and that is best applied by (support) groups of normal people (see again the contribution by Illouz). In other words, we have a psychology that does not need therapists – a religion that does not need priests. So when critics decry the victimology of the Holocaust, they are decrying people who treat historical events as personal rather than collective experiences, which is simply an everyday choice in a decollectivized society. In the final analysis, they are decrying the way people describe their personal experiences in 'uneducated' clichés. They call it 'trivial', or 'Americanized'.

Concluding Remarks

I believe we can say that the emergence of 'global memory' is closely related to processes of globalization at the end of the twentieth and the beginning of the twenty-first century. If the nineteenth and the first half of the twentieth century emphasized the invented (and imagined) dimension of collective memory, the second half of the twentieth and the beginning of twenty-first century reveal a shift to a more reflexive type of collective memory that self-consciously combines the universal and particular and extends its scope beyond the national. To be sure, this shift is neither inevitable nor is it the sole proprietor of contemporary memory types. Rather it is the product of broader historical processes simultaneously leading to the proliferation of particularistic memories and the emergence of a universal 'global memory' challenging the primacy of national narratives. No longer is the nation state the uncontested privileged site for the articulation of collective identity. The hegemonic state has been supplanted by society. This also means that our recent preoccupation with memory might express a transformed need for temporal anchoring, when, in the wake of the information revolution, the relationship between past, present and future is being transformed. Temporal anchoring becomes even more important as the territorial and spatial coordinates of our early twenty-first-century lives are blurred. This is amply demonstrated by the recent memory boom expressing the basic human need to live in extended structures of temporality.

'Global memory' indicates that there is not one apprehension of time, but rather that different groups have distinctive memories organizing meaningful structures of temporality for them. In the cosmopolitan global project, historical time is no longer conceived as 'national culture of memory', with individual recollections enclosed within it, but as fragmented and plural; in other words, a cosmopolitan and therefore optional remembrance and memory with all the resulting contingencies, complexities and contradictions of individual memory. This, as I have tried to show, is a project coming out of America and its ethnic minority groups, such as African-Americans, Jews and others. They have broken the spell of national memory. In these 'Black' and 'Jewish' forms of memory and remembrance, a variety of loosely connected, boundary-transcending layers of memory emerge, unfold, are being invented, at times in tune with the interests of the state and at times in competition with it (Gilroy 1993).

In addition, what so many call the banalization and trivialization of the Holocaust can be seen as a process that makes its history more accessible to larger groups of audiences (Rabinbach 1997). The recontextualization of the Holocaust as an American story reaches, indeed, beyond America's borders. The links between state, nation and culture are becoming increasingly disentangled. Hannah Arendt, in an almost lone cosmopolitan voice, claimed in 1945 after her emigration to the USA that 'the problem of evil will be the fundamental question of postwar intellectual life in Europe – as death became the fundamental question after the last war'. Who would have thought that

Steven Spielberg would carry her torch fifty years later? Can this be considered the revenge of civil society over the state? If so, it might be the true fitting answer to the horrors of the Holocaust.

References

Albrow, Martin (1996), *The Global Age*. Stanford, CA: Stanford University Press.

Anderson, Benedict (1983), *Imagined Communities: Reflections on the Origin and Spread of Nationalism*. London: Verso.

Beck, Ulrich (2000), 'The Cosmopolitan Perspective: The Sociology of the Second Age of Modernity', *British Journal of Sociology* 51(1): 79–105.

Berenbaum, Michael (1990), *After Tragedy and Triumph: Essays in Modern Jewish Thought and the American Experience*. Cambridge: Cambridge University Press.

Cheah, Pheng, and Bruce Robbins (eds) (1998), *Cosmopolitics: Thinking and Feeling Beyond the Nation*. Minneapolis: University of Minnesota Press.

Cole, Tim (1999), *Images of the Holocaust: The Myth of the 'Shoah Business'*. London: Duckworth.

Finkelstein, Norman (2000), *The Holocaust Industry*. London: Verso.

Flanzbaum, Hilene (1999), 'The Americanization of the Holocaust', *Journal of Genocide Research* 1(1): 91–104.

Gillespie, Mary (1995), *Television, Ethnicity and Cultural Change*. London: Routledge.

Gilroy, Paul (1993), *The Black Atlantic: Modernity and Double Consciousness*. Cambridge, MA: Harvard University Press.

Halbwachs, Maurice (1980), *The Collective Memory*. New York: Harper and Row.

Hannerz, Ulf (1995), 'Cosmopolitans and Locals in World Culture', in Mike Featherstone (ed.), *Nations and Nationalism in a Global Era*. Cambridge: Polity Press: 237–51.

Hansen, Miriam Bratu (1996), 'Schindler's List is not Shoah: The Second Commandment, Popular Modernism, and Public Memory', *Critical Inquiry* 22: 292–312.

Junker, Detlev (2000), 'Die Amerikanisierung des Holocaust'. *Frankfurter Allgemeine Zeitung* (9 September): 11.

Linenthal, Edward (1995), *Preserving Memory: The Struggle to Create America's Holocaust Museum*. New York: Penguin.

Marrus, Michael (1998), 'The Holocaust at Nuremberg', *Yad Washem Studies* XXVI: 5–41.

Nederveen Pieterse, Jan (1995), 'Globalization as Hybridization', in Mike Featherstone, Scott Lash and Roland Robertson (eds), *Global Modernities*. London: Sage: 45–68.

Novick, Peter (1999), *The Holocaust in American Life*. Boston: Houghton Mifflin.

Rabinbach, Anson (1997), 'From Expulsion to Erosion: Holocaust Memorialization in America since Bitburg', *History & Memory* 9(1–2): 226–55.

Robertson, Roland (1995), 'Glocalization: Time–Space and Homogenity–Heterogenity', in Mike Featherstone, Scott Lash and Roland Robertson (eds), *Global Modernities*. London: Sage: 25–44.

Rosenfeld, Alvin H. (1997), 'The Americanization of the Holocaust', in Alvin H. Rosenfeld (ed.), *Thinking about the Holocaust: After Half a Century*. Bloomington and Indianapolis: Indiana University Press: 119–50.

Shandler, Jeffrey (1999), *While America Watches: Televising the Holocaust*. New York: Oxford University Press.

Smith, Anthony (1995), *Nations and Nationalism in a Global Era*. Oxford: Polity Press.

— (1998), *Nationalism and Modernism: A Critical Survery of Recent Theories of Nations and Nationalism*. London and New York: Routledge.

Tomlinson, John (1999), *Globalization and Culture*. Cambridge: Polity Press.

Young, James Edward (1993), *The Texture of Memory: Holocaust Memorials and Meaning*. New Haven, CT: Yale University Press.

CHAPTER 10

From the Lisbon Disaster to Oprah Winfrey: Suffering as Identity in the Era of Globalization

Eva Illouz

On 1 November 1755, an earthquake shook the city of Lisbon. The news of the disaster quickly reached the French *philosophes* and sparked one of the most famous philosophical and theological controversies of French intellectual history. As tens of thousands of people had perished in the disaster, philosophers frantically debated on the role of Providence in human affairs. Voltaire, who responded to the disaster most swiftly, wrote in his *Poème sur le Désastre de Lisbonne*:

> Misled philosophers who shout 'all is well', come here, run and contemplate these horrible ruins, the wrecks, these carcasses, the pitiful ashes, the women, the children piled on each other under the broken marble, dismembered, one hundred thousand unfortunate people devoured by the earth, people covered with blood, torn apart, and yet still throbbing with life, buried under their own roof, they die without any help, in horror and agony. (Voltaire 1949, my translation)

Voltaire further drives his point and clarifies what is philosophically unacceptable in the event: 'which crime, which mistake have these children committed, crushed on their mother's breast in their own blood? Was Lisbon, which is no more, more corrupt than London or Paris full of delights? What? Lisbon is destroyed and we dance in Paris?'

Let me make a few preliminary observations. To the best of my knowledge, Voltaire's intervention marks the first time that a philosopher directly addresses his community of fellow philosophers *and* the general public about a contemporary but distant disaster, and the first time that a philosopher does this by questioning the role of Providence in human affairs.[1] Voltaire's bold conceptual

1 London's great fire in the previous century had not spurred the same sense of theological disquiet.

move consists in refusing to view suffering either as the punishment for a hidden sin or as the incomprehensible but just decree of an unfathomable God (Neiman, 2002; Baczko 1997). Voltaire claims that suffering ought to be submitted to the realm of human intelligibility and reason and that as such we can and ought to apply ordinary criteria of justice to suffering, *wherever it takes place*. In so doing, Voltaire breaks not only with traditional religious theodicy, but also with the eighteenth-century literary cult of suffering which had made tears synonymous with virtue and the spectacle of heroines' misery into a sweet sentiment supposed to elicit gentle compassion (see Boltanski 1999). Not only is his setting global rather than domestic, but the confrontation with the suffering of distant others does not soften or uplift or make us feel more virtuous. On the contrary, once suffering is disentangled from theology and from sentimental literature, it can become what it is here: a scandal. And it is a scandal not only because the innocent suffer meaninglessly but also because they suffer when others, in London and Paris, are merry and happy. The engagement of the philosopher with the suffering of distant others takes place in the present and goes hand in hand with the compression of spatial and national boundaries: what happens in Lisbon is scandalous from the standpoint of what happens in London and Paris and vice versa; we should feel uncomfortable dancing in Paris when people are buried alive in Lisbon.

Moreover, even if Voltaire might be making here an ordinary use of synecdoche, it is interesting to note that he refers to cities rather than to countries, perhaps suggesting a subtle solidarity between cities beyond their respective countries. By placing Lisbon's disaster into the perspective of the moral intelligibility that guides the world, Voltaire manages a double tour de force: he creates a proto-global public sphere – that is, a space of discussion about the moral coherence of *the world as a whole* – and places the question of the immanent rationality of the world squarely at the centre of the relationship that links Lisbon, Paris and London. Lisbon gets destroyed while Paris continues to dance: it is this moral scandal that marks the emergence of one of the central world images of secular global consciousness (Weber et al. 1946). While Christianity might have played an important role in the development of the consciousness of the world as a whole, I would argue that a global consciousness was never better served than when traditional theological accounts of Providence collapsed. Indeed, the weaker the explanations accounting for the disparity between principles of (divine) justice and the worldly fate of men and women, the more a world consciousness of (and solidarity with) misfortune was enabled.

Indeed, Voltaire's involvement with the Lisbon disaster is paradigmatic of what would become one of the central axes of the global public sphere, namely that the calamities of some become the problem of others, across territorial and national boundaries. In such a public sphere the relation to the suffering object is established through imagination, compassion and the forgetting of one's religious and ethnic allegiance. The imagination used and invoked by Voltaire combines sentiment and cognition, pathos and logos, and invites one to reflect on the order and principles that organize the world through the simultaneous use of philosophical debate and emotions such as empathy, compassion and guilt.

Thus the project of the global public sphere contained from the start two languages, each aiming at a different kind of universality. One is the rational impulse that there be a correspondence between merit and fate, and that the absence of such correspondence be accounted for and be accountable (see Weber et al. 1946; Neiman forthcoming). The other would appeal to what many eighteenth-century philosophers thought of as a universal capacity of the imagination, compassion and sympathy (Hutcheson 1742; Smith 1759). The public sphere as Voltaire constructs it here plays on both dimensions, inviting one to join in a rational discussion on the intelligibility of the world as well as to identify with a distant victim based on the assumption of a commonly shared humanity.

When we turn to contemporary global media it would seem – at least if we believe sociologists– that they have radically moved away from the disquieting vocation Voltaire had assigned to the public sphere. For example, Bob Connell, in an article entitled 'Sociology and World Market Society', suggests that

> we get global systems of mass communication dominated by commercial fantasy – Hollywood, TV soaps, consumer advertising, celebrity gossip, the major content of mass culture … We now live in a world where the normal content of mass communication is lies, distortions, and calculated fantasies. I don't think it is any wonder that the last 20 years have seen a steady decline in political party membership, a deepening public disillusion with politicians and the collapse of citizenship. (Connell 2000: 292)

Indeed, according to many, global media recruit us through the same global utopia of consumption which in turn distributes worldwide the same icons – of youth, beauty, glamour, abundance and happiness. Arjun Appadurai has best theorized the possibilities that such utopias have in store for global consciousness. As he suggests, transnational culture has opened new spaces for the imagination, thus making fantasy an intrinsic part of global social and cultural practices: 'ordinary lives today are more often powered not by the givenness of things but by the possibilities that the media (either directly or indirectly) suggest are available' (Appadurai 1991: 55). In this view, global consciousness is characterized by the play of the imagination, the open-ended character of one's conception of one's life, and deterritorialized fantasies. I would like to

191

suggest, however, that the global imagination is no less dystopic than it is utopian. From photojournalism to soap operas via the evening news, global media are ridden with the spectacle of private and public misery. Icons of agony – no less than icons of glamour – are the regular staple on which the global imagination feeds itself.

In what follows, I would like to offer one direction to start thinking about the role of the image of suffering in what has become a fully fledged global public sphere. Does such representation hold the promise of a cosmopolitan consciousness? Is the representation of, and identification with, 'scandalous suffering' the way to achieve transnational solidarity?

The Oprah Winfrey Talk Show

Talk shows are the latest comer in the competitive arena of media genres documenting, discussing and giving voice to suffering. The *Oprah Winfrey Show* is probably the best representative of the genre, not only because it was the first to offer the formula in which people came to discuss the countless ways in which they were unhappy, but also because Winfrey has explored the cultural possibilities of her show in the most exhaustive and most global way. To quote her website, the *Oprah Winfrey Show* is 'the highest rated talk show in television history, is seen by 15 to 20 million viewers a day in the United States and is in 132 countries ... So powerful is the talk show hostess that her influence extends beyond her daily one-hour gabfest into everything from the publishing industry to the agricultural commodity markets'. The *Oprah Winfrey Show* is global not only because of the scope of its audience and because it is distributed in 132 countries, but also because the format in which Winfrey has presented and processed human misfortune uses a global cultural form. It is this cultural form that will preoccupy me here.

The *Oprah Winfrey Show* is distributed in a dizzying list of countries: Israel, India, Bahrain, China, Slovenia, Singapore and Thailand are only a few haphazardly picked examples. In the span of a decade, Oprah Winfrey and her show have become global cultural forms. It is indisputable that the show bears little affinity with the social and cultural conditions of some of the countries in which it is distributed (Afghanistan being one such example). In other countries, however, it is quite possible, and even likely, that the show's moral and cultural project – the performance of private 'suffering' – resonates and bears an affinity with the cultural materials at work in those societies. My question will thus be: What makes the story of the suffering and of the self changing the self cross-cultural? In what sense can we characterize the *Oprah Winfrey Show* as a global cultural form?

In trying to answer these questions, I will try to show that Winfrey and her guests use a 'deep' cultural structure to make sense of their lives and that this structure is enacted by and embodied within institutional frameworks that have become transnational. This cultural structure explains not only the mechanism by which autobiographical discourse is routinized in the television format, but also how concepts of suffering and self-change can organize and process a wide variety of personal narratives.

The *Oprah Winfrey* formula is quite simple: one or more individuals come to tell their story – usually a story denouncing an injustice, recounting a misfortune, or telling a heartbreaking experience; the story is told in cooperation with other guests, the audience, the host of the show, and finally with one or more experts specializing in the difficult art of resolving the ways in which people make others and themselves miserable. Even if the time allotted to the experts is relatively short, they are nonetheless crucial to the show because they are the ones who bring to a resolution – or a pretence of it – the various predicaments narrated by the guests. The *Oprah Winfrey* formula is thus dual: it is about the uncanny variety of sad biographical experiences that saturate the polity as well as about experts' – mostly psychologists' – authority to adjudicate the conflicts presented by the guests of the show. Thus the *Oprah Winfrey Show* is about the myriad disputes, dilemmas and conflicts that constitute private life. And private life, if we examine the topics of the *Oprah Winfrey Show*, is far from being dull, harmonious, or heartwarming. Family feuds, marital quarrels, the betrayal of friends and lovers, the devastating effects of lack of self-esteem, quirky sexual relations, children who denounce their parents, parents who abuse their children, women battered by their husbands, husbands battered by their wives are the chief topics of the *Oprah Winfrey Show* and offer an image of private life as ridden with conflict and what I suggest calling 'low-intensity' forms of suffering. In short, one may say that the *Oprah Winfrey Show* is the cultural genre par excellence of failed identity and failed sociability in the realms of marriage, love, parenthood and sexuality.

This is all the more arresting given that the demographic of the show is clearly patterned. It is essentially composed of a high proportion of women, members of ethnic minorities, and members of the working classes, thus making the genre a clearly populist, feminine and at times even feminist one. Conspicuously under-represented in talk shows is the highly successful white male – except when he occasionally assumes the position of expert.

Let me now work through my argument by presenting a typical Oprah Winfrey story. This guest has written an autobiography, and has been the subject of a documentary aired on national (US) TV, and thus can be said to resonate with deep and significant aspects of American culture. I quote Oprah

Winfrey presenting her guest:

> This small baby girl was born whole, but was not allowed to remain safe for
> very long ... because at the age of two, Truddi Chase was brutally raped by
> her stepfather and was continually abused until she ran away at the age of
> 16. But her nightmare did not end there because, as a result, some of the
> most horrific abuse, the most horrific things you can ever in your conscious-
> ness imagine, Truddi Chase dealt with her pain by splitting into several
> personalities. Eventually all those personalities – which has been docu-
> mented – totaled 92 distinct people living in one mind. She calls them her
> troops ... Where is she now? Truddi Chase – the real Truddi Chase – under-
> went years of therapy and most of the therapy – stop [Winfrey cries] was
> videotaped because Truddi says that she wanted others to some day be able
> to understand that they are not alone in their abuse. And that is why we are
> doing this show.[2]

Like so many other guests of the *Oprah Winfrey Show*, Truddi is a victim. In
fact, Truddi might be said to be a super-victim. But she is not the victim of
brutal mass murder, natural disaster, or gross socio-economic injustice. She is
92 times victim of severe psychic damage done to her by a man, who belonged
to her familial circle. In contemporary parlance, this woman suffers from past
abuse and from trauma syndrome. Like many other guests of the *Oprah Winfrey
Show*, her life story is interesting and worthy to be presented on television
because she has been violently victimized in and by her family.

It is easy – almost trivial – to see how this way of exposing suffering in the
public sphere radically differs from Voltaire's proto-global public sphere. First,
the children crushed under their own roofs on their mothers' breast have been
replaced by a beautiful childhood crushed by neglectful or abusive parents, the
destruction of a city replaced by the destruction of families and psyches. Where
Voltaire discussed the large-scale, visible, objective physical destruction of
human lives, we are here made the witnesses of the psychic suffering of one
single person, a suffering that is by definition intimate, subjective and situated
in the private sphere.

Second, if Voltaire's clever philosophical and rhetorical construction consisted in juxtaposing the moral closeness of Lisbon and Paris with the irredu-
cible phenomenological distance separating Lisbon from Paris – the problem
of theodicy being precisely to account for that distance – talk shows on the
other hand are structured on the principle of immediate presence and intimacy
and on the mirroring of the experience and life stories of guests, audience
present in the studio, viewer and host. Indeed everything in the talk show is

2 *The Oprah Winfrey Show*, 'Truddi Chase – Multiple Personalities', 10 August, 1993.

designed to suppress the distance between the happy and the unhappy and to make all of us into victims or incipient victims. As an eminent commentator on American culture – Robert Hughes – put it, 'talk shows are only the most prominent symptom of an increasingly confessional culture, one in which the democracy of pain reigns supreme. Everyone may not be rich and famous but everyone has suffered ...' (Hughes 1993: 17).

Third, while in Voltaire's public sphere, the suffering person was indirectly apprehended – through the mediation of somebody else's speech and eye – here the suffering person has assumed a direct agency, witnessing directly to her own story, drawing us into the radical subjectivity of her speech and feelings.

Fourth, whereas Voltaire's speech was 'referential' – talking about a disaster that took place somewhere – in talk shows speech is essentially performative. To reveal in public the dark secrets of family life is the 'event' reported on and staged by the show; this is because to speak is already to heal. Like so much of American culture, the *Oprah Winfrey Show* is a deeply therapeutic genre in that it is predicated on the belief shared by the host, the guests and the experts that revealing and talking about emotions 'liberates' and generates change.

Fifth, where Voltaire's victims are simply the victims of an absurd disaster, Truddi's victimhood and suffering are different because they are endowed with a meaning that was absent from Voltaire's victims. The suffering person is now summoned to work on her pain, to make it into a meaningful life project. Concurrently, the victim has become sacred; she has come to acquire a unique moral status: not only is moral judgement normally suspended from the person who suffers but her very suffering entitles her to a special status and dignity.

Finally, and perhaps most importantly, where Voltaire referred to the theological chaos that makes the innocent suffer, Oprah Winfrey discusses almost exclusively the worldly chaos that saturates families and identity. Where Voltaire asked what were the meaning and moral coherence of a world in which suffering was haphazardly distributed, Winfrey's show asks mostly how identity and psychic coherence can be built when families, love and marriages no longer provide a reliable source for the formation of identity. To be more precise: I suggest that the *Oprah Winfrey Show* is about a certain form of social suffering that originates in the family and that is articulated from the experience and point of view of women inside the family. This social suffering is about the endless haggling and bargaining that take place in families; it is about the fact that, as Andrea Dworkin put it, 'you cannot separate normal and abusive' relations between women and men (quoted in Nussbaum, 1999: 245); and finally it is about the ways in which the contemporary family fails at accomplishing its function of producing and reproducing identity.

There is a certain irony here. If the genre of photojournalism and the evening news regularly import images of war, famine and natural disasters mostly although not exclusively from the non-Western to the Western world, the talk show represents the first television genre that exports American forms of suffering to the rest of the world – a suffering that differs significantly from the 'imported suffering' in that it is individual, is located in the private sphere, has a psychic character and concerns the self. Where imported suffering is mostly visual, this kind of American exported suffering is mostly narrative. Where the first is a daily and perhaps by now routinized reminder of the inequality in the distribution of collective resources across the globe, the second is more democratic in that it includes all and invites all of us to join in the community of sufferers.

In the remainder of this chapter, I try to clarify the ways in which the *Oprah Winfrey Show* presents two seemingly contradictory properties. One is the fact that it represents a uniquely American phenomenon. The second is that Winfrey has invented a cultural form that offers an example of what Beck dubs 'infra-globalization', or 'globalization from within', that is, a form that emerges from the very gaps and contradictions created by economic and political globalization (Beck 2000).

An American Story

As a genre that relentlessly deconstructs the family, the *Oprah Winfrey Show* derives from and represents the distinct social experience of Afro-American women. This is because throughout the nineteenth century the structure of the black family was systematically 'deconstructed' to fit the economic and geographical imperatives of the white slave owners. Furthermore, as Patricia Hill Collins and others have suggested, black women worked in great numbers in the domestic sphere, thus giving them a unique point of view on the family, which may be characterized as that of an 'outsider within' (Collins 1990). This point of view – of an inside outsider – is that into which the viewer of the talk show is drawn, and which, because of the processes of intense individualization which the American contemporary family has undergone (Beck and Beck-Gernsheim 1995; Beck 2000), has become the 'normal' point of view on the family.

Second, because the US welfare state has played very little role in providing support to individuals and communities, the USA developed early on a strong ethos of self-reliance which has made the self the paramount site of social identity. The *Oprah Winfrey Show* is a genre par excellence in which the self is staged, displayed, improved and transformed. The therapeutic ethos, which relies on the basic faith of the malleability of the self, has become a very powerful discourse in American culture at large, and in the *Oprah Winfrey*

Show in particular, precisely because in the US context, the self was responsible for acting out and reproducing social institutions. This begins to explain why the spectacles of chaotic families and of failed biographies play such an important role in the *Oprah Winfrey Show*. They articulate two powerful social sites and utopias of American culture: the family and the self, which are both severely strained and destructured under the pressures of individualization.

To a great extent, the spectacle of psychic pain represents a radical compression of the world: it is not only Lisbon and London that are telescoped together, but also a single individual biography with the world. From the exposure of stained dresses to difficult childhood via lack of self-esteem, talk shows have radically transformed the meaning of intimacy by compressing and telescoping individual biography with the world. Through the show, viewers in India, England, Israel or the USA are made the daily witnesses of the murky secrets of individuals and families. What enables such compression is not cheap voyeurism but rather the process of 'standardization of biography'. Oprah Winfrey's cultural inventiveness lies in the fact that her show provides a format in which to tell, process and transform biographical discourse. One of her most creative moves consisted in packaging her *own* biography on her own show in a way that followed the format of the show and mirrored closely her guests' stories. For example, in one of her first shows on the agonies of being overweight, she discussed her own – then heavy – weight, referring abundantly to her ample body as the result of her anxieties and lack of self-esteem, itself the result of a dysfunctional childhood. In fact, the three or four milestones of Oprah's career were the revelations that she made about herself: her difficulties in dieting, her history of sexual abuse (again, on a show about sexual abuse), her abortion and her problems with self-esteem – all revelations that have had a significant impact on the popularity of her show. But what is even more interesting here is that after these revelations Oprah's life changed. She became ever more thin, successful and full of a newly found self-confidence – thus becoming her own ideal typical guest in that she showed repeatedly in her own body and psyche that television can and does change lives.

With a certain irony, Oprah Winfrey is the first to provide an example of the ways in which social experience and social relations are increasingly mediated by the nexus of media and expert knowledge, mostly psychological knowledge. In contradistinction to Hollywood stars, who are essentially visual icons, Oprah Winfrey is a biographical icon created, so to speak, by and for the television studio. She is known for the major episodes that structure her life – episodes that all involved the story of a failed self – and for how she has transformed such a failed self into a highly successful one, by using the combined powerful effects of her talk show and of therapeutic knowledge.

What has enabled Oprah to package her own and her guests' life stories is what I call a therapeutic narrative. For example, on 20 June 1990, ABC aired an Oprah special. Her biographer George Mair summarized this interview: 'This program focused on what Oprah felt was the cause of most of the problems of the world. Because of lack of self-esteem, Oprah believed people abused others who were weaker; wars were fought; crimes were committed ... Oprah wanted to explain how important self-esteem is to everyone's happiness' (Mair 1998: 204). A therapeutic narrative is a story about the self, which connects a present suffering to a past event – often called a trauma – or to the ordinary and repetitive relations one had with one's kin. The trauma might have been triggered by an external event, but its meaning is purely internal. Like all narratives, the therapeutic narrative is structured by the tension between a goal and the obstacles encountered on the way to that goal. In the therapeutic narrative, the goal is psychic well-being, while obstacles to that well-being constitute what narratologists call a complication – what gets the action going. Therapeutic narratives structure biographical discourse, by guiding the selection of the events that are significant to one's life ('My father did not show much interest in me'), the ways in which they create causal relations between past and present ('therefore I tend to choose emotionally unavailable men') and the goals to which one's life should aspire ('not to crave my father's attention', 'choose the right man').

It is easy to see how therapeutic biographies become centred on suffering: suffering is the complication in a broader narrative aiming at well-being. Selves that fail to accomplish the many tasks that are required to manage and orchestrate the complicated score of work and family in the late modern era are likely not only to experience real social suffering – loneliness, stress, depression, anxiety – but also to look for the early wounds that made them fail at these tasks. Because biography has become (to use the words of Ulrich Beck and Elisabeth Beck-Gernsheim [1995]) a self-made biography, a project to achieve reflexively, through a Sisyphean work of self-observation, self-analysis and self-understanding, therapeutic narratives become the mental, linguistic and emotional structures most likely to shape biographies – precisely because they make (or seem to make) the self the sole orchestrator and legislator of social biography. The point here is a double one. First, Oprah's own biography and the biographies of her seemingly endless pool of guests represent the main commodity she has produced and from which she has extracted a tremendous surplus value. Second, she has commodified biography by using a therapeutic format to rewrite her own and her guests' life stories.

Therapeutic narratives have a paradoxical property which is in a way a property of globalization at large: they constitute highly particularized and individualized identities, and yet they also standardize biography. Standardized therapeutic biography is thus at once individualized and rationalized. At the same time that Oprah has offered a wide variety of singular stories, telling singular forms of pain and staging individual voices, these particular stories have been processed within a standardized cultural form, which we may call, following an expression coined by John Tomlinson (1999), 'standardized intimacy'. The narrative of suffering is a standardized cultural form that decontextualizes the image of the storyteller through five cultural devices.

1. The first device concerns the visual technique of camera and studio style. The genre of the talk show decontextualizes its characters by presenting people and stories in the abstract and neutral context of the TV studio. Abundant close-ups and almost exclusive focus on the human face make the genre simultaneously intimate and highly decontextualized. As Daniel Keyes puts it, 'Producers attempt to stage and capture traces of live spectacle while erasing most signs of locality and temporality in order that the programs can be syndicated nationally if not internationally' (Keyes 1999: 2). The talk show takes place in a highly abstract space, devoid of any spatial or cultural marker. The abundant close-ups contribute to one of its most original features: that it combines highly particular and individualized stories by locating them in an abstract and 'decontextualized' context.

2. In Giddens' terms, we may say that on the talk shows, personal relationships and intimacy are 'lifted out' of their spatio-temporal contexts to be processed by a visual and cultural form that is 'abstract' in the sense given to that word by Marx or Simmel in reference to the circulation of money. In the same way that money converts a concrete value (for example, shoes are for walking) into an abstract one (these shoes cost $200 and are therefore equivalent to a plane ticket), the talk show converts the concrete and singular experience of a person into a decontextualized narrative of suffering, equivalent to other singular narratives. The victim of sexual abuse becomes equivalent to the victim of 'emotional abuse', who becomes herself equivalent to the victim of emotional neglect. Unlike the many commentators who have claimed that talk shows make the public sphere into an intimate space, I argue that it is exactly the other way around: the *Oprah Winfrey Show* makes intimacy highly decontextualized and abstract.

3. The temporality of the trauma narrative – which is the most outstanding cultural example of the therapeutic narrative – is 'structurally' standardized. Traumatic time characteristically 'freezes' the self into a singular point in time, the point at which trust in the world collapsed. Traumatic time 'stands still' in consciousness because it is cut off from the past as well from the present. Immobilized, it becomes a sort of inaugural moment in which a 'new' self

emerges, a self cut off from its history as well as from its projection in the future. This time thus congealed in turn makes all traumatic biographies look the same. Whether the trauma was provoked by sexual abuse, rape, betrayal, or an earthquake, the traumatized psyche revolves around a traumatic time that is homogeneous because it is atemporal. This atemporal time in turn generates a narrative of self that, although a 'memory narrative', is also an atemporal one.

4. The temporal abstraction of trauma narratives is heightened by the fact that they are by definition abstract narratives of self: they frame the self in standardized analytical and narrative categories such as 'lack of self-confidence', 'anxiety', 'obsession' and 'self-destructiveness'. Paradoxically, it is the cultural availability of such standard concepts that can generate a wide variety of personal stories. This variety of forms of suffering and stories of suffering derives precisely from a standardization of emotional life through models and norms of mental and psychological health.

5. The therapeutic narrative leans on a highly standardized conception of the individual institutionalized in modern polities through the modern legal and state apparatus. As John Meyer et al. (1997) have extensively and persuasively shown, models of the individual are based on scripts that are abstracted from institutions, such as the welfare state and the market, which in turn have rationalized the individual through such notions as 'rights', 'mental health' or 'self-interest'. The discourse of therapy has been institutionalized in most Western polities, and this discourse has in turn rationalized individuals' self-conceptions, as well as their biographical trajectory.

This rationalization is sustained, I believe, by the fact that psychology has been institutionalized in many – perhaps most – countries of the world through what John Meyer et al. (1997) call worldwide models constructed and pro-pagated globally – through university degrees, academic knowledge, global publishing and international professional associations. In an increasing number of countries models of selfhood that have a psychological inspiration are propagated globally through the state, the academia, global media and now the Internet. Psychological knowledge is institutionalized in social services provided by the welfare state; it caters to families and standardizes parent–child relation-ships and couples' relationships through similar therapeutic models of 'communication'. Finally, psychologists have also widely penetrated the corpora-tion, through their large presence in industrial relations (Baritz 1960; Illouz 1997).

The form of the therapeutic narrative exerts a structural constraint on the ways in which a life story is told: through the diffusion of therapeutic know-ledge through publishing, state services and clinical practice, people can use the therapeutic narrative as a standard narrative to explain their own and others' failings and misfortunes, as well as to guide themselves in the complexity of the contemporary social world. I suggest that the *Oprah Winfrey Show* is part and parcel of the process of standardization of biographical discourse through the worldwide diffusion of therapeutic knowledge.

At the same time that the *Oprah Winfrey Show* developed as an economic empire and as a tentacular media structure, it has concomitantly further segmented and individualized its biographical formula. In 1995, the scope and reach of the show dramatically expanded. Not only did Oprah Winfrey continue to assume her role of moral entrepreneur, psychotherapist and public confessor, but she also became a successful lobbyist in Congress; set up college programmes and fellowships for ethnic minority students; created the Book Club which, according to representatives of the book publishing industry, has given the most significant boost to their industry for several decades (for example, a single appearance of Toni Morrison on the *Oprah Winfrey Show* has generated three times as many sales of her books as the Nobel Prize); created a magazine for women; and, more interesting perhaps for this discussion, created a very active website.

Through the website, the *Oprah Winfrey Show* has become far more interactive (soliciting ever more viewers to tell their stories, which are then selected to appear on the talk show) as well as more segmented (compartmentalizing the talk show and the website according to different kinds of stories and different kinds of expert advice: the 'Angel Network', 'Heal your Spirit', and so on). The website not only enables the audience to continue discussion of topics raised during the show, and to discuss the stories and biographies offered by the books of the Book Club, but, perhaps more importantly, to discuss their own biographies, to continue the talk show after the talk show. The *Oprah Winfrey Show* no longer has just one site; it has become a striking illustration of Castells' claim that 'the unifying cultural power of mass television (from which only a tiny cultural elite had escaped in the past) is now replaced by a socially stratified differentiation, leading to the coexistence of customized mass media culture and an interactive electronic communication network of self selected communes' (Castells 1996: 371).

The point is that the *Oprah Winfrey Show* has become a tentacular media structure that reaches to the central institutions of late capitalism – TV, movies, the publishing industry, the Internet – but through the highly individualized and standardized cultural form of what I earlier called therapeutic biography. Precisely because therapeutic biographies are both standardized and individualized, they in turn can generate communities of suffering that are properly transnational. Let me give an example. In the 'Angel Network' on the Oprah website a woman who calls herself ladydi13 addresses, like many other users, one of Oprah's regular experts, Phil McGraw:

My birth father left when I was just five years old. He was an alcoholic and my mother had a violent marriage ... parts of which are burned in my brain ... The man she married turned out to be a pedophile and I was ripe for the picking when he adopted us four kids ... Being a child of alcoholics, it was not uncommon for me to choose one for a husband who looked like my father ... I was never able to have a good relationship with a man ... I still am not healed of all the trauma ... I can't afford Dr Phil's books or tapes but am going to crounge [sic] the libraries. God bless him and make more like him. We injured spirits need his kind of guidance. (29 December 1999)

This story is written as a standard therapeutic narrative: she chose a man like her father, the main axis of her biography is centred on psychic wounds and her suffering, the goal of her life towards inner healing. And this woman, like many others, generates around her further support and advice from other viewers – advice that is strikingly similar in content and structure to that provided by Dr McGraw. If we have all become sufferers we have also all become experts and one another's therapists, precisely because therapeutic language has standardized life trajectories that are at once more individualized and more rationalized. The talk show and the website provide a scripted language and structure through which suffering can be shared. And it can be shared because it is organized around what I call the transnational therapeutic and media-based biography of trauma, which bypasses differences of nationality and territorial boundaries. Sexual abuse, divorce, obesity or anorexia nervosa might be said to create new lines of demarcation inside countries and new lines of connection with others across traditional national and territorial divisions. Thus communities of suffering have become institutionalized, for example, in such transnational organizations as AA and Overeaters Anonymous, which have exported their techniques for the management of the self. Like the *Oprah Winfrey Show*, these organizations are based on the combined effects of suffering, biography and standardized management of the self through therapy. This is a form of organization of social pain that cuts through the kinds of sufferings mapped and covered by the state as well as by traditional NGOs.

These communities can be thought of in terms of what David Held has called 'communities of fate' (2000: 423), communities that crisscross traditional lines of political demarcation and bypass conventional lines of class, ethnic or national distinctions. Communities of suffering at once reach 'below' (they are biographical) and 'above' the nation state. Thus, even if the *Oprah Winfrey Show* clearly represents an American genre, the process I have just discussed has no origins, and is circular, in the sense that these narratives at one and the same time point to a process of infraglobalization – how we become globalized from 'within' – and to the ways in which narrative structures are circulated worldwide.

202

Conclusion: Suffering or the Royal Road to Cosmopolitan Solidarity?

Do such communities of suffering have anything of value to offer to a democratic project of globalization or to what Appadurai and others have dubbed 'globalization from below'? Can such communities of suffering open up the global imagination and, if so, to what?

To the extent that cosmopolitanism implies, as David Held suggests, access to diverse political communities, it requires that political agents 'reason from the point of view of others' (Held and McGrew 2000: 425). I believe that talk shows succeed remarkably well in fostering such multiple perspectives because they develop, perhaps more than any other cultural genre, biographical imagination, the capacity to imagine other lives and to understand their predicaments. In that respect, talk shows seem to increase and enable a kind of mediated connectivity (Tomlinson 1999).

Yet, even though the 'communities' created by these shows no doubt increase connectivity, I want to express a scepticism towards their ability to be a source of cosmopolitan consciousness. This scepticism does not have to do with the standard critique of commodification or with the fact that entertainment and pain inhabit the same memory space. Rather it hinges on a question that seems to me most acute in the context of a discussion on globalization: how much distance from or closeness to the suffering of another is needed for cosmopolitan solidarity?

In her book *On Revolution* (1963), Hannah Arendt has warned us against what she calls the politics of pity. She suggests that when approaching the oppressed and the exploited, we should not use what she calls the politics of pity, that is, a politics based on compassion for the suffering of another person. Her claim is that we should do it as equal partners in human dignity. Her call here is on justice rather than sympathy, on principle or 'virtues' rather than on emotion. Her critique is that compassion does not act on the basis of an egalitarian relation (that demands justice and solidarity), but is predicated on the intrinsic asymmetry between the sufferer and the one who gives pity, and that it distracts us from cultivating the virtues that lead to genuine solidarity. In another text, a famous lecture she gave on Lessing (Arendt 1968), Arendt makes a further point: she argues that compassion reduces distance between people. Compassion abolishes what Arendt views as vital to the political bond, namely what she calls 'in-between', that is, a distance within which discourse about the world can flow. Compassion, in Arendt's view, is not discursive – perhaps precisely because compassion is based on an immediate identification with the sufferer. This is even more true about the bearer of psychic pain: inasmuch as one is the only legislator of one's own trauma, inasmuch as, quite frequently, psychic pain is not observable and is not arguable, it is not something that invites discourse about the world.

Standardized biographies of suffering might provide a way to organize trans-national communities of suffering around trauma; I believe that they might be an example of Ulrich Beck's globalization from within, but I am not sure that they can produce what we conventionally call cosmopolitan solidarity. For such solidarity precisely requires a fine dynamic of recognition of sameness and difference, a distance across which to talk about the world – a distance lacking in communities in which the commonality of suffering is the main structuring principle.

Globalization is 'both the compression of the world and the intensification of the consciousness of the world as a whole' (Robertson 1992: 8) – a definition that aptly describes Voltaire's denunciation mentioned at the beginning of this chapter. Oprah Winfrey provides powerful techniques – both visual and linguistic – to compress the world, but she does this without promoting a consciousness of the world as such. Rather, her show seems to provide an example of cultural standardization and homogenization without an awareness of the world 'as a whole' (Ritzer 2000). Precisely because they suppress distance, these communities of viewers lack the moral force of Voltaire's point of view and make us unable to see the scandal of suffering, the simultaneity of suffering *and* happiness.

Moreover there is something intrinsically paradoxical in these communities, for the 'success' of their members would mean the disintegration of the community. Once they have provided support for the reflexive monitoring of one's biography, one can and in fact should stop being a member, thus condemning these virtual biographical communities to be stitched together by a narrative of suffering but not by a narrative of hope, which ought to be, as Rorty (1999) suggests, at the centre of any project of globalization from below. Finally, I believe that such communities of suffering lack the *glocal* (Robertson 1992) ethical force of Voltaire's cosmopolitanism because they lack a point of view from which they could see what Voltaire made us see, namely the scandal of the lack of moral coherence of the world as a whole.

References

Albrow, M. (1996), *The Global Age: State and Society Beyond Modernity*. Stanford, CA: Stanford University Press.

Appadurai, A. (1996), *Modernity at Large: Cultural Dimensions of Globalization*. Minneapolis: University of Minnesota Press.

Arendt, H. (1963), *On Revolution*. New York: Viking.

— (1968), *Men in Dark Times*. New York: Harcourt Brace & World.

Baczko, B. (1997), *Job, mon ami: promesses du bonheur et fatalité du mal*. Paris: Gallimard.

Baritz, L. (1960), *The Servants of Power: A History of Social Science in American Industry*. Middletown, CT: Wesleyan University Press.

Beck, U. (2000), *What is Globalization?* Cambridge: Polity Press.

Beck, U., and E. Beck-Gernsheim (1995), *The Normal Chaos of Love*. Cambridge: Polity Press.

Boltanski, L. (1999), *Distant Suffering: Morality, Media and Politics*. Cambridge: Cambridge University Press.

Castells, M. (1996), *The Rise of the Network Society*. Cambridge, MA: Blackwell.

Collins, P.H. (1990), *Black Feminist Thought: Knowledge, Consciousness, and the Politics of Empowerment*. Boston: Unwin Hyman.

Connell, R. (2000), 'Sociology and World Market Society', *Contemporary Sociology* 29(1): 291–96.

Decker, J.L. (1997), *Made in America: Self-styled Success from Horatio Alger to Oprah Winfrey*. Minneapolis: University of Minnesota Press.

Greene, B., and O. Winfrey (1996), *Make the Connection: Ten Steps to a Better Body – and a Better Life*. New York: Hyperion.

Hannerz, U. (1996), *Transnational Connections: Culture, People, Places*. London: Routledge.

Held, D., and A.G. McGrew (2000), *The Global Transformations Reader: An Introduction to the Globalization Debate*. Malden, MA: Polity Press.

Hughes, R. (1993), *Culture of Complaint: The Fraying of America*. New York: Oxford University Press.

Hutcheson, F. (1742), *An Essay on the Nature and Conduct of the Passions and Affections; with illustrations on the moral sense*. Gainesville, FL: Scholars' Facsimiles & Reprints.

Illouz, E. (1997), *Consuming the Romantic Utopia: Love and the Cultural Contradictions of Capitalism*. Berkeley: University of California Press.

Keyes, D. (1999), 'The Imaginary Community of the Live Studio Audience on Television', *Studies in Popular Culture* 21: 3.

Lowe, J. (1998/2001), *Oprah Winfrey Speaks: Insight from the World's Most Influential Voice*. New York: Wiley.

Mair, G. (1998), *Oprah Winfrey: The Real Story*. Secaucus, NJ: Carol Publications Group.

Meyer, J.W., John Boli, George M. Thomas and Francisco O. Ramirez (1997), 'World Society and the Nation-State', *American Journal of Sociology* 103: 144–81.

Neiman, S. (2002), *Evil in Modern Thought: An Alternative History of Philosophy*. Princeton, NJ: Princeton University Press.

Nussbaum, M. (1999), *Sex and Social Justice*. New York: Oxford University Press.

Richardson, S. (1821), *Pamela; ou, La vertu récompensée*. Paris: De l'Imprimerie de Plassan.

Ritzer, G. (2000), *The McDonaldization of Society (New Century Edition)*. Thousand Oaks, CA: Pine Forge Press.

Robertson, R. (1992), *Globalization: Social Theory and Global Culture*. London: Sage.

Rorty, R. (1999), 'Globalization, the Politics of Identity and Social Hope', in R. Rorty (ed.), *Philosophy and Social Hope*. London: Penguin: 229–42.

Smith, A. (1759), *The Theory of Moral Sentiment, or, An essay towards an analysis of the principles, by which men naturally judge concerning the conduct and character, first of their neighbours, and afterwards of themselves*. London: Printed for A. Millar; Edinburgh: A. Kincaid and J. Bell.

Tomlinson, J. (1999), *Globalization and Culture*. Chicago: University of Chicago Press.

Voltaire (1949), 'The Lisbon Earthquake', in B.R. Redman (ed.), *The Portable Voltaire*. New York: Viking Press.

Weber, M., H.H. Gerth and C.W. Mills (1946), *From Max Weber: Essays in Sociology*. New York: Oxford University Press.

CHAPTER 11

Global Media, Cultural Change and the Transformation of the Local: The Contribution of Cultural Studies to a Sociology of Hybrid Formations

Rainer Winter

To the memory of Karl Hornung (1903–1971)

The US-dominated mass culture is mainly viewed in a negative light. From time to time, it is even damned apocalyptically as one of the principal threats to modern society. Looking at it in this way, mass culture can cause conformity, passivity, political apathy, racism and violence. The globalization of products, coming primarily from the USA, is said to bring about the creation of a standardized and stereotyped culture by spreading the same ideas and myths across the world. This is emphasized by the process within the culture industry of focusing on American lifestyles, which are offered as a model for self-presentation to the entire world. Beyond this, it is said that the worldwide diffusion of mass culture is destroying the uniqueness of regional cultures. As far as Europe is concerned, according to Stefan Müller-Doohm in his overview of this pessimistic evaluation, this is destroying the broad base of the European culture of Enlightenment, whose place is being taken by the internationally standardized mass production of popular culture (Müller-Doohm 1993: 593ff).

New theoretical works and empirical investigations contradict this understanding of popular culture as mass culture, which was largely marked by a nostalgic understanding of the modern age. My thesis is that the current global media culture cannot be adequately understood within this negative framework. It loses sight of the dynamism, differentiation and pluralization of popular culture spread by the media as well as the practices and productivity of the consumers. Recent works emphasize that global culture is not simply a standardized culture across the world (cf. Featherstone 1995; Kellner 1995; Winter 1995; Tomlinson 1999; Lull 2001). They point out that consumption of media products often leads to the opposite of this standardization. In the following, I would like to show, using a cultural studies approach, how the reception and appropriation of global media products in various local contexts is shaped by difference, syncretism and hybridity.

Rambo and the Ideology of 'Global America'

When the globetrotter and writer Paul Theroux (1992) visited the Solomon Islands, he found that Rambo was a folk hero on one of the islands and that even isolated villagers used a generator to power a video recorder to show the films. Even in Burma and in many other parts of South and East Asia, Rambo has become a popular figure (cf. Iyer 1989). At first sight, these examples could be corroboration that the global cultural industry is homogenizing culture in the South. This suggests that if *Rambo* is an imperialistic text representing the values and ideologies of American capitalism, it leads, like Coca-Cola, Donald Duck or *Dallas*, to the American way of life becoming the standard throughout the world. Through the circulation and availability of media, local cultures will, according to this argument, be levelled by consumer products and advertising and consumers manipulated. In this interpretation, the globalization process leads by and large to a stereotyped, common world culture.

Strong objections have been raised in recent years to this theory of cultural imperialism. The main criticism is that the actual reception of a product has too quickly been judged by an analysis of its content alone. This means that there has been no investigation into how consumer goods and media are actually received and appropriated in everyday contexts (cf. Thompson 1990; Winter 1995). First, Rambo, a manly hero who defeats countless enemies and overcomes all sorts of dangers, is naturally a figure who is attractive in many cultures. However, are the interpretations in Burma, the Solomon Islands, Illinois or Munich really the same? In the framework of cultural studies, we learned from early on to investigate various local reception processes more thoroughly. The American anthropologist Eric Michaels (1991) stated that Rambo is very popular, even among tribal Aborigines in the deserts of Central Australia. They see him as a Third World hero, defeating the white officer class. This reflects their own negative experience of the 'whites' in Australia, in particular those in authority. Moreover, they suppose that Rambo holds tribal or kinship relations with the prisoners he frees in Vietnam. In contrast, in the USA (for example in the case of former president Ronald Reagan) Rambo was viewed as an individualistic lone soldier with nationalistic inclinations, fighting for what is right. The Aborigines, in their analysis of the media text, find interpretations that are appropriate to their own experience as subordinate population groups. For them, Rambo becomes a figure with whom to identify, a figure that asserts itself to represent them in ethnic conflicts.

In John Fiske's (1989) analysis, the Aboriginal versions resist by contradicting the hegemonic interpretations suggested in the text. The Aborigines' social standing in Australian society leads to a productive reinterpretation of Hollywood texts. In a certain way, they create their own opposition culture in their enthusiastic reception of Rambo. Hence, Michaels' and Fiske's descriptions should not be misunderstood as depicting the standard form of reception. Not every appropriation of global products in the South acts as resistance or opposition. These options are more suitably termed 'moments of freedom', as the anthropologist Johannes Fabian (1998) wrote in his examination of popular culture in Africa. Marginalized and suppressed groups can use cultural resources to create meaning, form identity and develop their own interpretations. In the following, I would like to broaden this perspective, looking at the example of the reception of American media products. I will discuss various culturally shaped forms of interpretation and consumption in which popular culture is expressed as difference, resistance and hybridity. Finally, I will show how these processes can be interpreted within the cultural studies framework.

Difference, Syncretism and Hybridity in Media Reception

Daniel Miller (1994) made an interesting study of the example of the reception of *The Young and the Restless* in Trinidad. In it, he shows how a media product disseminated worldwide is interpreted in the South. His analysis clearly indicates that this process is misunderstood if it is only viewed as the exporting and consumption of American culture. He is able to show how the soap opera is subjected to a localization process where it is integrated into local practices and interpretations, into 'the world of gossip, scandal and confusion that generates the constant narrative structure of community life ... the soap opera is not just Trinidadian, but, as in a popular local expression "True True Trini"' (Miller 1994: 253). The reception of *The Young and the Restless* is a community activity like telenovelas in Brazil or Portugal. The viewers create a relationship between the series and everyday life, for example, by talking about the programme, in particular gossiping about sexual relations and incidents in the series. The scandals find great resonance because in the popular culture of Trinidad there is the idea that 'truth' can be brought to light through scandalous exposure. Viewers are also interested in clothes and fashion in the series, and discuss this intensively. This provides a direction for their own self-presentation. Miller attributes this to the fact that public image is very important in Trinidad for the formation and preservation of personal identity. His study clearly shows, therefore, that it is not enough to analyse the formal characteristics of media texts. It is just as important to investigate the local reception processes, which cannot be predicted beforehand, and are contingently and contextually specific. A similar interpretation applies to *Dallas*.

For many critics, *Dallas* was a synonym for cultural imperialism in the 1980s (cf. Tomlinson 1991: 45ff.). While the Texan soap opera enjoyed worldwide popularity, many cultural critics responded with hostility to its success. The ostentatious presentation of riches and luxury, the expensive clothes and automobiles, the plush apartments and so forth, were interpreted as having strong ideological meaning. The critics did not, however, examine how the programme was actually received. In an early study of reception, Ien Ang (1985) was able to show that enjoying *Dallas* is a complex phenomenon which cannot be reduced to the ideological power of the scripts. She found that many of the female viewers she interviewed, among them one committed feminist, enjoyed the emotional realism seen primarily in the depiction of personal conflict. On the other hand, these viewers considered *Dallas* to be unrealistic in its representation of American society. Furthermore, Ang reached the conclusion that some of the female viewers even saw the series in the context of a tragic, melodramatic emotional structure which was not so much present in the script but rather in their own female experiences. The cultural ability to place oneself within a melodramatic fantasy is shaped particularly by women who, in the course of their lives, have had to interpret events and situations psychologically and to cope emotionally. According to Ang (1985), these fantasy strategies arise from a vague, unarticulated dissatisfaction with personal existence and are an attempt to give meaning to everyday life. The example shows that there is room to play with meaning and to enjoy popular entertainment products which viewers can actively use to express their own perspectives and to fulfil their needs.

Tamar Liebes and Elihu Katz came to similar conclusions in their study, *The Export of Meaning* (1993), in which they examined the reception of *Dallas* in a variety of national and ethnic contexts. They expressed initial scepticism about theorists of cultural imperialism who attempt to deduce the effects of television programmes based on content analysis. The purpose of their comprehensive study was an empirical examination of this theory from the position of the viewer. They began with the fact that watching television is not an isolated activity but that social interaction, such as conversations with others, is an essential part of the interpretation and assessment processes, especially when the television programme comes from another culture. The study is based on group discussions following a standardized set of guidelines which, alongside a questionnaire, were carried out after participants from a variety of ethnic backgrounds had each watched an episode of *Dallas*. The various groups were constructed in such a way that they all had a similar class background ('lower middle class with high school education or less'), but were all from different ethnic backgrounds. Each group itself, however, was 'ethnically homogeneous': 'Accordingly, we assembled small groups of family and friends, each group consisting of three married couples of like age, education, and ethnicity. Forty-four such groups were chosen from among Israeli Arabs, newly arrived Russian Jews, veteran Moroccan settlers, and members of kibbutzim (typically second-generation Israelis)' (Liebes and Katz 1993: 6).

The interpretations by these groups were compared with those of American viewers in Los Angeles and Japanese viewers who had been most critical in viewing *Dallas*. The complex conclusions of this study cannot be comprehensively presented here. Of particular interest in our context are the divergent interpretations, already evident in the discussion of the episode's content. These interpretations were governed by the viewers' cultural background. For instance, an Arab group arrived at the following 'misreading'. In one episode, Sue Ellen left her husband, J.R., with her baby and fled to the house of her former lover and his father. The Arab group convinced one another in their discussion that the correct interpretation was that she had left her husband to live in the house of *her own father*. Katz and Liebes showed that the ethnic groups criticized the values within the programme in terms of their own cultural background. The Arab groups rejected the Western decadence, which in their opinion was manifest in the series in broken family structures, sexual immorality and the display of riches and luxury. Some of the Russian groups even developed conspiracy theories, believing that the producers were intentionally depicting a distorted reality to influence the viewer. The Americans, the kibbutzniks and the Japanese were also partly critical, but more often of the programme's aesthetics and the producer's competence.

The results of Liebes' and Katz's study show that the reception and appropriation of global media products are an active social process. Even regular viewers have the ability to regard American media in a complex and productive way. Their cultural background is not simply suppressed, but rather is often the basis for critical analysis of *Dallas*. They do not let themselves be so easily and completely manipulated as many critics believe, suggesting that the theory of cultural imperialism is, in many ways, a polemical exaggeration. A cultural sociological analysis must not be satisfied with an analysis of media texts or the strategies of the entertainment industry, important as these are. The task is to show how people react within local contexts to the strategies of the culture industry. This is illustrated, for example, by the current debate over the marketing by the American firm Warner Brothers of the Harry Potter character created by Scottish author, J.K. Rowling. Warner Brothers is trying for commercial reasons to enforce a worldwide, standardized image of Harry, but its efforts are being undermined and obstructed by the tactics of fans who have made Harry Potter their own by means of lovingly created homepages, translations, parties and so forth.

The next example I would like to examine in more detail comes from the field of popular music. In the American ghettos, primarily the Bronx, hip hop arose in the 1970s and 1980s. This, like earlier forms of Afro-American music culture, expressed the experience of humiliating living conditions, oppression, racism and struggle. At the same time, hip hop was a synonym for productivity and creativity, emanating from poverty, deprivation and need (cf. Rose 1994). Twenty years on, however, hip hop has become a global product spread by the American culture industry. Does the globalization linked to this lead to a trivializing of hip hop? Does it, as a part of the media 'white noise', become an empty symbol which has lost its original significance and its strength as a collective form of self-expression by marginal groups? Or can the underlying characteristics – such as those of young people tackling social problems and their position in life – be expressed in form and practice if they are usurped by local contexts and loaded with meaning from them? I would now like to examine these questions in the light of ethnographic research I have carried out. To do this, I will first look at some characteristic features of hip hop.

The hip hop culture (consisting of a variety of forms of cultural expression such as rap music, breakdance, graffiti, the DJ club scene, b-boy and wild-style fashions) first found success as performance art at rap parties and on the club scene before becoming popularized by records, CDs, music videos, a regular programme on MTV and films such as *Wild Style*. At its core is rap, rhythmical speech set against a musical background, which, from a drumbeat to a collage of riffs, can consist of drum breaks and diverse songs. The background music is produced in discos or clubs by using turntables. DJs produce a soundtrack on record players by choosing and combining parts of previously recorded songs. This basic technique of appropriating music (or musical history) is essentially refined by two technical acts, namely scratching and punch phrasing, techniques by which sounds of various turntables are overlaid or mixed. As Richard Shusterman (1992) has shown, rap deconstructs the traditional idea of originality and uniqueness because of these self-reflexive processes of usurpation. In this popular art form, there is no longer anything original but only the usurpation of other usurpations. This is because every DJ borrows from other sources. Recycling of 'tradition' and rearrangement can lead to complete transformation. They can be viewed as 'tactics of the weak', as defined by Michel de Certeau (1984), and can undermine the division between the artist

211

and the audience, producing something personal from those resources provided by the culture industry.

The reworking of existing compositions is supplemented by rap lyrics, which are often critical, giving a voice to social reality and the problems of the ghetto inhabitants and of other fringe groups. Such issues include unemployment, prostitution, violence or drug addiction. Many rap songs stand out because of clever and witty colloquial expressions, including the use of mottoes and clichés, gaining new significance in the rap context because of multiple levels of meaning, making them complex, polysemous texts. They outline alternative interpretations of social events and offer counselling, giving moral accounts of sexuality, drugs or alienation. Studies to date show that rap music can take on an important function for cultural and social identity (cf. Dimitriadis 2001). Therefore, hip hop leads to the construction of Afro-American identity first at a local level in the ghetto, a process also shaped by rivalry. There is also national rivalry, for instance between Los Angeles and New York rappers. Due to media circulation and the marketing of resistance by the record industry (cf. Dyson 1996), these identity models become globally significant.

The results of my ethnographic investigation, carried out mainly in Aachen, Cologne and Trier, show that the majority of interviewed hip hoppers use this musical style to define their own personal identity and, hence, for individualization. Hip hop for them is primarily an arrangement of consumer merchandise, consisting of CDs, XXL clothing, baseball caps, trainers, chains, and so on. At the outset, the use of these has no subversive or resistance connotations, apart from their perceived role of dissociation from adult culture. Hip hop is instead used to create an identity because it differs from mainstream youth tastes. This is clearly revealed in the reception of music focusing on beat and groove. Lyrics are only of minor importance to this scene, rarely gaining great attention. It is not the content of rap music that is decisive but the sounds. Therefore, rap in English is often more popular than rap in German because it flows better. The different fans, mainly coming to the scene through friends, know a lot about the history of hip hop. Most of those performers I interviewed first listened to hip hop in the mid-1980s and have remained loyal ever since. Accounts of the history of the music are often used to reconstruct their own past and that of their circle of friends. Marco describes community experience generated by the hip hop feeling in the following way:

> Not feeling alone, living hip hop, celebrating hip hop with other hip hoppers, with other mates. You know, like at a jam together, even though you don't know each other, you feel like you're in the group somehow. You just feel like you belong. (Extract from interview)

The group experience is defined as having fun together. It creates affective conditions for like-minded aesthetic communities to construct and confirm their own identity. Moreover, some recipients become active themselves, as Andy did:

> Actually, at first this began with paint spraying and then somewhere I heard hip hop, like *Public Enemy* and stuff and there was already trouble brewing. I heard it again and again and thought it's boring spraying day after day and in the evening, you've to do something about that, yeah, I thought, bought a mixing table, two record players, yeah and then it really got started with hip hop, scratching and stuff. (Extract from interview)

My results led to the conclusion that appropriation takes place in three phases. First is the reception of consumer products disseminated by music and the purchase of global merchandise. Most hip hoppers remain at this stage. In the second phase, the creative practices of the Afro-Americans using records are taken over as models. These are transformed through personal performance as a DJ and then creatively developed further. Almost all those interviewed distanced themselves from the ghetto feeling of the music. The appropriation process gains a reflexive character in the third phase, through examination of one's own life and social problems and through personal rap lyrics. For instance, the lyrics of an Aachen rap group deal with racism and alcoholism whose spread among young people is attributed to their circumstances, unemployment and lack of hope. The rappers relate their normal, concrete life, their wishes, hopes, hurts and suffering in their songs. Through this, they voice their own views, analyse their reality and become, according to de Certeau (1984), 'poets of their own affairs'. Thus, these young people even prefer to rap in German because in their opinion this provides a more authentic account of their own everyday life with its predicaments large and small.

Thus, my ethnographic study of the scene shows that hip hop, using music, group rituals and performances by DJs and rap singers, creates a community, providing identity and social cohesion. However, in the case of those I interviewed, hip hop did not emerge from everyday practices as it did in the ghettos in the USA. Rather, it was initially received as a global consumer product, and its identity models were taken over. Only a fraction of the hip hoppers then try to use it as a cultural resource to voice their own experiences and their own views. The significance of hip hop, like other popular texts, alternates between commercial trivializing and creative reinterpretation. The global marketing of an American product is confronted with local forms of appropriation. On the one hand, hip hoppers use hip hop for individualization, and on the other hand, they use it to create a community and sensibility that approach hip hop's original meaning and purpose.

In this context, the reception of rap in Africa is also interesting. In the early 1990s, rap was fashionable and mostly restricted to the better-off young people who could afford the latest consumer products from the USA. Today, however, it is popular among young people from a variety of social backgrounds (Servant 2000). Musicians from different African countries combine rap with their local traditions, practices and various languages. In the crossover, new arrangements arise from traditional and electronic music. The success of African rap even led to a renaissance of African music. Dakar, the new world capital of rap, is said to have about 2,000 rap groups, who were inspired by the urban Afro-American culture and who have made rap their lifestyle. The lyrics of African artists depict the bitter reality of their world, including poverty, environmental destruction, ethnic conflicts, AIDS and so on. Thus their productive examination of rap lends a popular foundation to their social criticism.

In addition, the music ethnologist George Lipsitz concludes in his study, *Dangerous Crossroads* that '[hip hop] expresses a form of politics perfectly suited to the post-colonial era. It brings a community into being through performance, and it maps out real and imagined relations between people that speak to the realities of displacement, disillusion, and despair created by the austerity economy of post-industrial capitalism' (Lipsitz 1994: 36). Moreover, Lipsitz shows that there are still more 'tactics of the weak' in the realm of popular music. For example, ethnic minority immigrants in big cities negotiate their identity by making music, combining their own cultural experiences with forms of global mainstream culture, which they change into a cultural resource. The examples that he gives of these inter-ethnic musical re-creations are Puerto Rican boogaloo in New York, Algerian rai in Paris, Chicano punk in Los Angeles, Aboriginal rock in Australia and swamp pop in New Orleans and Houston. Lipsitz takes these examples to show how musicians from oppressed minorities express their ethnic differences by using, and at the same time enjoying, mainstream music. One of the tactics, in Michel de Certeau's (1984) terminology, is anti-essentialism. This is an attempt by individuals and groups to construct, in a limited time-frame, a united front to defend common interest, feelings and needs. This is done by repelling any heterogeneous features. This commonality is not voiced directly, but rather is disguised or uses another medium. For example, in the late 1980s Maoris in New Zealand began to identify with Afro-American popular culture. They usurped Afro-American styles of self-depiction and the slang associated with them. What a superficial examination criticized as the success of American cultural imperialism and the destruction of local traditions, the Maoris themselves believed was a veiled effort to voice their own marginalized and lost position in the homeland, using Afro-American elements.

For Lipsitz, this tactical anti-essentialism[1] is the key to understanding the various inter-ethnic music juxtapositions. He writes:

> The key to understanding each of these groups is to see how they can become 'more themselves' by appearing to be something other than themselves. Like many members of aggrieved populations around the world, these strategic [*tactical*] anti-essentialists have become experts in disguise because their survival has often depended on it. (Lipsitz 1994: 63)

However, this treatment of music is just one empirical example of a creative everyday practice under global conditions. Theatrical productions also gain central significance. These are important both for identity formation and for community constitution. Performance politics can be interpreted as an answer of 'the weak' to social tension and difficult circumstances. A new and important task for research is therefore to examine how new identities and unforeseen links and alliances are created in the use of global media products rather than searching for cultural origins or foundations. For example, this can be examined from the perspective of diaspora. Related examples show that hybrid cultural forms arise that can result in an alternative public sphere. Difference is expressed from a marginal position and must be constantly renegotiated. Paul Gilroy states that '[the] seemingly trivial forms of youth sub-culture point to the opening up of a self-consciously post-colonial space in which the affirmation of difference points forward to a more pluralistic conception of nationality and perhaps beyond that to its transcendence' (Gilroy 1993: 62).

The public sphere transfiguration caused by globalization and migration provides opportunities to form personal lifestyles and cultural identity. As Homi Bhabha (1994) shows, these processes break up unambiguous cultural identity, revealing discursive constructs, ambivalence and ambiguity. In the gaps newly formed by cultural displacement and social discrimination, tactics can be developed to form communities and identities. These are no longer based on essence but on ambivalence and hybridity. In this field of cultural liminality, residual and newly arisen practices, according to Raymond Williams (1980) are discovered and expressed. Stuart Hall also seeks a new definition of the concept of ethnicity. This is no longer associated with nation and 'race'. The fact that we all have ethnic roots and speak from an ethnic position must not repress the reality of other ethnic groups forced out, dispossessed or excluded from representation (Hall 1992). Instead, the new ethnic politics must begin from the point of difference. In the case of identity politics, this

---

1 Lipsitz uses the phrase 'strategic anti-essentialism', following a study by Gayatri Spivak (1993). However, after de Certeau and Fiske (1989), it seems to be more accurate to refer to 'tactical anti-essentialism'.

means that essential and universal structures of identity must be surrendered and replaced with the concrete, non-essential and non-universal experience of the weak (Anzaldúa 1988). Room for cultural exchange must be thought of as a process, as Trinh T. Minh-ha puts it (1991), in which difference and identity are continually redefined and expressed. The question arises as to what consequences the development of 'new' collective identities will have. Roland Robertson (1992) shows in his studies on globalization that this process began at the latest in the early fifteenth century and is closely linked to the modernization process. Over the last twenty years there have been many signs that a qualitative leap has occurred, developed through a coincidence of migration and the globalization of electronic media. The flow of images spread by the media and the flow of people occur simultaneously and produce a 'public sphere Diaspora' (Appadurai 1996), but one in which individuals partake of more than just the products of the American culture industry. Japanese in San Francisco borrow Japanese films in their quarter, an Afghan taxi-driver in Chicago listens to religious cassettes from his homeland, Punjabis in London or Turks in Germany watch videos from their countries (Gillespie 1993). In Nigeria, a real boom in local videos has occurred (Servant 2001). Since 1997, 1,080 video productions were approved by the Nigerian Censor Board. At least 300,000 copies might be made of a successful film. Nigerian videos are increasingly seen in other African countries and also in the USA. About three million people make up the Nigerian diaspora in the USA. In New Orleans, the American rapper Master P. produced his own videos based on the model of the Nigerian dream factory and these are very popular in the American ghettos.

In contrast to modernization theorists' accepted belief, religion is not disappearing in the globalization process, since it is not shaped in essence by Western cultural imperialism. The ethnologist Appadurai writes: 'There is growing evidence that the consumption of the mass media throughout the world often provokes resistance, irony, selectivity, and, in general, agency' (Appadurai 1996: 7). Moreover, the media create possible 'emotional communities' (Maffesoli 1988; Grossberg 1997), specialized cultures (Winter and Eckert 1990; Winter 1999) and affective demonstrations of solidarity:

> Collective experiences of the mass media, especially film and video, can create solidarities of worship and charisma, such as those that formed regionally around the Indian female deity Santoshi Ma in the seventies and eighties and transnationally around Ayatollah Khomeini in roughly the same period. Similar solidarities can form around sport and internationalism, as the transnational effects of the Olympics so clearly show. Tenements and buildings house video clubs in places like Kathmandu and Bombay. Fan clubs and

political followings emerge from small-town media cultures, as in South India. (Appadurai 1996: 8)

Individuals and groups relate global flows to their everyday practices in the field of the imagination. This deserves a central role alongside the affective dimension. Shared imaginations are the prerequisites of transnational, collective behaviour. At the same time, they depend on the dynamic of the prevailing context, whether it is one that leads to new religiousness, to power or to greater social justice. Appadurai's approach also provides the opportunity to heighten the problems of 'global America'. If we do not identify America with the physical territory of the USA but see it as a global imagery, we can understand that there can also be a desire for the 'American style' within the context of local opposition. The global media, with their images of consumer products and lifestyles, create an imaginary geography which makes being in America or becoming American an ideal and a utopia. Hollywood films, soaps and adverts for Coca-Cola, Nike or McDonald's promise cosmopolitan and global alternatives to the locally available identities. Therefore, the appropriation of media can lead to a reflexive expression of cultural difference which contrasts real opportunities with imaginary ones. In order adequately to understand globalization, it is important to investigate the local contexts of reception and appropriation of media products. For instance, Ien Ang has argued for a radical contextualism modulated by ethnographic research. Only in this way can the locally based practices bound by contexts be understood. These are the practices by which television and other media are used in everyday life: 'The understanding emerging from this kind of inquiry favours interpretative particularisation over explanatory generalisation, historical and local concreteness rather than formal abstraction, "thick" description of details rather than extensive but "thin" survey' (Ang 1996: 71).

In conclusion, I would like to summarize what these cultural studies perspectives mean for research into the globalization processes.

Incorporating Differences and Radical Vagueness into the Global Postmodern Era

The discussion up to this point has shown that the power of the global must not be exaggerated. Global media products are of course locally re-expressed. This leads to processes of de-territorialization, syncretization and hybridization (cf. Nederveen Pieterse 1995; Chambers and Curti 1996; Lull 2000). Symbols, signs and ideologies are singled out of their original contexts and gain a new meaning by mixing with other cultural elements as, along with Lipsitz (1994),

Rowe and Schelling (1991) show in their study of popular culture in Latin America. For example, rap in Latin America is linked by artists with salsa, reggae and pop. Symbolic forms and their meanings are therefore continually subject to change. Throughout the world, people create their own versions of geographically distant cultures, as Tony Mitchell (1996) also highlights. This shows that globalization always implies processes of re-territorialization. Through productive and creative use of global resources, culture continually reconstitutes itself.

Thus Stuart Hall (1991) is right to describe the present globalization as a structure that is simultaneously global and local. The global flows of signs, information and images do not produce a standardized culture. The new culture, which Hall calls the global postmodern era, does not speak a single language and is not shaped by one dominant ideology, but rather is determined by difference and plurality. This culture is already characteristically a hybrid culture.[2] Now this must not lead us to exaggerate the power of the local and so think that the South could win the battle against the global postmodern era coming from the North. Hall even voices the supposition that a new form of homogenization is emerging through global commercialization processes. These would no longer try to overcome differences but would rather try to demand and incorporate differences. Therefore, it is appropriate to show scepticism towards over-optimistic judgements. However, here Hall is thinking – like the imperialist theorists – from the global point of view. If we turn to the side of the locals, a somewhat different picture arises.

With this in mind, it is even possible to see in the USA a rearticulation of the local in the form of a 'new regionalism' which is directed against cultural homogenization (Ostwald 2001). For example, the Lobsterburger in Maine, the vegetarian Californiaburger in San Francisco or the highly spiced Cajun catfish in New Orleans are set against the burgers of McDonald's. The trend towards cultural standardization is also undermined by the fact that the acceptance and popularity of TV shows and musical trends are regionally different.[3] The American entertainment industry must now be aware of regional peculiarities and local preferences in its own country. Given the waning – due to the progress of the globalization process – of state borders and national identity,

---

2 Admittedly, Renato Rosaldo (1989) has shown that every culture actually has a hybrid character. In his interpretation, hybridity reveals the fundamental experiences of earliest cultural encounters and contacts. James Clifford also argues along these lines in *Routes* (1997).

3 Ostwald (2001: 33) writes: 'The media market researcher, Sandra Kess, says that programmes with a certain degree of "edginess", such as detective series *Law and Order*, which was enormously popular in the North, would be rejected in the "Bible Belt", the religious South of the USA. In contrast, the series *Touched by an Angel* has its highest viewing ratings in the country in this area'. Even MTV reveals the trend towards local musical tastes.

consumers (re-)discover regional differences in history, customs, practices and identity.

The global postmodern era is marked by erosion and the diminishing significance of the nation state. Because this is not determined by cultural coherence, the global village is shaped by a 'realm of uncertainty', as confirmed by Ien Ang (1994). Thus, diverging subversive or reflexive uses and interpretations that are developed in cultural contexts are, on one hand, an expression of consumer freedom, and – even if it is restricted – an expression of individuality (Beck 1992; Beck and Beck-Gernsheim 1995). On the other hand, however, as the examples discussed above show, these uses and interpretations can be seen as contingent creations of meaning in a dynamic, conflict-rich and contradictory everyday life which is shaped by globalization. The global flows of signs, images and information (Lash and Urry 1994; Lash 2002) face a heterogeneous, unruly and uncontrollable game of difference within social practice. What meaning they acquire, how the global is expressed with the local, cannot be determined in the beginning. There are no firm structures of meanings; moreover, symbolic messages are arranged polysemously. In everyday communication processes which vary locally, culture is continually reconstituted in more or less hybrid forms. A cultural sociological analysis aimed at understanding the logic of power relationships in the global postmodern era must face this radical uncertainty of communication; it must acknowledge the breadth of opportunity, in particular in the South, without losing sight of the fact that there are dominant forces that are interested in profit, commercialization and incorporation.

As this analysis has shown, sociology can learn from cultural studies, if it considers this as a necessary completion. For many years, mainstream sociology did not satisfactorily consider the cultural dimension of social phenomena (cf. Long 1997). Therefore, a constructive dialogue with cultural studies should begin (cf. Kellner 1997; Denzin 1999; Winter 2001), one that questions the very foundations of the discipline and is willing to recognize its shortcomings. A revitalization of sociology can succeed if both culture and the processes of globalization are moved to the centre of analysis.

Translated by Andrew Terrington

References

Ang, Ien (1985), *Watching Dallas*. London: Methuen.
— (1994), 'In the Realm of Uncertainty: The Global Village and Capitalist Postmodernity', in D. Crowley and D. Mitchell (eds), *Communication Theory Today*. Oxford: Polity Press: 193–213.
— (1996), 'Ethnography and Radical Contextualism in Audience Studies', in Ien Ang

(ed.), *Living Room Wars: Rethinking Media Audiences for a Postmodern World.* London and New York: Routledge: 66–81.

Anzaldúa, Gloria (1988), *Borderlands/La Frontera: The New Mestiza.* San Francisco: Spinsters/Aunt Lute Press.

Appadurai, Arjun (1996), *Modernity at Large. Cultural Dimensions of Globalization.* Minneapolis: University of Minnesota Press.

Beck, Ulrich (1992), *Risk Society.* London: Sage.

Beck, Ulrich, and Elisabeth Beck-Gernsheim (1995), *The Normal Chaos of Love.* Cambridge: Polity Press.

Bhabha, Homi K. (1994), *The Location of Culture.* London and New York: Routledge.

Certeau, Michel de (1984), *The Practice of Everyday Life.* Berkeley: University of California Press.

Chambers, Iain, and Linda Curti (eds) (1996), *The Post-Colonial Question: Common Skies, Divided Horizons.* London and New York: Routledge.

Clifford, James (1997), *Routes: Travel and Translation in the Late Twentieth Century.* Cambridge, MA: Harvard University Press.

Denzin, Norman K. (1999), 'From American Sociology to Cultural Studies', *European Journal of Cultural Studies* 2(1): 117–36.

Dimitriadis, Greg (2001), *Performing Identity/Performing Culture: Hip Hop as Text, Pedagogy, and Lived Practice.* New York: Peter Lang.

Dyson, Michael E. (1996), *Between God and Gangsta Rap: Bearing Witness to Black Culture.* New York: Oxford University Press.

Fabian, Johannes (1998), *Moments of Freedom: Anthropology and Popular Culture.* Charlottesville: University Press of Virginia.

Featherstone, Mike (1995), *Undoing Culture. Globalization, Postmodernism and Identity.* London: Sage.

Fiske, John (1989), *Understanding Popular Culture.* London: Unwin Hyman.

Gillespie, Marie (1993), 'The Mahabharata: From Sanskrit to Sacred Soap. A Case Study of the Reception of Two Contemporary Televisual Versions', in David Buckingham (ed.), *Reading Audiences: Young People and the Media.* Manchester: Manchester University Press: 48–73.

Gilroy, Paul (1993), *Small Acts: Thoughts on the Politics of Black Cultures.* London: Serpent's Tail.

Grossberg, Lawrence (1997), *Dancing in Spite of Myself.* Durham, NC: Duke University Press.

Hall, Stuart (1991), 'The Local and the Global: Globalization and Ethnicity / Old and New Identities, Old and New Ethnicities', in Anthony D. King (ed.), *Culture, Globalization and the World System.* London: Macmillan: 19–39, 41–68.

— (1992), 'New Ethnicities', in James Donald and Ali Rattansi (eds), *Race, Culture and Difference.* Milton Keynes: Polity Press/The Open University: 252–60.

Iyer, Pico (1989), *Video Nights in Kathmandu.* London: Black Swan.

Kellner, Douglas (1995), *Media Culture.* London and New York: Routledge.

— (1997), 'Social Theory and Cultural Studies', in Dawid Owen (ed.), *Sociology After Postmodernism.* London: Sage: 138–57.

Lash, Scott (2002), *Critique of Information.* London: Sage.

Lash, Scott, and John Urry (1994), *Economies of Signs and Space.* London: Sage.

Liebes, Tamar, and Elihu Katz (1993), *The Export of Meaning: Cross-Cultural Readings of Dallas.* Oxford: Polity Press (2nd edn).

Lipsitz, George (1994), *Dangerous Crossroads: Popular Music, Postmodernism and the Poetics of Place.* London and New York: Routledge.

Long, Elisabeth (ed.) (1997), *From Sociology to Cultural Studies: New Perspectives.* Oxford: Blackwell.

Lull, James (2000), *Media, Communication and Culture: A Global Approach*. New York: Columbia University Press (2nd edn).

Lull, James (ed.) (2001), *Culture in the Communication Age*. London and New York: Routledge.

Maffesoli, Michel (1988), *Le Temps des Tribus*. Paris: Meridiens Klincksieck.

Michaels, Eric (1991), 'Aboriginal Content: Who's Got It – Who Needs It?', *Visual Anthropology* 4: 277–300.

Miller, Daniel (1994), *Modernity: An Ethnographic Approach. Dualism and Mass Consumption in Trinidad*. Oxford and New York: Berg.

Minh-ha, Trinh T. (1991), *When the Moon Waxes Red: Representation, Gender and Cultural Politics*. New York: Routledge.

Mitchell, Tony (1996), *Popular Music and Local Identity: Rock, Pop and Rap in Europe and Oceania*. London: Leicester University Press.

Müller-Doohm, Stefan (1993), 'Einführung in Eurovisionen – Wandlungstendenzen im europäischen Medienalltag', in B. Schäfers (ed.), *Lebensverhältnisse und soziale Konflikte im neuen Europa: Verhandlungen des 26. Deutschen Soziologentages in Düsseldorf 1992*. Frankfurt and New York: Campus: 587–95.

Nederveen Pieterse, Jan (1995), 'Globalization as Hybridization', in Mike Featherstone, Scott Lash and Roland Robertson (eds), *Global Modernities*. London: Sage: 45–68.

Ostwald, Sabine (2001), 'Schöne kleine Welt', *Neue Zürcher Zeitung (International Edition)* (27 February): 33.

Robertson, Roland (1992), *Globalization: Social Theory and Global Culture*. London: Sage.

Rosaldo, Renato (1989), *Culture and Truth: The Remaking of Social Analysis*. Boston: Beacon Press.

Rose, Tricia (1994), *Black Noise: Rap Music and Black Culture in Contemporary America*. Hanover and London: Wesleyan University Press.

Rowe, William, and Vivienne Schelling (1991), *Memory and Modernity: Popular Culture in Latin America*. London and New York: Verso.

Servant, Jean-Claude (2000), 'Rap – der Sound der Straße', *Le monde diplomatique* (German edn), 12/2000: 17.

— (2001), 'Video-Boom in Nigeria', *Le monde diplomatique* (German edn), 2/2001: 20.

Shusterman, Richard (1992), *Pragmatist Aesthetics*. Oxford: Basil Blackwell.

Spivak, Gayatri C. (1993), *Outside in the Teaching Machine*. New York and London: Routledge.

Theroux, Paul (1992), *The Happy Isles of Oceania: Paddling the Pacific*. New York: Putnam.

Thompson, John B. (1990), *Ideology and Modern Culture*. Cambridge: Polity Press.

Tomlinson, John (1991), *Cultural Imperialism*. London: Pinter Publishers.

— (1999), *Globalization and Culture*. Cambridge: Polity Press.

Williams, Raymond (1980), *Problems in Materialism and Culture*. London and New York: Routledge.

Winter, Rainer (1995), *Der produktive Zuschauer: Medienaneignung als kultureller und ästhetischer Prozeß*. Munich and Cologne: Herbert von Halem.

— (1999), 'The Search for Lost Fear: The Social World of the Horror Fan in Terms of Symbolic Interactionism and Cultural Studies', in Norman K. Denzin (ed.), *Cultural Studies: A Research Annual*, No. 4. Greenwich: JAI Press: 277–98.

— (2001), *Die Kunst des Eigensinns: Cultural Studies als Kritik der Macht*. Weilerswist: Velbrück Wissenschaft.

Winter, Rainer, and Roland Eckert (1990), *Mediengeschichte und kulturelle Differenzierung: Zur Entstehung und Funktion von Wahlnachbarschaften*. Opladen: Leske und Budrich.

221

CHAPTER 12

'Rockization': Diversity within Similarity in World Popular Music

Motti Regev

This chapter argues that a large part of the popular music produced and consumed in the world today is made under the influence and inspiration of Anglo-American pop/rock – or, to be more precise, it is based on the adoption and implementation of what I call the *rock aesthetic*. Popular music thus epitomizes the new forms of cultural diversity associated with the globalization of culture – diversities based on cores of shared practices and technologies, and on logics of eclecticism and hybridity. The chapter traces the cultural logic of the process that made the rock aesthetic the core practice of popular music in the world, provides some examples and discusses their implications. I turn first to a brief theoretical contextualization.

The globalization of culture, as process and condition, is associated with the intensification, in the final decades of the twentieth century, of the centuries-old phenomenon of inter-cultural flow of meanings and materials. It is most strongly linked to the worldwide dissemination of commodities and meanings associated with the international culture industry (films, television series, popular music and the hardware gadgets for consuming these art forms), all types of industrialized food, fashion garments, cosmetics, cars, buildings and furniture, glossy magazines, and the advertisements for all these commodities. The emergence of a world culture is also associated with 'domains of rationalized social life' (Meyer et al. 1997), such as business, public administration, law, medicine and science. The permeation of nation states by some or all of these components has sometimes been interpreted by stressing its homogenizing effects. Concepts such as 'Americanization', 'McDonaldization' (Ritzer 1993) and 'cultural imperialism' (Mattelart 1979) imply that, in many aspects of life and culture, people and societies around the globe are becoming 'the same', with most elements of 'sameness' being either 'American' and 'Western' or filtered throughout the prism of these two cultural formations. Other inter-pretations tend to stress the changing nature of cultural diversity resulting from the globalization of culture. Concepts such as 'mediascapes' and 'ideoscapes' (Appadurai 1990), 'cultural complexity' (Hannerz 1992), 'glocalization' (Robertson 1995) and 'cosmopolitanism' (Beck 2000) have been employed to demonstrate that the world flow of cultural materials is multi-directional, not only from the West to the rest of the world; and that the same cultural materials are used and decoded differently across and within countries. That is, they are localized or 'nationalized' by typical uses, interpretations and practices of hybridity.

The two approaches are not necessarily contradictory. As Meyer (2000) has indicated, the globalization of culture is a process in which collective actors, who tend to be increasingly similar in their structure and use of rationalized instrumental culture, are at the same time engaged in praising their tradition, and the production of their uniqueness (see Regev 2000), by using expressive culture. This is most obvious in the case of nation states:

> Standardized actorhood arises around the principle of actor unique identity. Thus, with globalization, actors systematically generate and expand their own self-conscious, unique bases. But they do this within global models of effective instrumental action. Robertson (1992) calls this Tocquevillian phenomenon 'glocalization'. Nations celebrate their unique heritages while moving into standardized models ... Uniqueness and identity are thus most legitimately focused on matters of expressive culture: variations in language, dress, food, traditions, landscapes, familial styles and so on ... (Meyer 2000: 245)

World or global culture is apparently developing through diversity within sameness. This logic works not only for the relationship between instrumental and expressive culture, but also within the realm of art and expressive culture itself. It works in the relationship between form and technology on the one hand, and content and meaning on the other. Cultural diversity, variations in content and meaning of expressive culture all involve the use of cultural and art forms. The globalization of culture renders all mechanically and electronically reproduced art forms available for use practically everywhere. The same art and cultural forms thus become the tools with which diversity and uniqueness are produced by different collective actors – nations or others. Films and novels, for example, have been adopted as contemporary forms of expression all over the world. Undoubtedly 'Western' in their origin as art forms, and therefore initially alien to many national, local and ethnic cultures, they have been localized in order to create unique national and local styles and genres –

not to mention individual works – of film and literature. Japanese films and French films all bear marks of Hollywood styles and genres, and in turn have influenced Hollywood films. Crucially, they have all become components of a global film art world.

Consequently, within the process of globalization, the circuits of production, dissemination, consumption and interpretation for each art and cultural form become networks, in the sense discussed by Castells (2000), or Bourdieuian fields. Hence, one way of better understanding the logic of the globalization of culture is through the study of particular cultural networks or art fields. The transformation, transmutation and permutation of art and cultural forms is an expressive tool used for the maintenance and invigoration of contemporary cultural uniqueness, yet at the same time it preserves the works, genres and styles of these forms, as well as their producers and audiences, interconnected and interrelated as components of social networks of information, and as actors in social spaces of power, hierarchy and prestige. Such studies might reveal the ways in which the globalization of culture takes shape in specific cultural realms, and not necessarily in nation states as whole entities.

Popular music is a good case here. It has already been demonstrated that, institutionally, popular music is a network of production and consumption (Wallis and Malm 1984; Robinson et al. 1991; Burnett 1996). In addition, several studies have discussed the problematics of stylistic diversity versus sameness (Mitchell 1996; Taylor 1997), as well as the discourse of the slippery concept of 'world music' as an all-encompassing term (Frith 2000). In what follows, I would like to add a dimension to this body of work, by focusing on the rock aesthetic as an essential element in the complex of diversity and sameness in contemporary world popular music.

The Rock Aesthetic

Let me start by defining what I mean by the term 'the rock aesthetic'. The rock aesthetic is a set of constantly changing practices and stylistic imperatives for making popular music, based on the use of electric and electronic sound textures, amplification, sophisticated studio craftsmanship, and 'untrained' and spontaneous techniques of vocal delivery. Central to the rock aesthetic is also an eclectic logic that encourages the application of these means to any musical style. In addition, the rock aesthetic tends to emphasize the authorship of performers. Let me stress that this definition includes within the rock aesthetic the styles of popular music largely based on sampling and electronics that emerged in the final decades of the twentieth century (hip hop, house, techno and so forth).

I term this set of music-making practices 'the rock aesthetic' because the socio-cultural context known as 'rock' was the locus in which these components were widely legitimized as creative and artistic means for making contemporary popular music. Their legitimization took place through the canonization of the so-called 'classic' Anglo-American rock albums and artists of the 1960s and 1970s, and their heirs. The canonization of rock artists and works has established the status of rock musicians as individuals whose work explores and expands the means of expression and the creative use of the set of components I call here the rock aesthetic. Much of this exploration was driven by an eclectic logic that applied electrification and amplification to various styles of black music, country music, traditional popular song, folk music, jazz, some elements of 'art' (i.e. classical) music, and to any combination of these styles or genres. Canonization was possible because of the connection between rock music and ideologies of rebellion and subversiveness (among other reasons). This connection ascribed 'serious' political, social and cultural meanings to rock music, beyond the traditional entertainment function typically attributed to popular music. Rock music came to be closely associated with the 'empowerment' of everyday lives of youth (Grossberg 1984), with implied 'resistance' to the dominant culture, and with active subcultural rebellion against hegemony (Hebdige 1979; Frith 1981; Wicke 1990).

The artistic and cultural status of rock pushed other actors in contemporary popular music to adopt the stylistic and sonic innovations explored by rock musicians and turn them into the conventional way of making music. In other words, the canonization of rock triggered the emergence of (in Bourdieu's terminology) an artistic field of popular music structured around a hierarchy of prestige (Regev 1994). In this field, the dominant positions are occupied by the already canonized 'avant-garde' of earlier periods and by the upcoming styles and musicians hailed as the new 'avant-garde' by power-holding critics and reviewers in the field (good examples of this continuous canonization can be found in Christgau 1981; 1990; 2000; and Larkin 1999). The rest of the field more or less follows the innovations and explorations of the avant-garde 'classic rock', the music made by the most highly valued rock artists of the 1960s and 1970s, functioned for the field of popular music just as the art cinema of the same period functioned for the field of film. It provided the works and the creative ideologies around which critics, reviewers and scholars could construct the analyses and interpretations of this music as an artistic achievement. The rock aesthetic was thus institutionalized as the taken-for-granted set of sensibilities, skills, dispositions and knowledge – in short, as the dominant habitus – for making contemporary popular music.

This logic was not confined to the original Anglo-American context of rock music. Rock music, as creative practice and as ideology, was successfully exported to many parts of the world. During the 1970s and 1980s, it was gradually adopted and embraced by musicians and audiences all over the world. The successful exportation of rock was greatly facilitated by the subversive meanings attributed to the music. Rock music was not necessarily perceived as another cultural form embodying blatant cultural imperialism. The rock aesthetic was accepted by musicians and audiences around the world as a way – as *the* way for some of them – to make local music that expressed rebellion against conservative traditional cultures and authoritarian regimes. Local hybrids of rock music often came to be perceived as authentic expressions of a modern and contemporary spirit within local or national cultures. The Eastern European bloc and the then Soviet Union were the most salient examples (Cushman 1995; Ramet 1994), although Argentina during the late 1970s provided another good example (Vila 1987).

Paradoxically enough, at least initially, an Anglo-American cultural form, associated with multinational media and culture industries, was absorbed into local cultures as a tool for expressing local cultural uniqueness. In addition, the hierarchization process repeated itself in other countries. The initial ideologically and artistically motivated adoption of the rock aesthetic had the effect of legitimizing it within local and national cultures. Soon enough, due to its artistic prestige, the rock aesthetic became the dominant mode for making popular music of any type.

Consequently, in the last quarter of the twentieth century, the rock aesthetic gradually became the conventional artistic context within which popular music is produced almost everywhere. That is, the use of electric and electronic instruments, and studio techniques that emphasize the clean amplitude of sound and accuracy in the putting together of sound fragments, not to mention techniques such as sonic collage and 'cut and paste', came to be perceived by musicians as legitimate practices for the creation of popular music. We should note that the star system, and in particular the construction of images that focus on certain gender and sexual characteristics of musicians, became a major conventional element in the packaging of music and in its marketing. The same holds for managerial practices in the music industry.

The Rock Aesthetic in the World

The extensive use of elements of the rock aesthetic in the production of popular music does not mean that all popular music in the world has become 'rock music'. Many of the styles that incorporate elements of the rock aesthetic within their creative practices are not conventionally counted as 'rock' – either by their own practitioners, or by rock aficionados. In this category fall for instance some sub-styles of Indian film music, especially the so-called 're-mixes'; some of the output of Brazilian musicians such as Caetano Veloso, associated with the *tropicalia* movement; and some of the Latin American styles grouped together under the general term of 'salsa'. In the latter there is occasionally even a hostility towards 'rock' in its conventional meaning as mostly electric guitar music (Roman-Velasquez 1995). The most notable 'non-rock' contexts of popular music that are nevertheless inspired and influenced by the rock aesthetic are those exemplified by the work of mainstream European pop musicians such as Italian singer Eros Ramazzotti, who come very close to the sonic idiom known as 'soft rock'. The hard-to-define and widespread musical idiom of the late twentieth century, which goes under such names as 'soft rock', 'middle-of-the-road', 'easy listening' or simply 'pop', is one of the best examples of the influence of the rock aesthetic. Ranging from the showy pop of Russian female star Alla Pugachova to that of Malaysian star Sheila Majid, these audio-visual commodities – although almost never called 'rock' – are deeply indebted to the rock aesthetic in their use of electric and electronic instrumentation, and some of the visual images employed for the marketing of stars.

One major emblematic case of this type of rock-inspired popular music is the Chinese musical framework known as Cantopop. Cantopop describes a contemporary category of popular music made in Hong Kong since the 1970s. Not really a musical style, but rather a cultural context of production and consumption of popular music, the one major element that defines Cantopop, according to Witzleben (1999), is the use of the Cantonese language (although many performers produce recordings in Mandarin, Japanese and English as well). The most important feature that makes Cantopop a striking example of world popular music is its vast popularity in mainland China, Japan, Singapore and in Chinese diaspora communities everywhere. Cantopop performers such as Anita Mui Yim-Fong, Faye Wong, Jacky Cheung Hok-Yau and Leon Lai Ming sell huge amounts of albums and concert tickets across South-East Asia and elsewhere. Soft electric guitars, gentle synthesizers, occasional full orchestration, romantic lyrics, good-looking performers who are not the authors, and, most importantly, clear and pleasant vocal delivery, are major elements of the core musical idiom of Cantopop that account for its perception – by Western ears – as 'soft rock' or 'easy listening'. Still, Witzleben (1999) argues that, given the political and cultural relationship between Hong Kong and mainland China, Cantopop should be understood, as its audiences perceive it, as a local authentic expression of identity and even opposition. Man (1997), analysing the music itself, insists that 'there are indications that hybridization processes were at work in Cantopop in the 1970s and that further analysis may reveal other ways in which Anglo-American and Chinese musical elements were re-deployed in the production of indigenous popular music in Hong Kong' (Man 1997: 54).

The point in discussing 'non-rock' styles is to stress that the use of aesthetic elements from rock gives a certain common denominator to all these different styles, rendering them familiar to alien ears. Thus, through exposure to local rock-inspired popular music, the attentive or the casual listener acquires an acquaintance with the sonic textures produced by electric and electronic instruments and the production values of the recording studio. Consequently, when people hear popular music from ethnic, regional or national cultures other than their own, which contains elements of the rock aesthetic, the sonic experience spontaneously has a certain familiarity. Even if we don't know the language, the melodic structure or the rhythmic patterns, we very often do know the types of sounds that are being used to convey these elements. In other words, the pervasiveness of the rock aesthetic has greatly reduced the sense of total strangeness, of 'otherworldliness', that radiated in the past from music from unfamiliar cultures. This feeling hardly exists any more. If this is true of genres that do not conventionally fall within the category of 'rock music', it is all the more so with music styles that fit squarely within the conventional notion of 'rock'.

On Ethnic Rock (or World Beat)

Styles or genres that are conventionally perceived as 'rock' by the musicians and audiences associated with them, as well as by the cosmopolitan community of rock cognoscenti, can be divided roughly into two categories. The first consists of styles highly imitative of Anglo-American pop/rock styles, sung in local languages. This includes Metal and Extreme Metal rock bands in many countries (Harris 2000), as well as hip hop and reggae styles (Mitchell 1996), female or male vocal groups modelled after the recent trends in mainstream pop, and local variants of electro-dance trends such as house and techno.

I believe, however, that the most culturally interesting genres are those that hybridize rock elements with local traditions, producing the category typically known as ethno-rock or world beat. This is the cultural context in which musicians and audiences in many countries embrace rock music as a tool for expressing their critique of and revolt against local conservative and traditional cultures, and against authoritarian regimes, yet with a commitment to indigenous styles and idioms (Regev 1997). They also adopt the rock aesthetic as the creative context for exploration of new patterns of music-making and innovation. Expanding the sonic vocabulary of traditional instruments through electrification and amplification, using electric guitars for playing music inspired by indigenous folk songs and hybridizing elements of local music heritage with rock styles are some of the creative practices legitimized by the rock aesthetic. The ethnic rock context is most clearly the one in which cultural diversity is consciously nurtured on a cultural platform of the rock aesthetic.

The list of styles, genres and musicians here is long and diverse. It covers styles and musicians such as Thomas Mapfumo from Zimbabwe, the Zaire/Congolese band Zaiko Langa Langa, Chinese rockers Cui Jian and Xu Wei, the Australian Aboriginal band Yothu Yindi, the early work of Yugoslav musician Goran Bregovic and his band Bijelo Dugme, the Thai *pleng phua chiwit* ('songs for life') movement, the musicians working within the Algerian genre of *rai* and its other North African derivatives, the vibrant scene of *Rock en Español* that flourishes from Mexico to Argentina and Chile, and the work of Hubert von Goisern und den Alpinkatzen, the Austrian band most associated with the term *Alpenrock*. Also worth citing in this context is the work of early British folk rock bands and musicians, especially that of Richard Thompson, as the initial point of departure for the practice of merging rock and ethnic styles. Not surprisingly, however, music governed by the same cultural logic is called 'folk rock' in the UK and Western Europe, and 'ethnic rock' when it is made in other countries. From its early start in the 1970s the logic of ethnic rock has grown to become a major creative practice for musicians in many countries, and it is still expanding. Even popular music in India that has been relatively resistant to the rock aesthetic has recently adopted it:

> Till but a few yawns ago, there were three distinct genres in music. They were the classical, the western pop and the filmi. And the three never quite mingled. You had to be the old nawabi kind to be a classical music buff. If you were young and trendy you went for pop. And well, to like Hindi film music you had to be desi and not quite hip. Today this caste hierarchy is crumbling. A new breed of singers with diverse singing styles is invading the not-so-nascent Indipop industry creating a whole new 'sound' which is in turn altering Hindi film music radically. This historical inevitability has engendered a new genre of mixed-breed music ... As Ash Chandler [one of the successful musicians of this trend] says, 'I used to listen to Deep Purple and Beatles as a child. Naturally that music had to influence my songs.' (*India Today*, 7 August 2000)

One recurrent element in the artistic ideology of musicians working within the wide context of ethnic rock or world beat styles is their insistence on perceiving themselves as rock musicians, and not necessarily as folk curiosities for Western ears. Counting rock music and the rock aesthetic as a major source of influence and inspiration, and as a social reference point, serves their self-perception as cosmopolitans. Adoption of the rock aesthetic is believed to be an act of joining modernity, of becoming an equal participant at the creative frontier of the art of popular music.

Take, for example, Angelique Kidjo, from Benin, who says that she grew up listening to James Brown, Santana and the sounds of her country's drums. The *Toronto Sun* (2 August 1996) describes her 1996 album *Fifa* as 'a heady brew of thick funk, pop, and indigenous rhythms from Benin'. Kidjo, in an interview, insists on her identity as a rock artist: 'I'm not going to play traditional drums and dress like bush people. I'm not going to show my ass for any white man. I don't ask Americans to play country music. They feel an African has to only do African music. They can't tell me what to do.' And in another interview she says:

> People will come to me and ask, 'Do you think that what you are doing is African?' But they have no idea of what Africa is, and they have no idea of what my background is. Most of the time African artists always have to explain why they are doing the music they are doing, but they never ask an Anglo-Saxon artist, or a French artist to explain what they are doing or why they are doing it. (*The Peak* [student newspaper, Simon Fraser University, Burnaby, British Columbia], 6 September 1996)

Taylor, writing on Kidjo and Senegalese musician Youssou N'Dour, adds that these two (like many other musicians)

> view Western demands for authenticity as concomitant with demands that they and their countries remain premodern, or modern, while the rest of the globe moves further toward a postindustrial, late capitalist, postmodern culture. N'Dour and Kidjo are concerned in becoming global citizens and do this by showing that their countries and their continent are neither backward nor premodern, that they can make cultural forms as (post)modern as the West's. (Taylor 1997: 143)

Nevertheless, despite the salience of rock elements in the various genres of world beat and the acknowledged Anglo-American influences, the music is also portrayed as authentic and indigenous. Attribution of 'local authenticity' to the music serves a double purpose. It places the music and musicians within the realm of individual creativity and authorship, so important to the artistic ideology of the rock aesthetic; and it places the music within the 'production of uniqueness' project of their collective identities, thus defending it from accusations of imitation. This is, for example, an appraisal of the song 'I Have Nothing' ('Yi Wu Suo You') by Cui Jian, the prominent Chinese rock musician, published in China's *People's Daily*:

What the song exposes, is the feeling of a whole generation: their sadness, their perplexity ... The song's use of the deep, desolate tone of the folk music of the Northwestern plateau, and its coarse rhythms are well suited for this purpose ... 'I Have Nothing' can also be called the seminal work of Chinese rock. It fuses European and American rock with traditional Chinese music, creating a rock music with a strong Chinese flavor. (quoted in Jones 1992: 134)

Contextualizing the song within the *xi-bei-feng* ('northwest wind') style, which is characterized as directly linked to Northwestern Chinese traditional folk music and as an 'integration of elements of Chinese style and that of Western rock music', musicologist Mao-Chun Liang says that the song is 'one of the most successful results of such integration, of rock music and Chinese music' (Liang 1997).

In some of the cases where ethnic rock musicians have been active for a long period, their prestige as exponents of local authenticity and cultural unique-ness has been canonized in a way similar to that of art or folk/traditional musicians. That is, ethno-rock musicians come to symbolize a contemporary sense of local or national uniqueness, defying any view of them as 'American-ized' or globally homogenized. Moreover, in the cases of Russian (in fact ex-Soviet) rock musicians (see Cushman 1995) and Argentinean rock, the local musicians are perceived as guardians of the original subversive spirit of rock, which has been lost or 'sold out' in Anglo-American rock.

One such example is provided by Argentinean musician Leon Gieco. Gieco's first album appeared in 1973. In the 14 albums that followed during the next quarter of a century he shifted constantly between acoustic folk and electric guitar rock, often combining the two. He became one of the pivotal figures of the *rock nacional* movement that expressed widespread criticism of the military regime of the late 1970s in Argentina. His name and music became widely known throughout Latin America when singer Mercedes Sosa recorded his anthem-like, anti-war song 'Solo le pido a Dios' ('I only ask God', originally on Gieco's fourth album, 1978). The following is an excerpt from a concert review that succinctly describes his stature:

Talking about him as a popular musician is not enough. It is also not possible to define him as a chronicler of our times ... Leon Gieco is, from his music, a defender of our collective memory ... Leon Gieco is a rocker and, as such, he imprints his songs with all that has been lost by this move-ment when it was incorporated by the market. That is: a way of looking at and reading the world without ever conforming ... The auditorium at Mar del Plata is full. It's more; there are many people that, having no seats, watch the show on their feet, leaning against the wall. Whole families, young couples and rockers lost in time are united in a popular fiesta like no other. (Daniel Amiano, *La Nacion*, 24 January 1997; author's translation)

I think it is obvious at this point that rockization does not amount to the homogenization of music of the world feared by so many commentators. The styles and genres grouped together under the category of world beat demonstrate that the pervasiveness of the rock aesthetic does not imply homogeneity. This is primarily because of the eclectic logic that lies at the core of the rock aesthetic. This logic of eclecticism encourages constant and continuous exploration of new sonic textures and of new patterns of hybridization. What we get therefore is a different, perhaps new kind of cultural diversity and musical variance, one that has more common ground to it, yet is far from homogeneous. Production and consumption of local styles of rock produce a sort of dual identity, one that is local and cosmopolitan at the same time. One feels connected to a vibrant transnational artistic field, yet at the same time feels connected to his or her own culture.

One way of portraying the rockization of popular music of the world is to interpret it as the emergence of an international field of popular music for which the rock aesthetic serves as a doxa. In other words, rockization implies the convergence of disparate social spaces for making music into one social space, spread across the globe. It means that the changing frontiers of sonic and stylistic innovations in rock have become the 'avant-garde' for popular music worldwide. In fact, ever since the global success of reggae in the 1970s, ethno-rock or world beat itself is perceived by many leading popular music commentators as one of the 'avant-garde' positions of the field of popular music; that is, as one of the loci in which sonic and stylistic innovation and exploration take place, in order to be adopted later by other positions in the field.

Obviously, local and traditional music were never 'authentic' in the way that people may want at times to believe. Ethnomusicologists have demonstrated time and again that folk styles of different countries and regions grew out of hybridization and merging of musical components borrowed from various sources. In this regard, rockization of popular music of the world continues a long history of hybridity and merging that has always existed in folk and popular musics. The major difference is that with the rock aesthetic a common platform is gradually being constructed, one that interconnects musical styles and idioms of the world into one web, governed by one cultural logic, by one habitus.

References

Appadurai, Arjun (1990), 'Disjuncture and Difference in the Global Cultural Economy', *Public Culture* 2: 1–24.

Beck, Ulrich (2000), 'The Cosmopolitan Perspective: Sociology of the Second Age of Modernity', *The British Journal of Sociology* 51: 79–106.

Burnett, Robert (1996), *The Global Jukebox*. London: Routledge.

Castells, Manuel (2000), *The Rise of the Network Society*. Oxford: Blackwell.

Christgau, Robert (1981), *Rock Albums of the Seventies: A Critical Guide*. New York: De Capo.

— (1990), *Christgau's Record Guide: The 80s*. New York: Pantheon Books.

— (2000), *Christgau's Consumer Guide: Albums of the 90s*. New York: St Martin's Press.

Cushman, Thomas (1995), *Notes from the Underground: Rock Music Counterculture in Russia*. Albany, NY: State University of New York Press.

Frith, Simon (1981), *Sound Effects*. New York: Pantheon.

— (2000), 'The Discourse of World Music', in Georgina Born and David Hesmond-halgh (eds), *Western Music and Its Others*. Berkeley: University of California Press: 305–22.

Grossberg, Lawrence (1984), 'Another Boring Day in Paradise: Rock and Roll and the Empowerment of Everyday Life', *Popular Music* 4: 225–58.

Hannerz, Ulf (1992), *Cultural Complexity*. New York: Columbia University Press.

Harris, Keith (2000), 'Roots? The Relationship between the Global and the Local within the Extreme Metal Scene', *Popular Music* 19: 13–30.

Hebdige, Dick (1979), *Subculture: The Meaning of Style*. London: Methuen.

Jones, Andrew F. (1992), *Like a Knife: Ideology and Genre in Contemporary Chinese Popular Music*. Ithaca, NY: East Asia Program, Cornell University.

Larkin, Colin (1999), *Virgin All-Time Top 1000 Albums*. London: Virgin Books.

Liang, Mao-Chun (1997), '"*Xi-bei-feng*" (Northwestern Wind): A Special Historical Period in the Stylistic Development of Chinese Popular Music', in Tarja Hauta-mäki and Helmi Järviluoma (eds), *Music on Show: Issues of Performance*. Tampere: University of Tampere: 203–04.

Man, Ivy Oi-Kuen (1997), 'Cantonese Popular Song: Hybridization of the East and West in the 1970s Hong Kong', in Tôru Mitsui (ed.), *Popular Music: Intercultural Interpretations*. Kanazawa, Japan: Kanazawa University: 51–55.

Mattelart, Armand (1979), *Multi-National Corporations and the Control of Culture: The Ideological Apparatus of Imperialism*. Brighton: Harvester Press.

Meyer, John (2000), 'Globalization: Sources and Effects on National States and Societies', *International Sociology* 15: 233–48.

Meyer, John W., John Boli, George M. Thomas and Francisco O. Ramirez (1997), 'World Society and the Nation-state', *American Journal of Sociology* 103: 144–81.

Mitchell, Tony (1996), *Popular Music and Local Identity*. London: Leicester University Press.

Ramet, Sabrina Petra (ed.) (1994), *Rocking the State: Rock and Politics in Eastern Europe and Russia*. Boulder, CO: Westview.

Regev, Motti (1994), 'Producing Artistic Value: The Case of Rock', *The Sociological Quarterly* 35: 85–102.

— (1997), 'Rock Aesthetics and Musics of the World', *Theory, Culture and Society* 14: 125–42.

— (2000), 'To Have a Culture of Our Own: On Israeliness and its Variants', *Ethnic and Racial Studies* 23: 223–47.

Ritzer, George (1993), *The McDonaldization of Society*. Thousand Oaks, CA: Pine Forge Press.

Robertson, Roland (1992), *Globalization: Social Theory and Global Culture*. London: Sage.

— (1995), 'Glocalization: Time–Space and Homogeneity–Heterogeneity', in Mike Featherstone et al. (eds), *Global Modernities*. London: Sage: 23–44.

Robinson, Deanna, Elizabeth B. Buck and Marlene Cuthbert (1991), *Music at the Margins*. Newbury Park, CA: Sage.

Roman-Velasquez, Patria (1995), 'Discotheques in Puerto Rico: Salsa vs. Rock', in Will Straw et al. (eds), *Popular Music, Style and Identity*. Montreal: The Centre for Research on Canadian Cultural Industries and Institutions: 285–91.

Taylor, Timothy (1997), *Global Pop: World Music, World Markets*. New York: Routledge.

Vila, Pablo (1987), 'Rock Nacional and Dictatorship in Argentina', *Popular Music* 6: 129–48.

Wallis, Roger, and Krister Malm (1984), *Big Sounds from Small Peoples*. New York: Pendragon.

Wicke, Peter (1990), *Rock Music: Culture, Aesthetics and Sociology*. Cambridge: Cambridge University Press.

Witzleben, J. Lawrence (1999), 'Cantopop and Mandapop in Pre-Post-Colonial Hong Kong', *Popular Music* 18: 241–58.

CHAPTER 13

The Internet: An Instrument of Americanization?

Rob Kroes

Once a year the Netherlands celebrates the Week of the Book. Every year an author is commissioned to write a book, usually a novelette or short story, as a gift to everyone buying books during the week. So far, for obvious reasons, the authors have been Dutch. In 2000, however, the theme for the week was 'Writing between Cultures', and the author invited was an avatar of inter-cultural writing, Salman Rushdie. The book he wrote was translated and came out under the Dutch title *Woede* (Fury). It is the story of a man haunted by his private version of the Greek Furies of old, cut adrift from his past, his friends, his wife and son, and ending up in self-imposed exile in New York. There, in an attempt to restore his creative powers, he invents an imaginary world, called *Galileo-1*, peopled by human beings and their cyborg replicas, who in a complex saga of war and ultimate victory replay the primal sagas as every culture in the world knows them. With the help of an odd assortment of computer whizz-kids, the narrative is turned into a cyberspace story, accessible through a website. It becomes an instant, worldwide hit. Immediately, the characters break out of their fictional cages and begin to people the streets of the world. Messages come from all over the world about gigantic representations of the story's heroes scaling the walls of high-rise buildings. They turn up at celebrity events, sing the national anthem at baseball games, publish cookbooks and are invited to be on the David Letterman show. As the book's protagonist, Malik Solanka muses, in an ironic aside:

Everywhere in the world ... people were obsessed by the theme of 'success in America.' In India people took exaggerated pride in the achievements of fellow-Indians, living in the US, in areas such as music, the publishing world ... Silicon Valley and Hollywood. The British hysteria was, if anything, even greater. British journalist finds job in the US! Unbelievable! British actor plays supporting role in American movie! Wow, what a superstar! British comedian in drag wins two Emmy's! Fantastic, we always knew that British travesty was the best! Success in America was the only true sign of a person's mettle. (Rushdie 2001: 220; my translation)

Now it has happened to him. With all the hype and attendant merchandising the saga of Galileo-1 sets new records. Only this time the global mania is not triggered by film or television, but by a website.

Rushdie's story provides us with a highly topical illustration of, and ironic comment on, the theme of this chapter. It positions the USA as the centre of global mass culture, and as the focus of a worldwide quest for success and celebrity. The culture of consumption and entertainment emanating from this hub may have characteristically American features, in its unabashed commercialism and marketing prowess, yet anyone from anywhere in the world may creatively contribute to it. America in this view is a hungry omnivore, indiscriminately devouring what reaches it from foreign shores, digesting it, and regurgitating it in an Americanized version, ready for global consumption. The story also shows us America in its mastery of the media of mass communication, such as film, television, and more recently the World Wide Web. Suggestive as the latter name may be of global reach and equal access, silent as it may be on the issues of cultural agency or cultural hegemony, the web of all current communication tools is arguably the most American. Does that mean that it is therefore necessarily an instrument for the further Americanization of an emerging global culture? This question I propose to explore in the following.

From one perspective, the Internet can be seen as the new Supermall for those shopping around for communities of like-minded spirits, allowing them to break out of available frameworks for affiliation in their real-life settings, especially when these are felt as imposed from outside and stifling. In this view the Internet is the new global site for the construction of imagined communities that are literally virtual, coming to life only on people's computer screens. Yet, from a different perspective, rather than liberating in the sense of offering endless variety for the construction of new forms of cyberspace affiliation, the Internet may be only the latest medium for the global transmission of a culture crucially cast in an American mould. Rather than being a vehicle for a multiplication of people's affiliations, it may narrow their options, subjecting them to an Americanization by stealth. My central question, then, will be that of how American the Internet is in the way it may affect its users.

It is still too early to give a definitive answer. The Internet as it is developing

236

now is too recent, and the impact on its users keeps changing as it spreads around the world. My exploration therefore is of the Internet's potential, its promise and possible threats, as seen by its community of users. I shall look at the Internet's potential in terms of the dreams that it holds out for Americans and non-Americans alike. They are all dreams of perfect information as these have informed classic views of *Homo politicus* and *Homo economicus*, if not of *Homo universalis*, of the fully informed citizen, consumer, and cultured human being. In relation to the latter, I focus on the dream of the Internet as potentially restoring the full body of human knowledge – the dream of perfect intertextuality, or in other words the dream of the lost library. First, let me explore the way in which the Internet may affect our political and economic dreams, while keeping in mind the possible American slant that these dreams may receive from the Internet.

Dreams of Democracy

Given its auspices and early history, the Internet may appear as a paradox, if not an oxymoron. It originated as a Cold War instrument, a military ploy to prevent the opposition from wiping out the command and communication structure of the US government in one devastating blow. It did this – and here is the paradox – by an act of pre-emption. Rather than allowing the enemy to destroy its vital centre, Pentagon planners chose to take away the centre themselves, opting for a Hydra-like, many-centred web of communication. The evolving network technology of interlinked computers allowed them to do this. The Arpanet, as the early, and secret, military version was called, shared many of the same crucial features with the later public version that came to be known as the Internet. It was a decentred, if not entirely centreless, system – a web that would simply re-route communication flows if parts of it had been damaged. The paradox, as I pointed out, is in the act of government decentring itself, creating a structure that was in essence anarchic, doing away with structures of hierarchy, of super- and subordination, potentially making for an equivalence of senders and receivers and for an equality of flows of information. This potentiality of the system came fully into its own once the net was opened up, to universities first, to the general public later.[1]

Once emancipated from its military/strategic rationale, the Internet became the chosen terrain for an academic community of mostly young intellectuals, who infused the system with an ideology of late 1960s libertarianism. In spite of the more recent growth of the Internet, driven by commercial motives, the

---

1 I am aware that I emphasize one particular reading of the origins of the Internet. There are rival views. For a good discussion of these alternative readings, see Rosenzweig 1998.

early view of the Internet as a realm of liberty and equality, and anti-authoritarianism, if not anti-government feelings, is still with us today. A blatant instance of this libertarianism turning to anti-government subversion is the work of the so-called hackers, cracking the codes that protect secret government data banks: they turn the net against government itself. It is an extreme case, yet illustrative of a more general underlying attitude shared by a population of Internet users. Jointly they have given a peculiarly American flavour to the Internet, a cultural imprint redolent with the long-standing rhetoric of American republicanism. They conceive of the Internet – and of the World Wide Web – not as a virtual community but rather as a virtuous community.

Admittedly, this idealistic view of the Internet community represents a dream rather than a reality. For one thing, many are the users of Internet facilities who participate for reasons totally unrelated to, if not actually at odds with, the republican impetus. But more importantly, if the dream of republicanism assumes a community encompassing all of humanity, as the very concept of a World Wide Web would seem to suggest, it is a far cry from reality. In fact, on a worldwide scale, users of the Internet constitute a small and privileged group. As such, they are representative more generally of the way in which the fruits of Western civilization are divided up among the world population. Undeniably, though, as access to the Internet gradually extends to formerly excluded groups, it may well give them a taste of civic participation in a virtual community that in their own life situations had always been withheld from them. I heard, in a variety of settings that brought together young academics from Second and Third World countries, ample testimony to the liberating effect of Internet access – for example, on young women scholars in Islamic countries, or young academics in stifling bureaucratic and hierarchical university structures in parts of the former Soviet Union.

As the catchment area of the web extends to become more representative of humanity across the world, it is one of the central forces of a process commonly referred to as globalization. From this perspective the question then arises – as it does in other discussions of globalization – whether it is also a force of the Americanization of the world. In other words, to what extent can we see the web as a carrier of cultural values and a mental habitus that are recognizably American?

How American is the Internet?

There are various ways of tackling this question. One pragmatic way is to look at the differential density in the use made of the Internet. In a graphical representation of the density of traffic along the channels of communication provided by the Internet, the USA clearly appears as the pre-eminent nodal point, with minor nodes showing up elsewhere in the network. They are interconnected, in the sense that traffic does flow along the lines connecting these nodes, but with nothing like the density that characterizes the nodal points. This is to say that the actual use of the Internet for interpersonal communication still tends to centre on national societies as our present-day world knows them. Americans tend to communicate via the Internet among themselves more than with the outside world, and the same pattern seems to hold for national societies elsewhere. It may actually be the case that among these other societies the access to the Internet per capita – let us call it the degree of 'wiredness' – may be higher than in the United States. Finland, for example, is 'wired' to a higher degree than the United States, yet in terms of the absolute density of traffic along the Internet it constitutes only a minor node compared with the United States. Thus, our imaginary exercise in graphical representation highlights a position that America holds in many other ways as well, and which we might appropriately call its imperial position. In this, as in many other respects, America constitutes a centre in structures of communication that span the world, relegating other participants to a relatively peripheral place. It is a sender more than a receiver, in much the same way that Rome constituted the centre of its imperial order.[2]

From this perspective, then, the Internet is still very much a tool of communication that Americans avail themselves of more than any other nation in the world. They were the first to use it and they still contribute the bulk of communication flowing along the net. Given their originating role and the American auspices under which much current communication along the net proceeds, does this mean that Americans have also been able to set a tone characteristic of conversations via the net? In other words, have they been able to leave a cultural imprint on the use that others, outside America, make of the net? This question suggests a second way of exploring the Americanness of the Internet.

As regards the tone and mode of messages spread via the net, I would like to suggest two features that might be seen as signs of an American imprint. One is the increased informalization of communication; the other is what we may call the greater democratization or de-hierarchization of communication that the

2 A recent book-length study of telecommunications and the Internet confirms the picture as briefly sketched here. The study, *TeleGeography 1999*, was written by the Washington-based research firm TeleGeography Inc. and was produced as an analysis of today's communication landscape for companies in the industry. For a summary of its main findings, see Shannon 1999: 7. As John Carr, in an interesting article on these issues, points out, 'In the Internet's own organization, and in the values and assumptions which underpin it, one thing stands out: the net is American ... more than half of internet users today are in the US' (Carr 1999).

net appears to bring. A comparison with two older forms of communication helps to highlight what I have in mind: the art of letter writing, and the telephone conversation. Clearly, in terms of forms of address and linguistic mode, letter writing is far more stylized and formal than the average communication via the net. The latter often reflects the informality of speech more than the formal code of written letters. It is in that sense closer to the directness of spoken telephone conversations. On the other hand, precisely because of its directness, if not its character of a social intrusion, people may be hesitant to use the telephone in situations of social inequality, such as structured hierarchical settings. As recent research has shown (van den Hooff 1997), in such situations people may be less hesitant to avail themselves of email. Recipients of their messages will read them and respond at a time of their own choosing. In this sense email communication makes for a lowering of social thresholds and an easier exchange across hierarchical boundaries. Thus, email messages find themselves between the older modes of communication provided by the written letter or the telephone. They resemble the latter in their greater informality of tone and style, while they are more like the former as a means of communication across hierarchical lines, only faster and therefore more efficient.

If informalization and democratization of communication do indeed characterize email exchanges, can we then decide to see them as having arisen under American auspices? Couldn't we argue, in a McLuhanesque way, that the medium is the message, or in other words that the nature of the medium makes for its own social and cultural impact, irrespective of who first set the tone? As in so many other instances of modernization, it is probably impossible to disentangle the two alternative explanations. We can only guess at what the typical mode of email exchanges would have been had the idea and its implementation come from France or Japan rather than the United States. Yet, as the history of many modern inventions (such as the motor car, the camera or the cinema) illustrates, America tended to diverge systematically from European countries in the way it always aimed at making these novelties available and accessible to the many rather than the few. It went for user-friendliness, mass marketing and mass advertising, whereas in Europe these inventions were made to function in ways that would confirm rather than upset established social hierarchies. Many were the anguished observers from Europe who noticed the slackening of social restraints in the ways that Americans used their motor cars, or flocked to watch the latest movies. More often than not they felt they were observing the ominous contours of Europe's future, and in many cases they were right. The joys of mass consumption would indeed come to Europe later, eroding the initial use of technical inventions for buttressing the symbolic capital of social elites. It was never solely a matter of Europe catching up with America in a parallel development towards becoming a consumption society. More often than not, before the average citizen in Europe could afford the luxuries of mass consumption, they had already acquired a taste for it, and for its democratic joys, under the impact of views of the good life reaching them from America, through film, through photographs, through journalistic reports, and through letters from friends and relatives who had migrated there. If this was the case for inventions that were introduced more or less at the same time on both sides of the Atlantic, how much more strongly, then, would it seem to apply to a novel means of communication such as the Internet, invented by Americans, imbued with their spirit of egalitarianism, and reaching others with its American imprint firmly established?

But surely the other reading – of the medium being the message – cannot be entirely discarded. A mode of communication does in certain ways set the form and tone of its own use. A telephone conversation will never end with the words 'Sincerely yours', nor will letters as a rule open with a phrase such as 'Hello, this is so-and-so writing'. It may well be, then, that a logic inherent to the medium has made for the greater informality and equality of exchange of email communication. If this is true, email in its own right, then, will serve as a force of informalization and democratization in the world. As Sellar and Yeatman (1930) might have put it, this is of course A Good Thing. But if email can affect the quality of communication in positive ways, does it also have less positive consequences?

One worrisome consequence in this respect is the transient, ephemeral quality of email communication. Unless properly stored, electronically, or in the old-fashioned way as a print-out on paper, email messages leave no trace. Here again, they are like telephone conversations. From a historian's perspective, this cannot but affect our sense of history as well as our capacity to reconstruct the past. Of course, traditional archives can be shredded, or Oval Room conversations can be taped, as active manipulations by the parties involved, often in attempts to control the way they will go down in history. But as active interventions they do not logically follow from the inherent nature of the medium of communication. This is different in the case of email or telephone exchanges. The medium does in these cases affect the historical status of the message.

In terms of our discussion, there is an irony here. Yes, the medium may inherently and independently determine the transience of the messages exchanged. But the massive way in which American society has embraced this particular means of communication, with all its implied amnesia, may in the eyes of outsiders seem to confirm what older forms of cultural critique of America had argued all along: that American culture is essentially ahistorical, lacking a sense of the present as adding to the store of history. Again, this leads us to the question of how American the Internet is. A recurrent theme in European critical observations of American culture is its lack of a sense of history, and its blithe orientation towards the present and the future. The Internet, carrying everything before it in its advent as the preferred tool of communication among Americans, might well have struck such earlier observers as 'typically American'.

There is one more consequence, logically following from the inherent nature of Internet exchanges, that might seem to confirm negative views of American culture. It appears as the negative side of the democracy of exchange that the Internet provides. From this perspective there is an equivalence of all messages, regardless of their truth content. There are no gatekeepers in the way that more responsible older forms of news dissemination, such as the press, know them. Anything goes, anyone can join. Truth now would seem to find its confirmation in the very repetition of messages more than in the traditional tests of checking sources, comparing views and versions, and the like. Thus, communities of like-minded users of the Internet arise, sharing a consensus view of reality that borders on a conspiracy view. On a surprising scale, for instance, Black Americans have come to believe in a conspiracy view of the AIDS epidemic as the result of a white racist ploy. Similarly, individuals, using their renown, can lend their alleged authority to the wildest rumours, seemingly confirming as truth their quasi-authoritative reading of certain events. Thus, Pierre Salinger made the news with his wild assertions on the Internet that a missile shot down a TWA civilian aircraft off the coast of Long Island in July 1996. Another infamous example is the *Drudge Report*, an electronic newspaper disseminating a wild hodge-podge of selections from established newspapers, mixed in with rumour and gossip. As its editor, Matt Drudge, himself defends his editorial policy, gossip and rumour are simply information that has not yet been substantiated. Yet another, and to some more worrisome, trend is the emergence of chat groups and websites specializing in hate speech and right-wing bigotry.

These are only a few examples of a certain view of the Internet that sees every user as a journalist, entitled to the free dissemination of his or her views on an equal basis with all other users. This has all the trappings of democracy gone haywire, and seems only the latest confirmation of de Tocqueville's more sombre views of the evil potential of a society geared to egalitarian principles. Yet, as more optimistic observers would hold, such societies have within themselves sufficient vitality and a variety of means of redress to stand up to such excesses. Older and more respectable voices of public opinion such as the printed press analyse and warn against such trends.[3] On the net, for every chat

---

3 The *New York Times*, for example, in an editorial piece, 'WWW.Internet.anarchy', denounced Drudge's journalistic style (quoted in *Le Monde, Sélection Hebdomadaire*, 2547, 30 August 1997).

group or website propounding a particular view, there are rival sites offering counter-views. Similarly, established legal institutions offer recourse to offended parties. For instance, in the autumn of 1997, Drudge was taken to court for slandering the former journalist and Clinton adviser, Sidney Blumenthal, whom he had accused of marital violence.

In all these ways a balance can be found between the freedom of the Internet and a set of rules of ethics, morality and responsible behaviour, as have previously applied to older public opinion media. In fact various attempts at regulating the Internet have been undertaken in the USA under government auspices. Much as the net may have been seen by early enthusiasts as a tool of anti-government libertarianism, government may now be striking back. Its first such attempt was centred around a concern shared by many Americans: the dissemination of indecent material via the net. It tried to exert control through the Communications Decency Act, but failed. In June 1997, the Supreme Court declared the act to be unconstitutional. Yet the very attempt at legislative intervention raised the hackles of those who had cast themselves in the role of guardians of the early libertarian Internet culture.

A Libertarian Strikes Back

One voice raised on behalf of the republican vision of the Internet is that of John Perry Barlow. He is clearly a member of the early generation of people who deserve the epithet 'cyberguru'. He represents the early Frontier enthusiasms of the 'cybercowboys', also known as 'cybernauts', the digital pioneers. He is co-founder of a computer civil rights organization whose purpose is to act on behalf of the interests of the citizens of cyberspace: the Electronic Frontier Foundation. From his self-chosen exile in Zürich he protested against the attempts of the US government to regulate the freedoms of cyberspace. He chose to do so by issuing, via the Internet, a *Declaration of the Independence of Cyberspace*.[4] It is a remarkable mélange of classic American political discourse, in the hallowed tradition of the American *Declaration of Independence*, and of anti-Americanism. It shows an anti-government cast of mind, so well entrenched in America, but now turned against the American government. A few quotations will give the reader an idea:

> Governments of the Industrial World, you weary giants of flesh and steel, I come from Cyberspace, the new home of Mind. On behalf of the future, I ask you of the past to leave us alone. You are not welcome among us. You have no sovereignty where we gather.

4 Http://numedia.tddc.net/scott/declaration.html

We have no elected government, nor are we likely to have one, so I address you with no greater authority than that with which liberty itself always speaks. I declare the global social space we are building to be naturally independent of the tyrannies you seek to impose on us. You have no moral right to rule us nor do you possess any methods of enforcement we have true reason to fear.

Governments derive their just powers from the consent of the governed. You have neither solicited nor received ours. We did not invite you. You do not know us, nor do you know our world. Cyberspace does not lie within your borders ...

We are forming our own Social Contract. This governance will arise according to the conditions of our world, not yours. Our world is different.

Cyberspace consists of transactions, relationships, and thought itself, arrayed like a standing wave in the web of our communications. Ours is a world that is both everywhere and nowhere, but it is not where bodies live.

We are creating a world that all may enter without privilege or prejudice accorded by race, economic power, military force, or station of birth.

We are creating a world where anyone, anywhere may express his or her beliefs, no matter how singular, without fear of being coerced into silence or conformity.

We believe that from ethics, enlightened self-interest, and the commonweal, our governance will emerge ...

In the United States, you have today created a law, the Telecommunications Reform Act, which repudiates your own Constitution and insults the dreams of Jefferson, Washington, Mill, Madison, Tocqueville, and Brandeis. These dreams must be borne anew in us.

Your increasingly obsolete information industries would perpetuate themselves by proposing laws, in America and elsewhere, that claim to own speech itself throughout the world. These laws would declare ideas to be another industrial product, no more noble than pig iron. In our world, whatever the human mind may create can be reproduced and distributed infinitely at no cost ...

These increasingly hostile and colonial measures place us in the same position as those previous lovers of freedom and self-determination who had to reject the authorities of distant, uninformed powers. We must declare our virtual selves immune to your sovereignty, even as we continue to consent to your rule over our bodies. We will spread ourselves across the Planet so that no one can arrest our thoughts.

We will create a civilization of the Mind in Cyberspace. May it be more humane and fair than the world your governments have made before.

In terms of the degree of Americanness of the Internet, Barlow's Declaration can be seen as recent, if paradoxical, testimony to the continuing imprint of American political dreams. It is paradoxical, because of its anti-American thrust, yet undeniably, in its view of cyberspace as a realm of republican virtue, populated by 'netizens' who constitute a community far transcending national borders, we recognize a language of unmistakably American coinage.

Yet, as I argued before, the Internet is American on entirely different grounds as well. Anyone who is surfing the net is drawn into a world of information, blending commercial and other messages, that in most cases is clearly of American origin, or is at least cast in an American mould. For all its potential egalitarianism, the Internet in its present use clearly represents the structure of a web with a centre dominating a number of peripheries. This view takes us back to the question of whether the process of globalization as facilitated by the Internet does not at the same time serve as an instrument for the Americanization of the peripheries by the centre. Given the openness of access of the Internet, are there no ways in which the peripheries can strike back, penetrating right into the centre of the dissemination of American mass culture?

Amstel Light – The Periphery Strikes Back

In the spring of 1997 an American friend sent me a clipping from, as he called it, an 'alternative weekly', published in Washington DC: the *Washington City Paper*. His description suggested a smallish readership sharing tastes and views at variance with mainstream opinions, a public in other words that one could address in ways inconceivable for the larger population. The clipping was of an alarmist message from a group calling itself 'Garrison Boyd and Americans for Disciplined Behavior'. It sounded like some offshoot of the Christian Coalition. In bold print the message shouted 'IMPENDING DOOM'. It went on, surprisingly, to attack the city of Amsterdam for its 'loathsome attitude of openness', and its 'spontaneous social intercourse'. In order to hammer the message home, it continued indignantly: 'Ask yourself: do you want Amsterdam's reckless "Open for Anything" culture here? No!' Yet the threat was imminent, doom was impending. For, as it turned out, the message was meant to warn Americans against Amstel beers as 'the true embodiment of Amsterdam's recklessly open-minded behavior ... You must resist their seduction. You must say no to the Amstels from Amsterdam.' The message finally referred to a website (www.g-boyd.com) which, once opened, gave further stern warning against the evils of the various Amstel beers.[5]

As I learned soon afterwards, this was not a small advertising ploy aimed tongue-in-cheek at a limited in-crowd of cultural sophisticates. In fact, it was a $20 million campaign addressing Americans of every walk of life. As a piece in the media section of the *Village Voice* made clear (Savan 1997), the campaign had penetrated as far as Times Square in New York, the iconic heartland of American billboard advertising. In addition to huge billboards, the marquees of cinemas on 42nd Street that until recently had shown XXX-rated movies were now marshalled for a campaign against moral corruption from Amsterdam. 'Do not look. Shield your eyes.' 'Openness is dangerousness.'

Casting its product in the light of evil seduction, admonishing the public to avoid its beer at all cost, a Dutch brewing corporation, in collaboration with an American advertising agency, had opted for the ironic inversion of usual advertising strategies, while parodying the tone of a moral crusade that had come to characterize much of American public discourse over the previous two decades. The case is interesting for several reasons. First, we should note the multi-media aspect of the advertising campaign: from classic newspaper advertisements, to billboards, to cinema marquees, to the World Wide Web, Amstel's advertising ploy had become well-nigh inescapable. In addition to this high-saturation approach to consumers, there are aspects of more direct relevance to my argument.

In recent years, many students of the reception of forms of American mass culture abroad have emphasized what we may call the freedom of reception. They have pointed to the many inventive and imaginative ways in which people at the receiving end have given twists to the meaning of American mass culture, redefining it in order to make it function within the larger cultural context of their own daily lives. The focus in all such reception studies is on the appropriation of American mass culture by publics exposed to it outside America's national borders. Thus, the study of problems of an alleged Americanization of national cultures outside America has served to redefine the problem in terms of the creative act of cultural translation. In terms of the many national contexts of reception, the research focus has thus become one of understanding the processes of what we might call the nationalization of American culture. Thus, for a country such as the Netherlands, the problem is not so much the Americanization of Dutch culture, but rather the Dutchification of American mass culture.

5 *Washington City Paper*, 27 June 1997.

Interestingly, the case of the Amstel advertising campaign takes us one step further. Here, the commodity to be sold is not American, but Dutch, and so are the backers of the advertising campaign. Rather than foreign publics being exposed to the seductive potential of American imagery, the Amstel campaign was aimed at Americans and based itself on prevailing images among Americans of Dutch culture as excessively open and permissive. The campaign then chose to recycle these images ironically, parodying the apocalyptic language of the moral majority constituency among the American public. It testifies to an uncannily accurate reading of American culture by outsiders who, rather than being the passive recipients of American cultural values, use them creatively in a parody of American cultural concerns, beamed back at the American public. It was a case, I might say, of the periphery striking back at the empire.

Dreams of the Perfect Market

As the example of Amstel beers shows, the Internet is being increasingly used for commercial purposes, for advertising, selling and buying, and for the very organization of business. The trend is very recent and its outcome hard to predict. Clearly, the Internet inspires not only dreams of democracy, but also dreams of a perfectly transparent market. If the Internet holds a promise of greater democratic participation, it also promises greater access to and openness of the economic market. Again, in the eyes of non-Americans, this may illustrate a peculiarly American tendency to conflate the spheres of politics and economics, conceiving of the public sphere of democratic politics as a market, not unlike the one where citizens meet as consumers.[6]

Yet another aspect of the net ties in with a different characteristic trait of American society: the geographic mobility of its population, or in economic terms, the flexibility of its labour market. The United States still far exceeds other societies in this respect. Such restlessness of movement across the national territory may find its perfect reflection in the Internet. As the CEO of a high-tech company that moved to Bozeman, Montana, put it, 'I'd [previously] run a business in New York and Silicon Valley. I realized that the Internet ultimately removes geography as a restraint to location.'[7] A de-localization of business has been made possible by the net, which allows for collaborative teams to be scattered across the nation, if not the globe. The driving force behind such a

---

6 I have argued this point at greater length in Kroes 1996, Chapter 5: 'The Fifth Freedom and the Commodification of Civic Virtue'. For an excellent survey of the way business is increasingly availing itself of the Internet, see 'Business and the Internet: The Net Imperative', a special survey published in *The Economist*, 26 June 1999, 44 pages following p. 72.

7 Bozeman, 'The Next Silicon Valley?', *Tributary*, April 2001: 10.

reconfiguration of business practices is the USA, precisely due to the *Wahlverwandtschaft*, or elective affinity, between an American mindset and the structural characteristics of the Internet.

Undeniably, the net has affected the way in which business organizes its production, distribution and marketing. It has made for greater transparency and efficiency in all such areas. It may have contributed to productivity growth and cost control during the 1990s. Yet at the same time the increasing commercialization of the net may negatively affect the free flow of information as we have known it. So far free communication along the Internet has been, as the jargon has it, 'end to end'. From any point of access any user can reach any site, irrespective of the routing of the messages. There are no toll roads or turnpikes that put a price on passage. With the demand for high-density downloading of items such as films or music videos increasing, though, the need for expensive broadband channels has grown. They constitute stretches along the net that providers may be unwilling to offer at no charge for transfers unrelated to their business. Thus the logic of commerce and the market may before long mark the end of the Golden Age of free communication, free of charge, free of constraints.[8] The market rationale may well lead people to wake up from their dreams of democracy. Yet inflated expectations of marketing opportunities provided by the net have led to a speculative bubble not unlike Dutch tulipmania in the seventeenth century. It may well be the case that people wake up from their dreams of economic gain before they give up on the freedoms of communication they now enjoy.

The Dream of the Lost Library

In what follows I intend to focus on a different dream, equally lofty as the dream of democracy and of a *res publica* in cyberspace. As well as other dreams, the Internet has inspired dreams of the return to a world of total intertextuality, the reconstitution of the full body of human thinking and writing. It would be the return to the 'City of Words', the labyrinthine library that, like a nostalgic recollection, has haunted human imagination since the age of the mythical library of Babylon. Tony Tanner (1971) used the metaphor of the city of words to describe the central quest inspiring the literary imagination of the twentieth century. One author who, for Tanner, epitomizes this quest is Jorge Luis Borges. It is the constructional power of the human mind that moves and amazes Borges. His stories are full of the strangest architecture, including the endless variety of lexical architecture to which human beings throughout history have

8 For a good discussion of these problems, see 'Upgrading the Internet', *The Economist Technology Quarterly*, March 2001: 30–35.

devoted their time – philosophical theories, theological disputes, encyclopae-dias, religious beliefs, critical interpretations, novels, and books of all kinds. While having a deep feeling for the shaping and abstracting powers of the human mind, Borges has at the same time a profound sense of how night-marish the resultant structures might become. In one of his stories, the narrator refers to the Library of Babel as the 'universe', and one can take it as a metaphysical parable of all the difficulties of deciphering human encounters in existence. On the other hand, Babel remains the most famous example of the madness in human rage for architecture, and books are only another form of building. In this library every possible combination of letters and words is to be found, with the result that there are fragments of sense separated by 'leagues of insensate cacophony, of verbal farragoes and incoherencies'. Most books are 'mere labyrinths of letters'. Since everything that language can do and express is somewhere in the library, 'the clarification of the basic mysteries of humanity ... was also expected'. The 'necessary vocabularies and grammars' must be discoverable in the lexical totality. Yet the attempt at discovery and detection is maddening; the story is full of the sadness, sickness and madness of the pathetic figures who roam around the library as around a vast prison (Tanner 1971: 41).

What do Borges' fantasies tell us about the Promethean potential of a restored city of words in cyberspace? During an international colloquium in Paris at the *Bibliothèque nationale de France*, held on 3–4 June 1998, scholars and library presidents discussed the implications of a virtual memory bank on the Internet, connecting the holdings of all great libraries in the world. Some saw it as a dream come true. In his opening remarks Jean-Pierre Angremy referred to the library of Babel as imagined by Borges, while ignoring its night-marish side: 'When it was proclaimed that the library would hold all books, the first reaction was one of extravagant mirth. Everyone felt like mastering an intact and secret treasure.' The perspective, as Angremy saw it, was extrava-gant indeed. All the world's knowledge at your command, like an endless scroll across your computer screen. Others, like Jacques Attali, spiritual father of the idea of digitalizing the holdings of the new *Bibliothèque nationale*, took a similarly positive view. Whatever the form of the library, real or virtual, it would always be 'a reservoir of books'. Others weren't so sure. They foresaw a mutation of our traditional relationship with the written text, such that new manipulations and competences would make our current reading habits as antiquated as the reading of papyrus scrolls would be to us.

Ironically, as others pointed out, texts as they now appear on our computer screens are like a throwback to the reading of scrolls, and may well affect our sense of the single page. In the printed book every page comes in its own context of pages preceding and following it, suggesting a discursive continuity.

On the screen, however, the page is the interchangeable element of a virtual data bank that one penetrates by the use of a key word that opens many books at the same time. All information is thus put on the same plane, without the logical hierarchy of an unfolding argument. As Michel Melot, long-time member of the *Conseil supérieur des bibliothèques*, pointed out, randomness becomes the rule. The coherence of traditional discursive presentation will tend to give way to what is fragmented, incomplete, disparate, if not incoherent. In his view, the patchwork or cut-and-paste approach will become the dominant mode of composition.[9]

These darker views take us back to my earlier discussion of the American imprint of the Internet. They are strangely reminiscent of an earlier cultural critique in Europe of the ways in which American culture would affect European civilization. Particularly, the perceived contrast between the act of reading traditional books and that of reading texts downloaded from the net recalls a contrast between Europe and America that constitutes a staple in the work of many European critics of American culture. Europe, in this view, stands for organic cohesion, for logical and stylistic closure, whereas America tends towards fragmentation and recombination, in a mode of blithe cultural *bricolage*, exploding every prevailing cultural canon in Europe. Furthermore, we recognize the traditional European fear of American culture as a levelling force, bringing everything down to the surface level of the total interchangeability of cultural items, oblivious to their intrinsic value and cultural hierarchies of high versus low.[10]

Yet, in the views summarized above, we find no reference to America. Is this because America is a subtext, a code instantly recognized by French intellectuals? Or is it because the logic of the Internet and digital intertextuality have a cultural impact in their own right, similar to the impact of American culture, but this time unrelated to any American agency? I would go no further at this point than to suggest a Weberian answer. It seems to be undeniably the case that there is a *Wahlverwandtschaft*, an elective affinity, between the logic of the Internet and the American frame of mind, which makes for an easier, less anguished acceptance and use of the new medium among Americans than among a certain breed of Europeans.

There is, it seems to me, a further way to explore this elective affinity. Most of the discussion at the Paris colloquium focused on the *use* of texts available via the Internet rather than on the *production* of texts, in other words on the act

9 For my summary of the proceedings at the Paris colloquium, I have used a report published in *Le Monde, Sélection Hebdomadaire*, 2589, 20 June 1998: 13.

10 For a fuller analysis of the metaphorical deep structure, underlying the European critique of American culture, may I refer the reader to Kroes 1996.

of reading rather than writing. At one point, though, the question came up as to whether the logic of the Internet might not also lead to new forms of literature. According to the report in *Le Monde*, no one can foresee the possible impact on creative writing. Yet one could venture a little farther than this. From a librarian's point of view the Internet can be seen as having generated a virtual library in cyberspace, linking all available texts ever produced by writers. Through the use of key words and related search techniques every visitor to this library can determine his or her own particular trajectory through the lexical labyrinth, producing a textual collage to fit the particular needs of individual readers. It is, in this case, individual readers who, on the basis of available texts, generate their own individual recombination and rearrangement of textual fragments. The logical next step, then, would be the production of precisely such a body of textual fragments, as an act of creative writing. This time, the author would provide the key words, known as hyperlinks, that would allow the reader to cruise through the textual fragments, and to arrange them in any number of combinations. The result would be what we might call a hypertext novel.

As it happens, the challenge has been taken up. Hypertext novels do exist, not on the shelves of real libraries anywhere in the world, but, as their logic dictates, in the virtual library in cyberspace. They can be downloaded as so many fragments and then, by clicking on any of the hyperlinks provided by the author, arranged by the individual reader sitting at his or her own computer.[11] This creative leap into cyberspace has something Promethean about it. It invites the reader to become his or her own individual author and to act out the dream that is so central to an age that has proclaimed the death of the author. No longer, it would seem, does the hypertext novel tie the reader down to forms of narrative flow and structure set entirely by the author. The very logic of the hypertext novel demands that readers actively construct their own texts.

Again, I would argue, this daring step was typically one for American writers to make first. Again, it does seem to fit in with a more generally American modularizing frame of mind, with a greater willingness to break up coherent wholes and to leave it to individual consumers to recombine the fragments as they please. Yet the idea of the hypertext novel seems more daring than any actual examples I have seen. The idea ties in with the dream of the lost library, where an author would do no more than set the reader off on a journey through the labyrinth of the human imagination, out into uncharted territory. The idea is one of a text that is structurally open, fraying at the edges, providing hyperlinks into the unknown. The hypertext in its present form is a far cry from

11 A site specializing in hypertext novels is www.eastgate.com

this, however. It is entirely self-enclosed, referring back to its own constituent elements only, allowing no escape beyond the structural closure set by the author. It is reminiscent of the attempts at building a robot that would not be a simple replica of a human being but an improvement on our present stage of evolution. The result has always been a Prometheus bound and shackled in retribution for his acts of hubris.

Similarly, the hypertext novel is no more than a clumsy replica of reading as we have always known it and done it. The act of reading texts in their traditional form has always been one of the active construction of hyperlinks. One book always reminds us of other books. Our mind produces its own links and associations. Reading one book we get up and open other books to verify our associative hunches. We hear voices of other authors reverberating in unison with the voice of any particular author we happen to be reading. Sometimes the reverberation is a matter of authorial intent, sometimes it is a case of the reader's mind wandering. But all reading is intertextual, all fiction a hypertext. Europeans have always produced fiction in a self-conscious awareness of its intertextuality, from Shakespeare and Cervantes to Julian Barnes and Julián Ríos. And so have Americans. In the cultural games that Americans play they may experiment in ways that strike Europeans as typically American, yet the dream of life in cyberspace is the contemporary version of dreams that we all share.

Or am I being too postmodern here, reducing human interconnectedness to the mental state of the individual, self-sufficient and erudite mind, to an intertextuality in our mind that connects us to other minds, past and present, no matter where we are or under what conditions? In response, I cannot help being reminded here of some of the great prison writings, by the likes of Arthur Koestler, Antonio Gramsci, or George Orwell. As they make clear, whatever the duress of isolation and torture, the mind may find resources for survival in its interconnectedness with the minds of fellow human beings, remembered through their words and works. Civilization, in this final analysis, is a state of mind, a fragile and precious work of culture. It sustains us, or shall we say the best of us, in the face of a breakdown of civil society, when we are confronted with whatever hardships are imposed on us by those who see salvation in totalitarian projects, trying to tear apart our bonds with the past and with a community of kindred spirits. Killing fields are all over this world, from Nazi gas chambers, to the Soviet gulag, Cambodian genocide, and the lethal pursuit of ethnic purity in the former Yugoslavia. Yet there have always been those whose minds never broke, and who remained citizens of the world when all that remained was their inner city of words.

References

Carr, John (1999), 'Age of Uncertainty: Anarchy.com', *Prospect* (June). (www.unnu.com/newhome/Gallery/etexts/anarchycom.htm, accessed 10 June 2003)

Kroes, Rob (1996), *If You've Seen One, You've Seen the Mall: Europeans and American Mass Culture*. Urbana and Chicago: University of Illinois Press.

Rosenzweig, Roy (1998), 'Wizards, Bureaucrats, Warriors and Hackers: Writing the History of the Internet', *American Historical Review* 103 (December): 1530–52.

Rushdie, Salman (2001),*Woede*. Amsterdam: Uitgeverij Contact.

Savan, Leslie (1997), 'Morality Plays on 42nd Street', *Village Voice* (16 June).

Sellar, W.C., and R.J. Yeatman (1930), *1066 and All That: A Memorable History of England*. London.

Shannon, Victoria (1999), 'What's Lurking Behind Those Slow Downloads', *International Herald Tribune* (27 May): 7.

Tanner, Tony (1971), *City of Words: American Fiction 1950–1970*. London: Cape.

van den Hooff, B.J. (1997), *Incorporating Electronic Mail: Adoption, Use and Effects of Electronic Mail in Organizations*. Amsterdam.

PART IV

EPILOGUE

Rethinking Americanization

Roland Robertson

The problems involved in analysing the degree to which the world is being Americanized are much more complex than we are frequently led to think by many intellectuals, politicians and journalists around the world. This applies also to those whom they influence and who are then strongly disposed to blame virtually every feature of the world of which they disapprove on 'America'. The latter word, of course, really covers all of the countries of North and South America from Canada in the north to Argentina and Chile in the south, and it is thus not a trivial matter to insist that, in using the term Americanization, we are in fact almost invariably speaking of *USAmericanization*. In any case, in this supposedly post-Cold War period in which, by conventional wisdom, the USA is the only superpower and enjoys an unprecedented degree of political muscle and economic leverage in the world as a whole, the claims about 'American-ization' are very intense. Indeed, some of this could well be called hysterical (complementing and mirroring much of the hysteria inside the USA itself in relation to the world beyond its own borders). This very pejorative attitude towards the USA was, at the time when the present contribution was first begun, being exacerbated considerably by the disturbing circumstances of the disputed presidential election of November 2000. The glee about these electoral escapades in the many commentaries outside the USA was very evident.

This situation was, of course, dramatically brought into even sharper relief by the attacks of 11 September 2001 on the World Trade Center in New York City and the Pentagon in Washington, DC, as well as the crash of a hijacked aeroplane near Pittsburgh, Pennsylvania. It seemed at that time that the some-what misleadingly named 'anti-globalization' movement had been morally damaged in a very serious way. This was apparently so because this movement was in certain ways an American movement, in spite of the anti-American sentiments expressed in much of the rhetoric and actions of the virtually world-wide protests against capitalistic globalization, as opposed to other forms and dimensions of globalization. Thus, the events of 9/11 occurred at a time of growing anti-Americanism. In many parts of the world, the latter was – as it turned out, only temporarily – diminished a great deal by 9/11.

My first intuition about the undermining of the anti-globalization movement proved to be less than prescient, since some strands of this movement quickly transformed themselves into a peace movement, while other elements moved, more slowly, to an ambivalently expressed conflation of views about the attacks in New York, Washington and Pennsylvania, on the one hand, and the more militant 'anti-US plus anti-global' sentiments on the other. More specifically, sympathy for the USA was very quickly attenuated – leading within two years or so to more or less worldwide anti-American sentiment.

Thus, although this short chapter was commissioned and written largely before 9/11, its contents have by now undoubtedly been deeply coloured by it. This is mostly because the events of 9/11 and its aftermath have brought to the fore the most salient of the features of both Americanism and *anti*-Americanism. This has, of course, greatly involved the extensive and intensive controversy concerning Iraq, which at the time of my concluding this (early March 2003) was at a crucial stage. My concerns here are, nonetheless, primarily methodological. More specifically, I am mainly interested in articulating the pivotal issues on which we must focus when speaking of Americanization, anti-Americanism, American imperialism, the USA as an exemplary society, 'global America', and so on. These issues are relevant regardless of particular historical circumstances, and indeed it might be said that they are even more relevant as a way of keeping our 'analytic cool' in the world-shaking period since 9/11.

In a sense, I deliberately attempt here to complexify these themes, precisely in order to reach, in the longer run, a more parsimonious set of formulations. Indeed, the proposition that it is necessary to indicate complexity in order to obtain a manageable degree of parsimony – or in the best sense, of simplicity, but still involving both ambivalence and ambiguity – is a leading theme in the present context. That this is not an obscure statement is illustrated by the variation between American embracement of unambiguity and the much greater degrees of toleration of ambiguity and ambivalence in other socio-cultural settings. We are here forced to confront a form of the Orientalism–Occidentalism divide, in the sense that US conceptions of Europe, Asia, Africa and Latin America largely centre on perceptions of lack of clarity, on the one hand, and quaintness and exoticism, on the other. And set against this is the pejorative view of much of American life as based on triviality, naivety, lack of subtlety and excess.

258

It is not my purpose here either to defend the USA against the many charges made against it, or to present a rosy picture of American society. As a person who has spent approximately half of his residential life in the UK and the other half in the USA and who has regularly shuttled back and forth, primarily between the USA and Europe but also to various parts of Asia, Latin America and Africa over the past thirty years or more, I am only too aware of my own ambivalence with respect to questions of nationality, loyalty and the like. My own biographical circumstances have undoubtedly provided me with some valuable experience of transnationality and a particular sensitivity to socio-cultural difference. In case these appear to be claims marked by hubris, I wish to emphasize that ambivalence is a central psychosociological feature of our time. But it is most certainly not without its drawbacks. While ambivalence is clearly a concomitant of the risk society (Beck 1992) – and a functionally necessary one at that – there is also a countervailing need for revisable or reflexive certainty in the face of the uncertainties increasingly generated in much of the world. This is so not just at the 'macro' level of world politics and 'terror', but also very evidently in the quotidian lives of individuals as they attempt to negotiate their way in and through rapidly increasing uncertainty (Beck 2001). Yet, necessary as it is, analytic confidence must not regress into fundamentalistic reduction-ism, meaning the adamant refusal to modify, let alone change, ideological or religious course. In fact, fundamentalism has – notwithstanding the rather sloppy use of the term as an analytic concept – become inexorably a feature of contemporary globalization, in the multidisciplinary sense of the latter theme.

The question of the degree to which the world is being Americanized requires a kind of sophistication that is rarely seen, not least since the conflation of the problem of al-Qaeda and 'the war on terrorism' with the issue of 'regime change in Iraq'. Not infrequently pro- or anti-Israeli sentiment has also been involved in this conflation. In any case, without declaring here my own position, I consider it analytically appropriate to describe the slogan of 'Peace' (in the absence of elaboration) as basically fundamentalistic, if not so funda-mentalistic as the crusading spirit of the more militant of the circle around President George W. Bush, as well as his dominant Christian Right supporters.

As a starting point in this quest for more analytic rigour, I present here an elemental typology of orientations to the USA, one that is as applicable to Americans themselves as to non-Americans. (Of course, both of the latter denotations, 'Americans' and 'non-Americans', are extremely simplistic and unstable.)

1. Pro-American: disagrees with the strong Americanization thesis (i.e. that the world is becoming Americanized).

2. Pro-American: agrees with the strong Americanization thesis.
3. Anti-American: disagrees with the strong Americanization thesis.
4. Anti-American: agrees with the strong Americanization thesis.

It is rather obvious that it is the second and the fourth of these that are most relevant in the present context. The first and third certainly cannot be neglected, but I am unable to address them here. Let me, then, concentrate on the orientations that involve, on the one hand, pro-Americanism combined with agreement that we are well on the way to 'global America', and on the other, anti-Americanism in combination with assent to the thesis that the world is quickly being Americanized.

Before doing this, however, it is in order to indicate some further analytic problems, as well as making a few relevant empirical observations. In the former respect, it must be pointed out that in considering the idea of Americanization – which is here seen very emphatically as conceptually distinct from globalization (see, for example, Robertson 1992) – we must distinguish between cultural, social-communicative, political, and economic dimensions. Thus when we interrogate the question of the degree of Americanization, we have to discuss separately these four aspects of the term, acknowledging in so doing that, in reality, the four dimensions are interpenetrative. They are not empirically, as opposed to analytically, distinct.

On the directly empirical side, we can, in a highly selective manner, look at some often neglected aspects of the Americanization thesis.[1] Currently the popular music making a strong impact within the USA is rather eclectic, with Britain, Latin America, Germany, France and even Iceland appearing in recent lists of best-selling CDs or DVDs. Europe clearly dominates the fashion scene; Britain has a great presence in Broadway theatre. While Hollywood seems to remain supreme in the world with respect to TV and film, its impact has been considerably exaggerated. Aside from the increasing significance of Latin American TV programmes in the USA, and the fact that many of them are broadcast in Spanish, there is much to suggest that the overall traffic is from Europe to the USA at present – and certainly that many, but not of course all, of the USA's most popular TV shows, particularly so-called 'reality TV', are, in fact, European in origin. Actually, however, the question of origins is extremely complicated. After all, Hollywood was largely founded and developed by immigrant Jews from Central and Eastern Europe, and few American studios these days are all-American in respect of their ownership (Gabler 1988;

---

1 This and the following paragraph rest in part on Micklethwait and Wooldridge 2000. In great contrast and for what I have indicated as hysterical (scholarly) anti-Americanism, see Galtung 2001.

cf. Portuges 1998). However, in spite of Hollywood's undoubted influence around the world, the producers and directors of actors in its films have, if anything, become increasingly 'cosmopolitan' (Robertson and White 2003). In fact, since much of this thesis concerning 'the Americanization of the world' so often centres on 'Hollywood', the recognition of the intriguing mixture of (in the loose sense) cosmopolitanism and 'gung-ho' Americanism poses problems of great importance for serious scholars dealing with the position of the USA in the world. It seems that each generation has to deal with this problem, from inside and outside the USA.

If we maintain the distinction between globalization and Americanization, as I believe we should, then it can be argued viably that globalization is a process involving the expansion of attention to a very wide range of cultural themes. In this connection a distinction should surely be made between American 'trash' and American influence of a much more sophisticated type, whether we are talking about ballet, opera, aesthetically praiseworthy films, architecture, fusion cuisine, or yet other kinds of cultural outputs. It would be verging on the perverse to argue, for example, that the Guggenheim Museum in Bilbao should fall into the same category as Sylvester Stallone (an *Italian-American*) as a case of Americanism in the all-too-usual sense of the word. In so far as the notion of Americanization is used to mean American *cultural* homogenization, the argument is far from clear. It is much more accurate to say that the world is becoming more hybridized (or, at least in mundane respects, cosmopolitanized), both resulting from globalization rather than Americanization. There is, of course, on the other hand, an argument to be made that the USA is the consummation of globalization. An essential point to bear in mind with respect to such ideas as Americanization and global America is that cultural diversity in the USA is rapidly increasing and that, in spite of superficial characteristics to the contrary, the USA itself is becoming ever more heterogeneous in cultural terms. In this respect, the idea of global USA or the world as an extrapolation of the USA makes a lot of sense.

These mainly empirical comments have dealt, for the most part, with the cultural dimension. Let me now turn briefly to the social, political and economic dimensions. In so far as there is much cultural Americanization, one might expect that there would be a similar Americanization of patterns of social interaction. There is, in my view, a fair amount of this but not to anywhere near the same degree. The world is certainly not being Americanized with respect to its religiosity, magical and millenarian tendencies (mainly cultural characteristics), rituals of greeting, expressions of the erotic (where the USA still stands out for its puritanism, including its *pornographic* puritanism), loudness of verbal interaction, and so on. Although it is possible that the so-

261

called global teenager has a very recognizable American social (as well as cultural) tinge, the same could be said of various other influences, mainly Western (including Latin American) in nature, but certainly not exclusively so. In any case, numerous examples could be produced of styles of social interaction that are becoming increasingly conspicuous in much of the world, but which are not 'American' in origin. One thinks here, for example, of the 'double kiss' which is a very common style of greeting, particularly between both men and women in Latin American countries, the Middle East, and more and more of Europe and elsewhere. In the USA this ritual has been slow to arrive – except, of course, among the fast-growing 'celebrity' subculture, as well as the Latin American and Middle Eastern fractions of the American population. In sum, *social* Americanization has not been particularly evident during the last few years. Indeed, there is much to suggest that, simply in social terms, the USA is actually being *de*-Americanized (see the article by Ulrich Beck in this volume).

When the economic dimension of the problem is considered, we enter somewhat more complex territory. For here we are addressing not merely Americanization in the sense of US-American influence or diffusion of American culture or social practices, but also – more clearly than in the cultural and social spheres – issues of power and domination. Obviously, to the degree to which the economic can be empirically separated from the cultural, the USA does have an extraordinary degree of hegemony. However, as Giddens has remarked, during the Cold War 'American economic power was backed by a global network of military alliances, by numerous forms of interventionism, and by the propagating of "proxy wars" in various places' (Hutton and Giddens 2000: 61). But the USA does not have these strategic interests or consequences now (although, here again, the post-9/11 circumstances have altered this somewhat). So the extent to which the USA has a high degree of control over what is often called the global economy is a debatable matter, in spite of old-leftist views to the contrary.

When the fourth of the most salient dimensions that I specified earlier – that is, the political – is addressed, we face an issue that has much resemblance to considerations of the economic dimension. This similarity consists in the fact that we must reflect on both the politico-military power of the USA in the contemporary world and, on the other hand, the degree to which other nation states are adopting or adhering to American models of governance and conceptions of self-interest. It is worth mentioning in the latter respect that *Realpolitik* was not an American invention. In fact, in its early years the USA was singularly uninterested in world politics.

Clearly, the USA has had an enormous impact on the world as a whole with regard to its constitutionality and the form (if not the content) of its democracy. The USA more or less inaugurated constitutionality as we now know it and, whatever its obvious flaws and the gloating commentaries on its clearly flawed presidential election of 2000, the USA has been a remarkably influential model for other countries to emulate. As to the politico-military strength of the USA, there can be little doubt that in the post-1989 period it has been by far the most powerful nation in the world. Nonetheless, recent developments with regard to the tentative creation of a European military formation, the increasing military strength of China, and the actual or potential proliferation of countries equipped with nuclear, biological and chemical weapons should give pause to those who speak blithely and dogmatically of American domination of the world. And this is, indeed, where the current circumstance as of early 2003 has become of vast, global importance.

Ever since the Second World War, the USA has been caught in a no-win situation. When it leans towards isolationism, as it was doing in the early months of George W. Bush's presidency, the USA is often criticized for not playing its full international role. When, on the other hand, the USA attempts to police the world or intervene in the affairs of other countries, it is often accused of imperialism. The latter has, of course, much to do with the authoritarian, expansionist views of most of the inner circle of Bush advisers, as well as the cowardice of the American Left and much of the American press.

In concluding this commentary, I would urge social scientists to be more circumspect and analytically careful in expressing their views about the important issue of Americanization. Among the numerous matters I have not had the opportunity to address is that of the ever-changing nature of the USA itself, with particular reference to its transnationality.[2] To speak of Americanization or global America one must surely know a considerable amount about the sociological characteristics of the USA itself. Yet very rarely is such knowledge exhibited by those employing such terms. One might reasonably say that 'anti-Americans' cannot have it both ways. They cannot, logically speaking, say, at one and the same time, that the USA dominates the world and that too much attention is paid to American society. The USA at present appears to be moving into a phase in which its various ethnic and cultural 'communities' are becoming less attached to 'core Americanism' and correspondingly more attached to their extra-USA origins (including 'roots of choice'). When people talk of the Americanization of the world, they would do well to reflect on this and related issues.

---

2 This notion has been inspired by Lind 1995: 259–98. However, I certainly do not subscribe to Lind's ideas *in toto*.

References

Beck, U. (1992), *Risk Society*. London: Sage.

— (2001), 'Living Your Own Life in a Runaway World: Individualisation, Globalisation and Politics', in W. Hutton and A. Giddens (eds), *On the Edge: Living with Global Capitalism*. London: Jonathan Cape/Vintage: 164–74.

Gabler, N. (1988), *An Empire of Their Own: How the Jews Invented Hollywood*. New York: Anchor Books.

Galtung, J. (2001), 'Americanization Versus Globalization', in E. Ben-Rafael with Y. Sternberg (eds), *Identity, Culture and Globalization*. Leiden: Brill: 277–89.

Hutton, W., and A. Giddens (2000), 'Is Globalization Americanization?', *Dissent* (Summer): 61.

Lind, M. (1995), *The Next American Nation*. New York: The Free Press.

Micklethwait, J., and A. Wooldridge (2000), 'The Cultural Guards Have Got It Wrong', *International Herald Tribune* (19 May): 5.

Portuges, C. (1998), 'Accenting L.A.: Central Europeans in Diasporan Hollywood in the 1940s', in E. Barkan and M.-D. Shelton (eds), *Borders, Exiles, Diasporas*. Stanford, CA: Stanford University Press: 46–57.

Robertson, R. (1992), *Globalization: Social Theory and Cultural Change*. London: Sage.

Robertson, R., and K.E. White (2003), 'Globalization: An Overview', in R. Robertson and K.E. White (eds), *Globalization: Critical Concepts in Sociology. Volume I: Analytical Perspectives*. London: Routledge: 1–44.

Index

Index

Index

Index

Index